Praise for *Hope in a Jar*

"Excellent . . . Peiss follows women as they move from the farm and drawing room to the mall and boardroom."
                    —*The New York Times Book Review*

"Peiss is that rarity: a historian who comes neither to praise the modern world nor bury it; she is, rather, genuinely interested in discovering how a society—and the people within it change."
                    —*Los Angeles Times Book Review*

"A fabulous book that shows how women made their way through minefields of advertising and moral commentary . . . An astonishing array of materials with loads of delicious tidbits."
                    —Susan Porter Benson, author of *Counter Cultures*

"A delight."   —*The Indianapolis Star*

"At once insightful and surprising as Peiss illustrates how the beauty culture is interwoven through so much of our social fabric."
                    —*The Hartford Advocate*

"*Hope in a Jar* is wonderful to read and consistently enlightening. Peiss brilliantly weaves the stories of the immigrant and African-American women who built the beauty industry into the larger history of women's changing lives."
                    —Susan Strasser, author of
            Satisfaction Guaranteed: The Making of the Mass Market

"Weaving together business history, history of women, history of advertising, and history of the body, Kathy Peiss illuminates both the hidden corners and visible theaters of American life. Big, bold, and captivating."
                    —Daniel Horowitz, author of *The Morality of Spending*

HOPE IN A JAR

HOPE IN A JAR

The

Making

of America's

Beauty

Culture

KATHY PEISS

An Owl Book
Henry Holt and Company
New York

Owl Books
Henry Holt and Company, LLC
Publishers since 1866
175 Fifth Avenue
New York, New York 10010
www.henryholt.com

An Owl Book® and 🅗® are registered trademarks of
Henry Holt and Company, LLC.

Library of Congress Cataloging-in-Publication Data
Peiss, Kathy Lee.
Hope in a jar : the making of America's beauty culture /
Kathy Peiss.
p.   cm.
Includes bibliographical references and index.
ISBN-13: 978-0-8050-5551-1
ISBN-10: 0-8050-5551-7
1. Beauty culture—United States—History. 2. Cosmetics—
United States—History.   I. Title.
TT957.P45   1998   97-42706
391.6'3'0973—dc21   CIP

Henry Holt books are available for special promotions and
premiums. For details contact: Director, Special Markets.

First published in hardcover in 1998 by Metropolitan Books

First Owl Books Edition 1999

DESIGNED BY KATE NICHOLS

Disclaimer: Cosmetics recipes as described herein are given for historical and reference purposes only, and may cause skin, eye, and other injuries. In no way should the reader attempt to create, mix, apply, or ingest any of the recipes.

Frontispiece: Helena Rubinstein, around 1920

Printed in the United States of America
10   9   8   7   6   5   4   3

FOR PETER

with gratitude and love

Contents

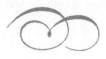

Preface

Some years ago, I sat in my aunt's kitchen, explaining to her my plan to spend the day at the Max Factor Museum of Beauty in Hollywood, not as a tourist, but as a researcher. A vital woman in her sixties who had sold cosmetics for a Los Angeles wholesale house, she was intrigued by my project, although perplexed that a scholar would find in beauty products a subject of any significance. Then the conversation turned. Scrutinizing my face, she said, "You know, a little blusher, a little eye shadow, they make you look and feel good. Don't you think cosmetics would make you look better?" I replied, "I think they would make me look different." "Different how," she persisted, "different good or different bad?" I smiled. "Just different."

This was, of course, an evasion. For women of my generation, born during the baby boom and coming of age in the 1960s, judgments about manufactured beauty changed with lightning speed. The counterculture and feminism came along just in time to turn my ineptitude with cake eyeliner and thick mascara into the natural look. At the same time, being a failed user has not exempted me from frequenting makeup counters, examining cosmetics ads, reading women's magazines, or looking in mirrors. Indeed, the idea for this book originated in a New Jersey outlet mall, during a running conversation with my shopping mate. Obviously, I live within the very culture of beauty whose history I have endeavored to write.

Still, my reply to my aunt's question declared the stance I have tried to take in this study. I write about cosmetics out of an interest in the world of appearances, in the ways women have fashioned their looks to express their own sense of selfhood and social role. I have wanted to understand women's intentions as they began to use these mass-produced items, as well as the social and cultural forces that influenced their use. To do so, I have tried to be open to the different values, meanings, and purposes women have attached to beauty preparations. How could such throw-away feminine objects be the stuff of serious investigation, my aunt wondered. This book is my answer.

I am grateful to many institutions and individuals who have sustained me as I worked on this project over the years. The American Council of Learned Societies, the National Endowment for the Humanities, the Smithsonian Institution, and the Rutgers Center for Historical Analysis generously funded my work, and the University of Massachusetts granted several research leaves. Many libraries and archives provided the source materials for a study that sometimes seemed boundless. I thank the National Museum of American History; Library of Congress; National Archives; New York Public Library; Indiana Historical Society; Procter and Gamble Company; Baker Library, Harvard University; Schlesinger Library, Radcliffe College; Sophia Smith Collection, Smith College; State Historical Society of Wisconsin; Chicago Historical Society; New-York Historical Society; American Medical Association Archives; Hagley Museum and Library; and the special collections libraries at Duke University, Cornell University, Rutgers University, University of Iowa, and Vassar College. I owe a special debt to archivists Vanessa Broussard-Simmons, Wilma Gibbs, Ellen Gartrell, Marian Hirsch, Russell Koonts, Amy Fischer, and the tireless reference and interlibrary loan staff at the University of Massachusetts Library. I am also grateful to A'Lelia Bundles, who kindly permitted me access to the Madam C. J. Walker Papers.

Many individuals sent me clippings, directed me to sources, or shared their work with me, including Joseph Arnold, Natalie Beausoleil, Patricia Brady, Margo Culley, Dana Frank, Kathryn Fuller, Paul Gaffney, Larry Goldsmith, Martin Greenfield, James Grossman, Michael Harris, Susan Johnson, Roland Marchand, Ellen Marlatt, Maureen Montgomery, Charles McGovern, Dorothy Moses Schultz, Susan Smulyan, and Ellen Todd. Others gave insightful comments on chapters and presentations, among them Anne Boylan, David Glassberg, Jennifer Jones, Bruce Laurie, Philip Scranton, and Christine Stansell. I have had invaluable research assistance from Marc Ferris, Kathleen Goudie, Kim Gunning, Pamela Haag, Laura Helper, Madeline Hunter, Margaret Lowe, Linda Shih, Susanna Yurick, and especially Judy Ruttenberg. Beth Duryea expertly managed photograph permissions. I am very grateful to Riva Hocherman for her helpful reading and careful attention to the manuscript, to Mark Aronson, and to the talented staff at Metropolitan books.

There are a handful of friends and colleagues to whom I owe special thanks. Susan Porter Benson, Daniel Horowitz, Roy Rosenzweig, and Susan Strasser all read an earlier version of the entire manuscript and generously gave me their criticism and advice. Steve Fraser also offered early support and a careful reading. I came to a better understanding of my work in lively conversations with Victoria de Grazia, spirited dinners with Barbara Clark Smith, Daniel Bluestone, and Hattie Smith, and an ongoing friendship with Judith Gerson. Thanks also to Larry and Maggie Malley, who took good care of me during research trips to Duke.

Two individuals gave an extraordinary amount of time and effort to helping me write the book I wanted to write. My editor, Sara Bershtel, is remarkable: Her close reading of the manuscript has challenged me as a writer, even as her enthusiasm has kept me going. I was dubious when she said we were going to have fun, but she was right.

My husband, Peter Agree, probably knows more about cosmetics than any man outside the beauty industry. Throughout he has been cornerman and wordsmith, adviser and soul mate. Every page of this book bears some trace of his commitment and involvement; these few words of acknowledgment cannot express the intensity of my gratitude to him.

Greenfield, Massachusetts
September 1997

HOPE IN A JAR

Introduction

In 1938 the cosmetics firm Volupté introduced two new lipsticks. *Mademoiselle* magazine explained that one was for "girls who lean toward pale-lacquered nails, quiet smart clothes and tiny strands of pearls," the other "for the girl who loves exciting clothes, pins a strass [paste] pin big as a saucer to her dress, and likes to be just a leetle bit shocking." One had a "soft mat finish" while the other covered the lips "with a gleaming lustre." The names of these lipsticks were Lady and Hussy. As *Mademoiselle* put it, "Each of these two categories being as much a matter of mood as a matter of fact, we leave you to decide which you prefer to be."[1]

The assumptions behind this promotion are arresting. For nineteenth-century Americans, lady and hussy were polar opposites—the best and worst of womanhood—and the presence or absence of cosmetics marked the divide. Reddened cheeks and darkened eyelids were signs of female vice, and the "painted woman" provoked disgust and censure from the virtuous. But by the 1930s, lady and hussy had become "types" and "moods." Female identities once fixed by parentage, class position, social etiquette, and sexual codes were now released from small swiveling cylinders. Where "paint" implied a concealing mask, the term "makeup," in common usage by the 1920s, connoted a medium of self-expression in a consumer society where identity had become a purchasable style. Women could choose the look of gentlewoman or prostitute—and apparently Hussy outsold Lady five to one!

Lady and Hussy lipsticks mark a sea change, not only in the meaning of cosmetics, but in conceptions of women's appearance and identity. How did this fundamental transformation take place? How did a sign of disrepute become the daily routine of millions? And how did a "kitchen physic," as homemade cosmetics were once called, become a mass market industry?

Small objects sometimes possess great moral force, and the usual answers to these questions have been charged with disapproval and criticism. Cosmetics have been condemned as symptomatic of all that is wrong in modern consumer society: Their producers create false needs, manipulate fears and desires, and elevate superficiality over substance, all to sell overpriced goods that do not deliver on their promises. Today the most formidable judgments about cosmetics often come from feminists who, since the 1960s, have argued that powerful male-dominated consumer industries and mass media have been a leading cause of women's oppression. In this view, the beauty industry has added to, even to some extent supplanted, the legal and economic discriminations that have for so long subordinated women. Manufactured images of ideal beauty and supermodel glamour have come to dominate women's consciousness. And the act of beautifying, though it seems enticing and freely chosen, is really compulsory work, so narcissistic, time-consuming, and absorbing as to limit women's achievements.[2]

To many critics, the story begins and ends there. But this view is partial and, in many respects, wrong. For one thing, this business for women was largely built *by* women. In the early stages of the developing cosmetics industry, from the 1890s to the 1920s, women formulated and organized "beauty culture" to a remarkable extent. The very notion of femininity, emphasizing women's innate taste for beauty, opened opportunities for women in this business, even as it restricted them elsewhere. And women seized their chances, becoming entrepreneurs, inventors, manufacturers, distributors, and promoters. Handicapped in pursuing standard business practices, they resourcefully founded salons, beauty schools, correspondence courses, and mail-order companies; they pioneered in the development of modern franchising and direct-sales marketing strategies. The beauty trade they developed did not depend upon advertising as its impetus. Rather, it capitalized on patterns of women's social life—their old customs of visiting, conversation, and religious observance, as well as their new presence in shops, clubs, and theaters.

Strikingly, many of the most successful entrepreneurs were immigrant, working-class, or black women. Coming from poor, socially marginal backgrounds, they played a surprisingly central role in redefining mainstream ideals of beauty and femininity in the twentieth century. Focusing new attention on the face and figure, they made the pursuit of beauty visible and respectable. In many ways, they set the stage for Madison Avenue, whose narrowly drawn images of flawless beauty bombard us today. But before the rise of the mass market, these early businesswomen served up a variety of visions of womanly beauty. Elizabeth Arden was a Canadian immigrant and "working girl" who remade herself into a symbol of haute femininity; she carved a "class market" for cosmetics by catering to the social prestige and power of wealthy and upwardly mobile white women. In contrast, such black entrepreneurs as Madam C. J. Walker and Annie Turnbo Malone promoted a form of beauty culture entwined in the everyday lives of poor African-American women. They consciously created job opportunities for women, addressed the politics of appearance, and committed their profits to their community. Indeed, the history of these businesswomen flatly contradicts the view that the beauty industry worked only *against* women's interests.

What about the women who bought and used beauty products? Cosmetics have often figured in the old stereotype of women as vain and foolish, a stereotype contemporary critics too often reinforce. How could a rational being eat arsenic to improve her complexion, spread hormones on her face, believe promises of a wrinkle-free future, and pay exorbitant prices for an ounce of prevention?

Answering these questions requires us to listen more closely to women's own voices and to consider how *they* understood beautifying in their own lives. Remarkably, women from across the country, from different social classes and racial-ethnic groups, enthusiastically embraced cosmetics—especially makeup—in the early twentieth century. This acceptance was no mere fad or fashion, but a larger change in the way women perceived their identities and displayed them on the face and body. For some, cosmetics use quickly became a self-diminishing habit: Women reported as early as the 1930s that advertising and social pressures to be attractive lowered their self-esteem. Others, however, boldly applied their lipsticks in public and asserted their right to self-creation through the "makeover" of self-image.

Today the possibility of transformation through cosmetics is often belittled as a delusion, "hope in a jar" that only masks the fact of women's oppression. In truth, women knew then—as they do now—precisely what they were buying. Again and again they reported their delight in beautifying—in the sensuous creams and tiny compacts, the riot of colors, the mastery of makeup skills, the touch of hands, the sharing of knowledge and advice. Indeed, the pleasures of fantasy and desire were an integral part of the product—and these included not only dreams of romance and marriage, but also the modern yearning to take part in public life.

Beauty culture, then, should be understood not only as a type of commerce but as a system of meaning that helped women navigate the changing conditions of modern social experience. "Modernity" is, to be sure, a slippery concept. It describes the paradoxical effects of an urban, capitalist order—its rationalized work, bureaucracy, and efficiency, on the one hand, its fleeting encounters, self-consciousness, and continuous novelty, on the other. Women's rendezvous with modernity brought them into a public realm that was not always welcoming.[3]

Their changing status as workers, citizens, consumers, and pleasure seekers was acknowledged cosmetically: During the nineteenth century, the "public woman" was a painted prostitute; by its end, women from all walks of life were "going public": Women crowded onto trolleys, promenaded the streets, frequented the theaters, and shopped in the new palaces of consumption. They found jobs not only in the traditional work of domestic service, sewing, and farming, but also in offices, stores, and other urban occupations that required new kinds of face-to-face interactions. A new "marriage market" substituted dating for courtship, and the dance hall for the front porch; a new sense of sexual freedom emerged.

For women experiencing these social changes, the act of beautifying often became a lightning rod for larger conflicts over female autonomy and social roles. Among white women, for example, popular concern centered on the morality of visible makeup—rouge, lipstick, mascara, and eye shadow. In the black community, beauty culture was explicitly a political issue, long before the contemporary feminist movement made it so. Skin whiteners and hair straighteners were the tokens in a heated debate: Against charges of white emulation and self-loathing, many black women invoked their rights to social participation and cultural legitimacy precisely through their use of beauty aids.

Still, for all the efforts to fix the meaning of cosmetics in relation to beauty standards, ideals of femininity, profit-making, and politics, the significance of these substances remains elusive. What do women declare when they "put on a face"? Is making up an act of deception, a confirmation of "natural" female identity, a self-conscious "put-on"? By the light of today's TV shopping channels, as celebrities hawk their cosmetic lines, it may seem that the promise of beauty is nothing but a commercial myth that binds women to its costly pursuit. Critics are not wrong to address the power of corporations, advertisers, and mass media to foster and profit from this myth. But they have overlooked the web of intimate rituals, social relationships, and female institutions that gave form to American beauty culture. Over the decades, mothers and daughters have taught each other about cosmetics, cliques have formed around looks, women have shared their beauty secrets and, in the process, created intimacy. Not only tools of deception and illusion, then, these little jars tell a rich history of women's ambition, pleasure, and community.

Masks and Faces

A sociable Victorian woman, just eighteen years old, developed a sunburn at a charity garden party, "when for a moment I stood without raising my sunshade to the direct glare of the sun." Her friend Abigail sent her a recipe to relieve the "troublesome redness," with the assurance "that she had tried it and that it had proved most satisfying." The instructions read: "To a pint of white wine vinegar put a full handful of well-sifted wheat bran, steeping it for several hours and adding the yolks of five eggs with two grains of ambergris. Distill and bottle for fourteen days." If she used the mixture, "a polished whiteness of the complexion will ensue." So wrote a proper young lady of the 1860s in her book of beauty secrets, marked "private papers" and found years later by her niece.[1]

The recipe captures much of what was distinctive about cosmetics in the nineteenth century, before the rise of a mass beauty industry. At that time, most American women did not wear visible face makeup, although they avidly sought recipes to improve their complexions and achieve the ideal of white, genteel beauty. Following her friend's instructions, this young woman would have found all the ingredients but one in the kitchen; a druggist would have supplied the ambergris, used in perfumes as a fixative. The recipe itself supposedly originated long ago in a Spanish royal court and, like many nineteenth-century "beauty secrets," boasted an old pedigree.

In contrast, "Mary C.," a St. Louis housewife, chose to lighten and beautify her complexion by "painting" her skin. At age twenty-four, she began applying a commercial skin lightener, Laird's Bloom of Youth, to her face, influenced, perhaps, by illustrated advertisements that promised beauty, wealth, and social power: "With this essential a lady appears handsome, even if her features are not perfect." In 1877, she was admitted to the St. Louis Female Hospital, her arms paralyzed from the elbows down. At first, she denied using hair dyes or cosmetics and was released, only to be readmitted sixteen months later in worsened condition. Finally she confessed that she had been applying Bloom of Youth for years. Moreover, she said that after her first hospital stay a lady had advised her to mix "a quarter of a pound of white flake and two ounces of glycerine" as a skin lightener. Alternating this mixture with a bottle of Bloom of Youth, she made the two preparations last "generally about three weeks." Not long thereafter, Mary C. died of lead poisoning. Publishing the case in a medical journal, her physician condemned women's vanity as he exposed a dangerous commercial product.[2]

These two women had much in common in their pursuit of beauty: They desired a lighter complexion, mixed their own preparations—and tried to conceal their behavior. Choosing a homemade whitening lotion or a commercially manufactured lead-based paint, however, carried different implications. In the nineteenth century, Americans insisted on a fundamental distinction between skin-improving and skin-masking substances. The word *cosmetic* usually referred to creams, lotions, and other substances that acted on the skin to protect and correct it. Paints and enamels, in contrast, were white and tinted liquids, mainly produced commercially, that covered the skin. "Paints must not be confounded with Cosmetics, which often really do impart whiteness, freshness, suppleness, and brilliancy to the skin," instructed one

George W. Laird Co., Bloom of Youth *Advertisement, around 1870.*

writer; "these consequently assist Nature, and make amends for her defects." Paints, however, masked Nature's handiwork to hide expression and truth behind an "encrusted mould," a "mummy surface."[3] Depending on their composition, face powders were identified either as paint or cosmetic; starch and rice powders were often used as skin protectors, while lead-based powders were classified as paints. Tinted powders and paints were highly controversial materials that aroused social, ethical, and health concerns. Skin-improving cosmetics were not: From urban ladies to farm wives, women were familiar with these substances as part of their knowledge of beauty and the body.

Nineteenth-century American women inherited a tradition of cosmetic preparation, which freely borrowed from a variety of sources and reached back through the centuries. Englishwomen in the 1600s and 1700s knew "cosmetical physic," as it was called, just as they understood how to cook, preserve, garden, and care for the sick. Blending housewifery, therapeutics, and aesthetics, cosmetic preparation was a branch of useful knowledge women were expected to master. They learned to identify herbs, gather roots, distill their essences, and compound simple skin remedies. Clearing the complexion, producing good color, or taking away the effects of smallpox, these cosmetics combined the arts of beautifying with the science of bodily care.[4]

Early cookbooks, household manuals, and medical treatises commonly included recipes for "Beautifying Waters, Oils, Ointments, and Powders," codifying formulas once circulated orally. Indeed, some of these household guides acknowledged the oral tradition by citing a "traveller," "a great professour of Art," or an "outlandish Gentlewoman" as the source of recipes. These works did not strictly distinguish between cures for disease and cosmetics for beautifying. Medicinal waters to treat dyspepsia and consumption differed little, in materials and preparation, from toilet waters to perfume the body or relieve sunburn. Nicholas Culpeper's popular *London Dispensatory*, for example, included "such Medicines as adorn the Body, adding comeliness & beauty to it." As Culpeper observed, "Beauty is a blessing of God, and every one ought to preserve it."[5]

Brought to the colonies by English immigrants, the cosmetic formulas of Culpeper and others blended with American Indian, French, Spanish, as well as African traditions in ways now difficult to disentangle. Native Americans used indigenous plants and their own systems of therapeutics to treat skin problems. Some of these cures became popularized as "Indian medicine." John Gunn, a doctor practicing on the Tennessee frontier and author of a book on domestic medicine, recommended puccoon root steeped in vinegar for skin disorders; known as "Indian paint," puccoon root was used in Algonquin remedies. Slaves followed simple cosmetic and grooming techniques that originated in West Africa but also borrowed from American Indian and European practices. They applied substances from the kitchen or garden, smoothing down hair with grease or reddening cheeks with crushed berries. Some continued to plait their hair, make cornrows, or use headwraps in the West African manner, while others tied their hair with string or used other methods to straighten it and then arrange it in Anglo-American styles.[6]

Similar practices sometimes surfaced in different folk cultures and distinct regions. For example, the custom of using the "warm urine of a little boy" as a cosmetic, recounted by several generations of Mexican Americans, also appears in early Anglo-American manuals as a cure for skin disorders and freckles. John Gunn, for instance, advised that a blue dye containing indigo and urine, "made by country people to color their cloth," would heal the skin.[7]

Like household hints and cooking recipes, cosmetic knowledge spread by word of mouth, within families and between neighbors. Women often compiled their own recipe books and passed them on to their daughters. Scattered among food recipes and medical formulas were instructions for compounding cosmetics. The cookbooks of two New England women, a Mrs. Lowell and Mrs. Charles Smith, for instance, contained recipes for making tooth powder, cold cream, and salve for soreness after breast-feeding, all preparations with a therapeutic or sanitary purpose. Occasionally a beauty recipe appeared: Mrs. Smith wrote down instructions for an almond paste to perfume the body, while Mrs. Lowell included a tinted lip salve, from a recipe dating back to 1694, that required "sallad oyl," redwood, and balsam. Eleanor Custis Lewis, the granddaughter of George Washington, often made pots of lip salve from wax, hogs' lard, spermaceti, almond oil, balsam, alkanet root, raisins, and sugar. "This was Grandmama's lip salve & I never knew any so good," she wrote.[8]

Recipes for cosmetics began to be published in the United States in the late eighteenth and early nineteenth centuries. By this time, methods of physical care formerly treated as a single body of knowledge had split into such distinct "disciplines" as medicine, cooking, and grooming. Physicians and pharmacists increasingly claimed the medical and pharmaceutical dimensions of health care as their own. But throughout the nineteenth century, natural healing recipes and hygienic practices remained women's domain. Indeed, women's authority in these areas may have been strengthened early in the century, as a popular health movement emphasizing self-help, prevention, and natural remedies gained ground.[9]

Women's access to information about cosmetics expanded even more with the publishing boom of the 1840s and 1850s. Ladies' guides to beauty and fashion self-consciously addressed bourgeois women— and all those who aspired to that rank. Like etiquette books, they explained how to navigate the genteel social world by cultivating a well-groomed face and form; cheaper paperback editions carried the same message to female millworkers and domestic servants. At the same time, household encyclopedias compiled cosmetic recipes in voluminous works that offered, as one put it, "anything you want to know." These peculiarly American creations promoted family self-sufficiency, good citizenship, and do-it-yourself virtue, even as they plagiarized one another. Sold throughout the United States, often by traveling agents and peddlers, the compendiums could be found in farming, artisan, as well as middle-class households.[10]

The two genres diverged in tone, reflecting different class and cultural orientations. Encyclopedias were haphazard acculumations of beauty knowledge, cataloguing page after page of recipes with only an occasional warning or moral judgment. Simple garden substances—the juice of elderberries or burned cork to darken lashes, for example—could yield satisfactory results with no one the wiser. The ladies' guides, in contrast, worried over questions of women's health and morality, but nevertheless recited harmful formulas for beautifying—and even painting—the face. Still, both genres point to the growing importance of maintaining a good appearance in an increasingly commercial and mobile society.

Recipes in such household manuals and beauty guides frequently presumed a notion of the body and health based on the ancient theory of the humors. In this view, four humors or bodily fluids—blood, phlegm, yellow bile, and black bile—exist in different proportions to determine a person's health. The humors in turn produce four human temperaments—sanguine, phlegmatic, choleric, and melancholic—that reveal themselves in the appearance and condition of the skin. Humoralism regarded the inner and outer aspects of the body not as separate, bounded entities but as elastic dimensions in flux. A good complexion thus was a matter of temperament, health, and spirit.[11]

Sir Hugh Plat in his 1651 cookbook, *Delights for Ladies,* illustrates the basic principle. An attorney with a red, pimpled face, who had spent freely on medicine to no avail, was told to line "double linnen socks of a pretty bigness" with bay salt "well dryed and powdered," then "every Morning and Evening dry his socks by the fire, and put them on again." According to Plat, the lawyer's face cleared in fourteen days: The salt had pulled out moisture and cooled the body through the feet, which modulated the flow of bodily fluids and reduced "exceeding high and furious colour" in the face. Although socks full of salt may have been an extreme measure, early English manuals commonly recommended barley water, vinegar, wine, and lemons to cool the blood or draw out ruddiness.[12]

Many cosmetic recipes also affirmed popular beliefs in the power of nature's cycles, astrology, and magic. They cautioned housewives to concoct simple compounds using only herbs, roots, and flowers. To remove freckles, Plat advised, "Wash your face in the wane of the Moon with a sponge morning and evening with the distilled water of Elder leaves, letting the same dry into the skin." Others instructed readers on how to gather May dew, considered the purest of waters, or invoked the curative powers of spring by insisting on strawberry-water, frog-spawn water, the juice from birch saplings, or the dew from young vines.[13]

These beliefs did not survive the new medical techniques and scientific discoveries of the Enlightenment. In the volatile struggle among apothecaries, barber-surgeons, chemists, and medical doctors, humoralism in particular was discredited as a framework for medical treatment. Nevertheless, these various therapeutic traditions persisted as a source of lore about health, hygiene, and beauty, and as a lexicon for reading individual character in the human face. Nineteenth-century American beauty guides and household encyclopedias warned that freckles were difficult to eradicate because it was "dangerous to drive back the humors which produce them." Recipes called for virgin milk and the first juice of spring plants. Some recipes even followed principles of medieval alchemy, like the "cosmetic juice" made by filling a hollowed-out lemon with sugar, covering it with gold leaf, and roasting it in a fire. A British journalist observed in 1838 that the "superstition" about bathing the face in May dew was "not yet quite extinct"; indeed, folklorists recorded such beliefs among Americans of different ethnic backgrounds as late as the 1950s and 1960s.[14]

One old tradition, also deriving from the humors, survived the Enlightenment intact: the importance of regular habits of breathing, eating, sleeping, excretion, and emotional control. These habits were known as hygienic regimen or the "non-naturals," so called because they did not form part of the living body but nevertheless affected bodily fluids, humoral balance, and complexion. Culpeper's *Pharmocopoeia* warned, for example, that applying external beauty preparations would do no good unless the bowels were clean. Hygienic regimen only became more important in nineteenth-century American culture, which especially endorsed cleanliness, diet, and temperance as the path toward a sanitized, well-regulated body and beautiful complexion. "If you mind these things," *Gunn's Domestic Medicine* noted, "you need care nothing about *cosmetics* and *lotions,* and such nonsense, which always sooner or later do immense injury." Experts advised bathing in various mineral waters of different temperatures and washing the face only in pure spring water. One writer declared, "It were better to wash twenty times a day, than to allow a dirty spot to remain on any part of the skin." Cool water baths and vegetable diets that did not "produce much animal heat" were recommended to people with ruddy complexions.[15]

The reciprocal relation of the inner and outer body became a staple of the burgeoning trade in drugs and elixirs. Warning against exclusive reliance on external treatments, one vendor advised ingesting arsenic wafers to improve a poor complexion, in addition to moderate diet, frequent bathing, and exercise. Nerve tonics and blood purifiers promised to cure "disfiguring humors, humiliating eruptions, itching and burning tortures, loathsome sores," and every other skin affliction by correcting internal imbalances. The Potter Drug Company hedged its bets, urging consumers both to swallow its Cuticura patent remedy and to apply it to the skin to relieve skin disorders.[16]

By the mid-nineteenth century, the expansion of the market began to transform women's knowledge of beauty preparations. A growing commerce in herbs, oils, and chemicals enabled women to secure formerly exotic and costly substances. Women continued to mix simple complexion recipes—horseradish and sour milk, lemon juice and sugar—but many now sought ingredients available only at pharmacies or general stores. A recipe for Turkish rouge, for instance, instructed women to "get three cents worth of alkanet chips at any druggist's." Although people living in the country's interior often could not afford or even acquire unusual ingredients, drug wholesalers and distributors used new transportation networks to extend their availability greatly. Domestic and imported drugs, spices, dyes, and essences, as well as commercially made beauty preparations, filled their catalogues. These businesses increasingly referred to visible powders and paints as cosmetics, to make them more acceptable by blurring the distinction between skin-masking and skin-improving products. Although paint continued to be a term of moral censure, cosmetics gradually became the general name for all beauty preparations.[17]

Women who did not make their own cosmetics had two choices. They could go to a pharmacist (or, less often, a hairdresser) who compounded preparations under a "house" label, or they could purchase commercial products made by perfumers and "patent cosmetic" firms. The distinction was not a trivial one, for it pitched local druggists using standard formulas against remote manufacturers of secret skin remedies and beauty aids.

Druggists' invoice records and daybooks suggest the small but perceptible place of cosmetics in nineteenth-century trade. Urban and small-town druggists alike kept collections of cosmetics recipes, drawing upon published formularies and testing their own inventions. Edward Townsend, a Philadelphia druggist, wrote down recipes for skin problems from many sources and frequently logged their effectiveness. One cold cream would "keep sweet during warm weather," a freckle lotion was "said to be a good article," he noted in his formulary. Townsend, like most druggists, compounded generic versions of cosmetics women knew by name, from old standbys like Gowland's Lotion to such newer brand-name goods as Miner's Cold Cream and Hunter's Invisible Face Powder.[18] George Putney and Bryan Hough, small-town pharmacists in New York and New Jersey, also had on hand ingredients to compound their own cosmetics. A few commercial preparations, including cologne, hair oil, shaving cream, pomades, and skin whitener, appeared on their shelves in the 1860s. Stock from wholesalers increased gradually in the decades that followed. In the 1880s, for instance, Putney offered a cold cream from the big wholesale drug supplier McKesson & Robbins in addition to the cream he put up himself.[19]

As Putney's and Hough's businesses suggest, it took commercial preparations a long time to establish themselves. There was no identifi-able "cosmetics industry" in the nineteenth century, no large and dis-tinct sector of the economy devoted to beauty products. In 1849, the value of manufactured toiletries throughout the United States totalled only $355,000. Although sales grew through the 1800s, they remained small in scale compared to the widespread popularity of such con-sumer goods as patent medicines and soaps. Still, the trade catalogues, advertisements, broadsides, and advice books of the period reveal a growing interest in these products.[20]

A variety of manufacturers made commercial preparations. Appar-ently, the most desirable came from abroad. Commercial agents im-ported precious cosmetics and paints to sell in fashionable American shops; these included English lotions, French perfumes, Portuguese rouge dishes, and "Chinese Boxes of Color," containing color-saturated papers of rouge, pearl powder, and eyebrow blacking. Some American drug wholesalers and retailers also began to branch into cosmetics manufacturing, and a small number of businesses whose primary prod-ucts were hair goods, perfume, or even house paint made cosmetics a sideline. The Philadelphia firm T. W. Dyott, for example, began in 1814 as an importer and wholesaler of drugs, chemicals, and dye stuffs, and soon produced a line of cosmetics, including cold cream, skin lotion, hair powder, and pomatum. The firm touted its Balm of Iberia, which swiftly "improves the skin to perfection; rendering it smooth, white, odoriferous and healthy." Dyott maintained a large warehouse, adver-tised in newspapers and broadsheets, and sold through agents, mainly concentrated along the Eastern seaboard but extending as far west as the Missouri Territory. The company was among the first merchandisers to develop a national market, but cosmetics were a fraction of its trade.[21]

Perfumers too played an important part in the early beauty busi-ness. Requiring specialized knowledge of essences and distillation, perfumery was considered a skilled craft distinct from the drug trade. According to several perfumers, American demand for fragrant creams and lotions was "general" and came from all social classes: "The pomade of the fashionable belle becomes . . . the bear's grease of the kitchen maid." In addition to importing cosmetics from Paris and London, American manufacturers, often emigrants from France, began to make cheap and popular imitations. By mid-century, the Philadelphia firms of Jules Hauel, Roussel, and Bazin not only dominated perfume manufacturing, but produced full lines of beauty products.[22]

The most controversial beauty aids on the market were made by patent cosmetics companies. Historically monarchs in early modern Europe had granted patent rights to encourage innovation and industry. In the nineteenth century, however, the term "patent" simply referred to medicines and beauty preparations sold through specific techniques of national advertising and distribution. By disseminating trade cards, almanacs, and handbills, patent cosmetic manufacturers often bypassed traditional distributors and retailers to address consumers directly. They competed fiercely with one another, using psychological appeals and before-and-after pictures, touting secret formulas and miraculous transformations. Dr. Gouraud's cosmetics and Jones's preparations, for example, sparred in the pages of the New York *Daily Tribune,* with such rhymes as this:

> Do you hear that lady talk?
> See her face destroyed by chalk;
> Once't was white, but now, 'tis yellow,
> Coarse and rough, and dark and sallow.

The themes of elite fashion and social contest often characterized the sales pitch for patent cosmetics. Thus Laird's Bloom of Youth, with its deadly ingredients, advertised itself through tableaux of high society—ladies at dinner, gossiping about a rival's face and form; a languid beauty gazing into her mirror; a fashionable woman the center of attention at a ball.[23]

City dwellers could purchase commercial cosmetics in a variety of outlets. In the mid-nineteenth century, hairdressers and specialty stores sold combs, perfumes, and toilet articles in New York, Philadelphia, and Boston. Carroll and Hutchinson, a New York fancy goods dealer whose motto was "we deal in the beautiful," invited ladies "to call during their promenade in Broadway," examine the shop's artwork, and browse the jewelry, stationery, and cosmetics for sale.[24]

Women in smaller cities and towns, far removed from the centers of fashion, also had access to these products. A sales agent sold Gouraud's in the factory town of Lowell, Massachusetts, and claimed that the "articles seem to be selling very well, considering there is no advertising done here." These complexion creams and rouges may have held a particular appeal for the Yankee women who worked in the textile mills and whose modish style expressed their newfound sense of independence and urbanity.[25]

Peddlers and traders even carried the cheaper brands into distant farming and frontier communities. Although the "patent-nostrum men have their head-quarters in the cities," warned one writer, "it is the shelves of country stores that they load with their quack stuff." Self-help manuals often advised would-be entrepreneurs to peddle cosmetics; these wares could "command a quick sale and insure a full pocket."[26]

Although the commerce in beauty aids remained limited, critical voices grew ever louder. While sellers claimed their wares rapidly improved and beautified the complexion, many advice writers and physicians argued otherwise, noting that the dramatic brilliance imparted to the skin was short-lived. At best, these goods covered up flaws, acting locally on the face rather than healing skin problems. Constant use, doctors warned, damaged the epidermis and internal organs and led to death.

The secrecy surrounding patent cosmetics, especially those "advertised with high-sounding names," heightened the alarm. Americans distrusted cosmetics sold in the market, and with reason: Mercury, lead, and arsenic appeared in the formulas of a number of fashionable beauty preparations. Moreover, the exorbitant price of these toiletries, "sold at twelve to fifteen times above the actual cost," contributed to the impression of hucksterism. It seems manufacturers had already

learned a cardinal principle of selling cosmetics: that consumers measured the value of "beauty secrets" not by how cheap they were but
how dear. Buyers also rightly worried that distant manufacturers
evaded responsibility for their products' defects. Actress Lola Montez
expressed the opinion of many: Women should become their *own
manufacturer*—not only as a matter of *economy,* but of *safety.*"[27]

These objections to patent cosmetics echoed the common view that
costly chemical compounds and mineral paints were dangerous, unlike
traditional homemade preparations. Patent compounds were also associated with social climbers and urban sophisticates concerned more
with making a good appearance than with living a virtuous life. For
many observers, the commodity form of cosmetics quite literally represented the corrosive effects of the market economy—the false colors of
sellers, the superficial brilliance of advertisers, the masking of true
value. Abolitionist and journalist Lydia Maria Child singled out
Gouraud's and Jones's shrill handbills as troubling signs of a new
"commercial age" in American life. She satirized patent cosmetics advertising—the exclusive beauty secret that everybody could purchase—but also observed how skillfully pitchmen appealed to human
vanity.[28] Warning against imitations, adulteration, deceitful advertising, and unfair pricing, advice writers began to address women not only
as household manufacturers but also as consumers who were increasingly negotiating the world of commerce.

The outcry over commercial beauty preparations focused especially on
the morality of masking or transforming features and raised anew longstanding questions about women's nature and social role. Powder and
paint had always been more identified with the feminine than the masculine in Anglo-American culture, but in the eighteenth century, their
use was as much a matter of class and rank as gender. In England,
enamel, rouge, white powder, masks, and beauty patches were instru-
ments of fashion that covered pockmarks, drew attention to good features, and served as props in the spectacle of court society and posh

urban life. Elite colonists of both sexes imitated the aristocratic mode and sought the grooming aids of apothecaries and hairdressers. Powder and paint proclaimed nobility and social prestige, as essential to fashionable high culture as ornamental clothing and tea drinking.[29]

A challenge to this view came during the American Revolution. In a republican society, manly citizens and virtuous women were expected to reject costly beauty preparations and other signs of aristocratic style. The transformation in self-presentation was most pronounced in men, who spurned luxurious fabrics, perfume, and adornments as effete and unmanly. In a personal declaration of independence, Benjamin Franklin discarded his periwig. The "great masculine renunciation," as fashion historians call it, replaced spectacular male display, once considered an essential symbol of monarchial rule, with a subdued and understated appearance. Republican ideals of manly citizenship reinforced the idea: Men need not display their authority, since their virtue was inherent. The democratization of American politics after 1830 further advanced the new view of male self-presentation. The point of no return may have occurred in 1840, when Representative Charles Ogle, in a speech before Congress, attacked Martin Van Buren's presidency *and* his manhood by ridiculing the toiletries on Van Buren's dressing table. Corinthian Oil of Cream and Concentrated Persian Essence no longer endorsed the gentleman of rank but intimated the emasculated dandy.[30]

As a mercantile and manufacturing class gained power, businessmen avoided artificiality in appearance in an effort to gain trust in the marketplace. In turn, men who adorned their features were treated with contempt. Novelist Sara Willis, for instance, disdained a "be-curled, be-perfumed popinjay"; Walt Whitman said of a "painted" man on Broadway, with "bright red cheeks and singularly jetty black eyebrows," that he "looks like a doll." Of course men continued to pay attention to the mirror. Shaving paraphernalia, hair dyes and "rejuvenators," bay rum and brilliantine were all sold on the market throughout the nineteenth century. Barber supply catalogues featured face washes, colognes, tinted talcum powders, and "cosmetique," a perfumed waxy substance used to touch up gray hair. Except for shaving and hair care, however, cosmetic practices among men became largely covert and unacknowledged.[31]

Women also were encouraged to shun paints and artifice in the service of new notions of female virtue and natural beauty. Early nineteenth-century literature bound the feminine to ideals of sexual chastity and transcendent purity. These views took root under the growing authority of the middle class, which perceived beautifying as the "natural disposition of woman," but only as it reflected those feminine ideals.[32]

A belief in physiognomic principles, that outer appearance corresponded to inner character, underlay these views and echoed the earlier belief in humoralism. Reinvigorated by Johann Kaspar Lavater in the 1780s, physiognomy and its nineteenth-century cousin phrenology claimed to reveal personality through the study of facial and bodily features. These pseudosciences classified men in terms of a diverse range of occupations and aptitudes. When it came to women, however, their subject was solely beauty and virtue. Thus physical beauty originated not in visual sensation and formal aesthetics, but in its "representative and correspondent" relationship to goodness.[33]

Assessments of female beauty, however, often unconsciously reversed the physiognomic equation, submerging individuals to types and reducing moral attributes to physical ones. Hair, skin, and eye color frequently stood as signs of women's inner virtue. The facial ideal was fair and white skin, blushing cheeks, ruby lips, expressive eyes, and a "bloom" of youth—the lily and the rose. Although some commentators disagreed, most condemned excessive pallor or coarse ruddiness. Nor was the ideal an opaque white surface, but a luminous complexion that disclosed thought and feeling.

If beauty registered women's goodness, then achieving beauty posed a moral dilemma. Sisters Judith and Hannah Murray neatly captured the middle-class viewpoint in their 1827 gift book, *The Toilet*, made by hand and sold for charity. Each page carried a riddle in verse and an image of a cosmetic jar, mirror, or other item typically found in a lady's boudoir. The pictures were pasted onto the page in such a way that when lifted, they revealed the answer to the puzzle. "Apply this precious liquid to the face / And every feature beams with youth and grace." A pot of "universal beautifier"? No, the secret lay in "good humour." In like manner, the only "genuine rouge" was modesty, the "best white paint" innocence. These riddles must have had a wide appeal. *Harper's Bazaar* described an "old-fashioned" fair in 1872, where a girl sold for a dime little packages "said to contain the purest of cosmetics"—the Murrays' moral recipes.[34]

The Murray sisters acknowledged the allure of cosmetics in elegant bottles, but maintained that only virtue could produce the effects they promised. Even so, their gift book reinforced the widespread belief that beauty was simultaneously woman's duty and desire. *Godey's Lady's Book,* the arbiter of middle-class women's culture, took up the theme, advocating "moral cosmetics" in tales of sad appearances transformed by plain soap and clean living. In "Lucy Franklin," an unattractive woman whose complexion combined the "colour of dingy parchment" with a "livid hue" becomes lovely under the guidance and friendship of an older woman. Happiness, the story concludes, is "a better beautifier than all the cosmetics and freckle washes in the world."[35]

Etiquette books addressed to African Americans, published later in the nineteenth century, similarly distinguished between cosmetic artifice and the cultivation of real beauty from within. Mary Armstrong, training Hampton Institute students to display signs of middle-class refinement and modesty, considered the use of visible cosmetics disgraceful. "Paint and powder, however skillfully their true names may be concealed under the mask of 'Liquid Bloom,' or 'Lily Enamel,' can never change their real character, but remain always unclean, false, unwholesome," she insisted.[36]

Nothing was more essential to beauty than self-control and sexual purity. "Those who are in the habit of yielding to the sallies of passion, or indeed to violent excitement of any kind," cautioned Countess de Calabrella, "will find it impossible to retain a good complexion." Management of emotion nevertheless coexisted with "management of the complexion," as one guide called it: pinching cheeks or biting lips to create a rosy hue, or wearing colors, especially in bonnet linings, to produce the optical effect of lightening the skin.[37] The ideal of pure, natural beauty disguised the way women's appearances were in fact dictated by middle-class cultural requirements.

The new feminine ideal challenged but did not entirely displace earlier perceptions of women as sexually corrupt, deceitful, and vain, vices that face paint had long signified. In his 1616 *Discourse Against Painting and Tincturing,* Puritan Thomas Tuke had endorsed the use of washes made with barley, lemons, or herbs, the cosmetics of domestic manufacture. But, he warned, "a painted face is a false face, a true falshood [*sic*], not a true face." Women who painted usurped the divine order, as poet John Donne put it, taking "the pencill out of God's hand." Indeed, some viewed the cosmetic arts as a form of witchcraft. The specter of "designing women" led the English Parliament in 1770 to pass an act that annulled marriages of those who ensnared husbands through the use of "scents, paints, cosmetic washes, artificial teeth, false hair, Spanish wool, iron stays, hoops, high-heeled shoes and bolstered hips." That a woman with rouge pot and powder box might practice cosmetic sorcery suggests both an ancient fear of female power and a new secular concern: In a rapidly commercializing and fluid social world, any woman with a bewitching face might secure a husband and make her fortune.[38]

Nineteenth-century moralists continued to view face paint as "corporeal hypocrisy," a mask that did not conceal female vice and vanity. They invoked Jezebel, the biblical figure who represented the dangerous power of women to seduce and arouse sexual desire. Painting her eyes with kohl and loving finery, "Oriental" Jezebel was "the originator and patroness of idolatry," whose arrogance and pride brought death and destruction. Her example taught that women had a duty to spurn adornment, submit to authority, and cultivate piety.[39]

To most Americans, the painted woman was simply a prostitute who brazenly advertised her immoral profession through rouge and kohl. Newspapers, tracts, and songs associated paint and prostitution so closely as to be a generic figure of speech. In New York, "painted, diseased, drunken women, bargaining themselves away," could be found in theaters, while in New Orleans, "painted Jezebels exhibited themselves in public carriages" during Mardi Gras. Mining camp balladeers sang:

> *Hangtown Gals are plump and rosy,*
> *Hair in ringlets mighty cosy.*
> *Painted cheeks and gassy bonnets;*
> *Touch them and they'll sting like hornets.*[40]

The older view of the painted woman informed the efforts of the middle class to distinguish itself from a corrupt upper class. In *Godey's Lady's Book*, face paint and white washes often appeared as the potent temptations of dissolute high society to be avoided by respectable young ladies. New York journalists at mid-century exposed the "ultra-fashionable" woman as all art and no substance. James McCabe offered a typically harsh assessment in 1872:

> She is a compound frequently of false hair, false teeth, padding of various kinds, paint, powder and enamel. Her face is "touched up," or painted and lined by a professional adorner of women, and she utterly destroys the health of her skin by her foolish use of cosmetics. . . . So common has the habit of resorting to these things become, that it is hard to say whether the average woman of fashion is a work of nature or a work of art.[41]

Lurid accounts described the "enamelling studio" as a den of female vice, where fashionable women could "get their complexions 'made up' by the 'quarter' or 'year.'" The enameller first "filled up the ugly self-made wrinkles and the natural indentations, with a plastic or yielding paste," wrote photographer H. J. Rodgers. "Then the white enamel is

Every one recognizes your ability to paint (Yourself).

Trade card satirizing the fashionable woman, around 1870.

carefully laid on with a brush and finished with the red." Fast women, it seemed, would do anything for beauty—paint their veins blue, powder the hands white, remove superfluous hair, expose their eyes to dangerous chemicals. Belladonna gave a "languishing, half-sentimental, half-sensual look," chemist Arnold Cooley noted, while prussic acid helped "fashionable ladies and actresses, to enhance the clearness and brilliancy of their eyes before appearing in public."[42]

Such descriptions of the "aesthetic side to vice" drew upon well-worn images of the painted woman to rein in contemporary women's behavior. Anxiety focused especially on the family, perhaps because the nascent feminist movement, the growth of women's wage work and migration to cities, even the rise of fashion itself all implied that women were loosening familial bonds and duties to pursue individual ends. Uneasy commentators described women who used their wits and beauty to gain advantage in the marriage market, wives more interested in dress than motherhood, and—the conclusive sign of female degradation—women who frequented both the enameller's studio and the abortionist's clinic.[43]

Occasionally a writer revealed the deeper psychic and cultural dread paint provoked, its power to attract and repulse. Richard Henry Dana came across painted women in the dance halls and saloons of Halifax in 1842. One prostitute in particular caught his eye. She was the "best looking at a distance," and Dana approached her, seeking to rescue her from sin, yet slipping into the role of virtuous seducer, a situation the prostitute herself sensed and manipulated. Upon closer in-

"FALSE FACES."—AN "ENAMELING" STUDIO ON BROADWAY.

From George Ellington, The Women of New York, *1869.*

spection of the woman, however, he wavered between fascination and loathing: "every sign of health, natural animation & passion had left her, & with a wasted form, hectic & fallen cheek, glassy eyes, & a frisette fastened to her head, she looked like a painted galvinised corpse." Despite his sympathy toward a fallen woman once "handsome and in better circumstances," he could not contain his fear of corruption from a woman whose painted face was a mask of death.[44]

Abolitionist William Lloyd Garrison exposed the sexual resonance hidden in the formulaic phrase *painted woman.* In 1829, before he had achieved fame in the antislavery movement, Garrison was engaged to be married. When a friend wrote him that his fiancée wore visible cosmetics, he replied, "So!—Mary Cunningham '*paints*'—does she?" Garrison imaginatively combined the art of seduction with that of a cosmetician:

> She shall buy her own brushes, *with her own money;* but, if she insist upon it, I'll be the painter—and a rare one I should make! Something, perhaps, after this sort: Hold your head steadily, dearest—so—very still—you shall look in the glass presently— a little more vermilion, a denser flame of health on this cheek—I like to see the *blood,* Mary, mounting up to the very temples, commingling with that lily whiteness—your eyebrows are hardly coal black—a little darker, in order to give a deeper brilliance to your starry eyes, or rather to their light—shut your mouth, and draw back that little saucy tongue, you pretty witch, for I'm going to put a ruby blush upon your twin (not thin) lips, *after I've kissed them*—there—softly—softly—smack goes the brush. . . .[45]

Garrison knew well the ideal of beauty in his time—the white skin, red blush, and dark brows—and played with these colors in what quickly evolved into a sexual fantasy. After disowning her expenditures on the tools of beauty, he asserted the conjugal prerogatives of his paintbrush. Painted women supposedly invited a sexual encounter; here painting the face *was* a sexual encounter.

Mary Cunningham may have sparked an explosion of desire in Garrison, but she soon disappeared from his life and letters. Five years later and now leader of the antislavery movement, he placed cosmetic artifice within a safe, moral, middle-class compartment. In letters to Helen Benson, soon to be his wife, Garrison praised her simplicity in "rejecting all tawdry ornaments and artificial aids to the embellishment of your person." He observed: "Truly, not one young lady out of ten thousand, in a first interview with her lover, but would have endeavored falsely to heighten her charms, and allure by outward attractions." What impressed him about Helen was the truthfulness of her self-presentation in the marriage market. Her tasteful, unadorned appearance indicated both her sexual purity and social respectability. "I know you do not paint—your fair cheeks; but can't you paint mine?" he teased, complimenting Helen's talents as an amateur portraitist as well as her natural beauty.[46] Garrison's musings took two directions: toward an expression of sexual desire, ultimately to be repressed in favor of the pure womanly ideal, and toward an elaboration of middle-class respectability and taste.

Cosmetics and paints marked distinctions between and within social classes; they also reinforced a noxious racial aesthetic. Notions of Anglo-American beauty in the nineteenth century were continually asserted in relation to people of color around the world. Nineteenth-century travelers, missionaries, anthropologists, and scientists habitually viewed beauty as a function of race. Nodding in the direction of relativism—that various cultures perceive comeliness differently—they nevertheless proclaimed the superiority of white racial beauty. Some writers found ugliness in the foreign born, especially German, Irish, and Jewish immigrants. Others asserted the "aesthetic inferiority of the ebony complexion" because it was all one shade; Europeans' skin, in contrast, showed varied tints, gradations of color, and translucence. And because appearance and character were considered to be commensurate, the beauty of white skin expressed Anglo-Saxon virtue and civilization—and justified white supremacy in a period of American expansion.[47]

Aesthetic conventions reinforced this racial and national taxonomy. Smithsonian anthropologist Robert Shufeldt, for example, classified the "Indian types of beauty" in North America in an illustrated 1891 publication. The women he considered most beautiful were posed as Victorian ladies sitting for their photographic portrait. In contrast, the camera rendered those he classed as unattractive in the visual idiom of ethnography: half-naked bodies, direct stare, and frontal pose.[48] Tellingly these women also used paint on their faces and hair, which to white critics illustrated the "lingering taint of the savage and barbarous." According to Darwinians, the use of paint even impeded evolutionary progress: If men used visual criteria to choose the best mate, cosmetic deception thwarted the process of natural selection.[49]

A light complexion preoccupied not only the educated in science and letters, but was the governing aesthetic across the social spectrum. Traveling to a "lonely, out-of-the-way place, where the people are all sunburnt and rough-skinned, and even the pretty girls are sadly tanned by exposure to the weather," itinerant photographers in the 1850s and 1860s discovered that customers expected a white face without wrinkles, blemishes, or freckles on their portraits. One woman, invoking

"A Belle of Laguna" and "Mohave Women" in Robert Shufeldt, Indian Types of Beauty, *1891.*

the facial ideal, demanded that her face be *"white* with a *blush* on it."
Sitters were especially conscious of skin color in group photographs
that invited comparisons. While middle-class patrons, schooled in the
conventions of portraiture, accepted the artistic use of half tints, country folk and working people resisted shading and contouring. An itinerant photographer's experiment with chiarascuro ended in failure in
Bennington, Vermont, for no one would buy pictures "where one side of
the face is darker than the other, altho it seems to stand out better and
look richer." One of H. J. Rodgers's clients refused his photograph with
the objection, "the face looks dirty, just like a nager."[50]

No one defined the antipode of the dominant American beauty ideal
more starkly than African Americans. Kinky hair, dirty or ragged clothing, apish caricatures, shiny black faces: White men and women had
long invoked these stereotypes to exaggerate racial differences, dehu-
manize African Americans, and deny them social and political participation.

In the antebellum period, slaves audacious enough to cross over
into the white mistress's "sphere" of beauty and fashion endured severe punishment. Delia Garlick, for instance, recalled the beating she
received when she imitated her mistress's cosmetics use: "I seed [her]
blackin' her eyebrows wid smut [soot] one day, so I thought I'd black
mine jes' for fun. I rubbed some smut on my eyebrows an' forgot to rub
it off, an' she kotched me." The mistress "was powerful mad an' yelled:
'You black devil, I'll show you how to mock your betters.' " Picking up
a stick, she beat Delia unconscious. For this Southern mistress, fash-
ionability, including the use of beauty preparations, underscored the
class and racial hierarchy of the plantation. Significantly, she refused
her slaves "clothes for going round," providing only "a shimmy and a
slip for a dress"; "made outen de cheapest cloth dat could be bought,"
such clothes were a badge of slavery.[51]

By beautifying herself, Delia had defiantly claimed recognition as an
individual and a woman as she burlesqued her mistress's feminine airs.
Continually made aware of the social significance of appearances, nineteenth-century African Americans understood the power and pleasures

of "looking fine" in the face of destructive stereotypes. Yet, observed antebellum author Harriet Jacobs, herself a former bondswoman, physical beauty contained a cruel irony, for it inflamed white men's sexual abuse of black women.[52]

Racist representations proliferated in the latter half of the nineteenth century. Evolutionary science fitted African-American bodies into new visual classifications of inferiority based on facial angles and physiognomic measurements. Trade card advertising and minstrelsy caricatured the plantation slave's appearance to negate black Americans' efforts to define themselves as modern and self-respecting. One minstrel song, "When They Straighten All the Colored People's Hair," mocked an increasingly popular form of hair styling. For white Americans, sustaining a visual distinction between white and black masked an uncomfortable truth, that Africans and Europeans were genealogically mixed, their histories irrevocably intertwined.[53]

In advice manuals and formula books, white fears of losing their superior racial identity underwrote old anxieties about cosmetic artifice. An etiquette book warned that the use of tinted lip salve gave the mouth a "shriveled, purplish" look "of a sick negress." One tale about cosmetic washes containing lead or bismuth appeared repeatedly. Intended to whiten the skin, these preparations produced the opposite effect when they came into contact with sulphur in the air. The setting for this story varied—a public lecture, a laboratory, a bath—but in each case the cosmetic-using woman was humiliated because her lily white complexion had muddied and darkened. The most explicit of these stories appeared in 1890, in a period of deepening racial tension. At a mineral-spring resort, a fashionable lady envied for her perfect and supposedly natural complexion decided to take a therapeutic bath. Advised by the attendant to wash her face of any cosmetics, she grew indignant at the inference, ignored the warning, and proceeded to the bathhouse. Tragedy ensued: "Suddenly there was a sound of sorrow from the little room, and our belle rushed frantically forth, with her face and neck about the color of those of a dingy mulatto." Responding to these fears an advertisement for Hagan's Magnolia Balm exposed the

BEFORE USING.   USING.   AFTER USING.

Detail, Lyon's Manufacturing Co., "The Secret of Health and Beauty," an advertising pamphlet for Hagan's Magnolia Balm.

class and racial overtones of products ostensibly sold simply to remove tan or diminish freckles: It crassly promised not only to lighten skin color but also to transform the stereotyped countenance of a backward, rural black woman to that of a genteel white lady.[54]

In answer, black writers unmasked white hypocrisy through narratives that turned upon deceptive appearances, mistaken identities, and passing. In a short story by Gertrude Dorsey Brown, for instance, wealthy white partygoers laughingly put on blackface for a masquerade ball, secure that it would wash off. But this is no ordinary preparation. Unable to remove the blacking, the revelers become black, forced to endure the indignities of Jim Crow. The internal purity of the white lady, without the sign of white skin, could not protect her from harassment. African Americans lived with these conditions daily, Brown observed. Appearance indexed the moral and social status of an entire population, but, she argued, complexion was not commensurate with character.[55]

Before the rise of a mass-market cosmetics industry, American women may not have been awash in cosmetics, but they were far from unfamiliar with them. Different approaches to attaining facial beauty—homemade preparations, diet and exercise, and nerve tonics—flourished in these years. Paints and patent cosmetics too had a small following. Even as a market for cosmetic preparations slowly materialized, however, older traditions of therapeutics and beautifying continued to inform American habits. Thus preparations to improve the quality of the complexion, made of safe organic substances by women in the home, caused little concern. Commercial preparations, especially paints, were literally another matter: Made from dangerous chemicals and secret formulas, they acted against the body, nature, ethics, and social order. Masking paint, wicked women, tarnished merchandise, sexual corruption, racial inferiority: The world of rouge pots and powder boxes was a very threatening one indeed. Still, some women purchased and painted. Advertisers and advice writers alike acknowledged as much. "As you ladies will use them," one "distinguished doctor" testified, "I recommend 'Gouraud's Cream' as the least harmful of all the skin preparations."[56] Embedded within the warnings about patent cosmetics was tacit recognition of a desire among women to enhance appearance, to possess cosmetic secrets, even to employ volatile, dangerous products in the pursuit of beauty.

Women Who

Painted

Nineteenth-century women who painted, who made visible what others condemned or concealed, left few traces for posterity. While they commented often upon dress and hair, Victorian women wrote only occasionally about their use of cosmetics in diaries and letters. Still, these fragments offer some insight into what it meant to wear makeup conspicuously at a time when Americans looked askance at the painted face. Even as the moral aesthetic continued to govern beautifying practices, a small but growing number of women backed the use of visible cosmetics. These painted women followed another logic of the self and appearance that presaged our modern usage of cosmetics.

Ellen Ruggles Strong was one such woman. In the mid-nineteenth century, she enjoyed the diversions of New York high society as wife of civic leader George Templeton Strong. When he founded the Sanitary Commission during the Civil War, Ellen, like many women of her social class, volunteered to do hospital relief work. She caught the eye of diarist Maria Lydig Daly, who caustically described Ellen's greater commitment to fashion than to nursing: "They say very kindly and charitably that Mrs. George Strong went down with rouge pot, crinoline, and maid to attend to the wounded and came home having washed the faces of seven men." Attending a reception, she observed Ellen "painted like a wanton . . . with a huge bouquet sent her by one of her little *beaux,* without her husband." Not long after, she again met Ellen Strong at a party, "painted as usual, looking, as Temple Prime said, however, very pretty and very young looking. 'It is well done,' said he. 'I can't see it.' " Daly's acid reply: "Put on your glasses and thank Providence you are near-sighted, then."[1]

Daly held to the traditional view of cosmetics as mask and deplored this display of female hypocrisy and vanity, especially at a moment that called for selfless duty. The rouge pot betrayed the simple, truthful appearance that all women ought to desire. George Templeton Strong, in contrast, had nothing to say about his wife's cosmetic practices in his diaries, nor would he have recognized the painted wanton sketched by Daly. "What must he think? What can he mean by thus leaving her so much to herself?" Daly had wondered. Although warned by friends that Ellen Ruggles was "fashionable" and "artificial," George Templeton Strong could see her only as the model of angelic, dependent womanhood—"poor, little Ellen in her ignorance and simplicity," "a noble little girl."[2]

As one of the fashionable elite women condemned by Victorian moralists, Ellen Strong skated the thin line between ill-repute and a measure of autonomy. It was an artful performance. The dutiful wife appeared at hospitals and charity events, gave up waltzing because her husband disapproved, and "turned away her eyes from beholding vanity" when the couple went to Tiffany's. When left to herself, however, Ellen played the fast woman in a world of fashion, seductive young men, parties, and pleasures. Her beauty secrets, unseen by men yet visible to women, undermined the ideal of natural beauty, and with it, a fixed sense of self.[3]

The strain between female appearance and identity—that women are not what they seem—is, as we have seen, age-old, but this tension deepened substantially in the latter half of the nineteenth century. One manifestation was the anxious response to the feminist movement, the

warning that women would "unsex" themselves by making public demands for equality with men. Another surfaced in the uneasiness about
urban life, where strangers mingled on the streets. Cautionary tales circulated about prostitutes disguised as shoppers, saleswomen posing as
ladies, and light-skinned "octaroons" passing into white society. Advice books gave bachelors hints on how to tell the authentic beauty
from the fake. "The Venuses and the viragoes," complained one writer,
"have all been concealed in a maze of crinoline and whalebone, cotton,
powder and paint."[4]

At the same time, another language of the body began to be spoken.
In a society in which appearances were fluid and social rank unstable,
the question of how to represent oneself was a pressing one. Strategies
of appearance—dressing for effect, striking a pose—became ever more
important. As writer N. P. Willis observed, "Some of us know better
than others how to put on the best look."[5] For some women, cosmetics
use was less a deception, a false face, than a dramatic performance of
the self in a culture increasingly oriented to display, spectatorship, and
consumption.

The ideal face, defined by pale skin and blushing cheeks, remained remarkably constant for most of the nineteenth century. Fashion generally upheld this ideal. Nevertheless, the antebellum image of natural,
transparent beauty briefly gave way to a more theatrical and artificial
look among the affluent in the Civil War era. Confederate partisan
Emma Holmes complained bitterly about the "rebellious" girls in
Charleston's high society, who defied their parents, danced as their
brothers died, and painted their faces. Young Sallie Bull and Lilly De-
Saussure, she declared, "have taken to *rouging* & Sallie won't submit
even to her grandfather's control."[6] Wealthy New York trendsetters
wore large bustles and deep décolletage, wove flowers and birds into
their curls, and, when a burlesque troupe called the "British Blondes"
became a popular sensation in 1868, bleached their hair to a golden
hue. For a short time, these women applied rouge, white paint, and eye

makeup to complement such extreme styles, but they quickly returned to a more "natural" look.[7]

For most American women, these cosmetic fads and fashions meant little. But the aesthetic of natural beauty imposed its own demands, paradoxically compelling women to use white powder and even apply "washes" and masking paints to achieve the desired look. Indeed, skin whiteners remained the most popular cosmetic throughout the nineteenth century. Women ranked white powder—typically ground starch, rice, or chalk—most acceptable on sanitary and practical grounds. Especially in the West and South, women used powder to protect the skin from the climate, prevent tanning, and reduce perspiration and shine. Even so, powdering went beyond hygiene. Concealing ruddiness, sweat, and exertion, it produced the proper pale shade of leisured gentility. "The ladies have strange ways of adding to their charms," Englishwoman Frances Trollope wrote during her antebellum travels in America. "They powder themselves immoderately, face, neck, and arms, with pulverised starch; the effect is indescribably disagreeable by day-light, and not very favourable at any time." Certainly many women viewed powdering as an unhealthy evil, a practice that blocked the pores but stimulated vanity. As late as 1900 in many Midwestern towns, only daring young women poured "some of the coarse grained powder into paper envelopes" and secretly applied it at dances. Still, beauty adviser Marie Mott Gage noted, powdering was akin to "charity balls, church fairs, corsets, décolleté gowns and other follies," often criticized but "so dear to the popular heart."[8]

Other skin lighteners, closer in definition to paints, also supported the aesthetic ideal. Known generically as lily white, white wash, and "white cosmetic," these products were used by some women irrespective of class and age. In 1879, Jessie Benton Frémont admired the "fresh *clean* faces of the girls & women" in New York and Boston, in contrast to the women who "powder & daub" in San Francisco and Prescott, Arizona. In the West, she wrote, "it is quite funny to see that smeared smooth white face, & red wrists emerging from one button pale gloves. But the creme de lis [a whitening paste] is sure to be on."

Even a widow in her sixties might be a customer: Ariadne Bennard purchased three or four bottles of lily white annually from an apothecary in Portsmouth, New Hampshire.[9]

Women applying dangerous lead-based whitening lotions like Bloom of Youth began to appear in medical case records after the Civil War. These women were often wage earners who had begun the practice as teenagers or young adults. Going to great lengths to conceal their cosmetics use, they initially were diagnosed with hysteria or reproductive disorders, the usual suspects in Victorian women's ailments. Only after repeated questioning, their condition worsening, would they admit the truth. Some may have fallen for patent cosmetic advertising, with its appealing images of fashion and high society, but most offered explanations grounded in the exigencies of their daily life. An umbrella maker stated a simple desire "to take the shine off the skin." Some used white paint specifically to improve their chances at work: A ballet dancer applied a lead-based wash supplied by her dance company; a milliner painted to look refined when she met her patrons; a young Irish-born copyist used different powders and pastes, applying them to her neck and shoulders when going to work. The white face, purged of the exertions of labor, simultaneously asserted bourgeois refinement and racial privilege.[10]

The use of powders and skin whiteners among African Americans received notice by the black press as early as the 1850s. The *Anglo-American Magazine* criticized African Americans who appeared with painted faces, lips "puckered up and drawn in," the hair "sleeked over and pressed under, or cut off so short that it can't curl." It decried the emulation of white beauty standards: "Beautiful black and brown faces by the application of rouge and lily white are made to assume unnatural tints, like the vivid hue of painted corpses." How common such practices had become, and among which groups of African Americans, is unknown. It may be that some black devotees of white powder were not so much emulating as parodying the style of white elites—making up the face and hair to complement the exuberant, "high-style" dress that black dandies and their lady friends wore.[11]

BLACK SKIN REMOVER.

REGISTERED IN PATENT OFFICE U.S.

BEFORE   AFTER

A Wonderful Face Bleach.

AND HAIR STRAIGHTENER.

both in a box for $1, or three boxes for $2. Guaranteed to do what we say and to be the "best in the world." One box is all that is required if used as directed.

A WONDERFUL FACE BLEACH.

A PEACH-LIKE complexion obtained if used as directed. Will turn the skin of a black or brown person four or five shades lighter, and a mulatto person perfectly white. In forty-eight hours a shade or two will be noticeable. It does not turn the skin in spots but bleaches out white, the skin remaining beautiful without continual use. Will remove wrinkles, freckles, dark spots, pimples or bumps or black heads, making the skin very soft and smooth. Small pox pits, tan, liver spots removed without harm to the skin. When you get the color you wish, stop using the preparation.

THE HAIR STRAIGHTENER.

that goes in every one dollar box is enough to make anyone's hair grow long and straight, and keeps it from falling out. Highly perfumed and makes the hair soft and easy to comb. Many of our customers say one of our dollar boxes is worth ten dollars, yet we sell it for one dollar a box. THE NO-SMELL thrown in free.

Any person sending us one dollar in a letter or Post-Office money order, express money order or registered letter, we will send it through the mail postage prepaid; or if you want it sent C. O. D., it will come by express, 25c. extra.

In any case where it fails to do what we claim, we will return the money or send a box free of charge. Packed so that no one will know contents except receiver.

CRANE AND CO.,
122 west Broad Street,
RICHMOND, VA.

Crane and Co. advertisement addressed to African Americans, in The Colored American Magazine, *1903.*

Still, the aesthetic dimension of racism—gradations of skin color, textures of hair—shaped work opportunities, marriage chances, and social life, giving advantages to those with lighter complexions and straighter locks. Early dealers in face bleach certainly exploited this prejudice in the 1880s and 1890s: One pledged that a "black skin remover" would yield a "peach-like complexion"; another vowed to "gradually turn the skin of a black person five or six shades lighter"; a third claimed that "the Negro need not complain any longer of black skin." In reality, those products often caused blotches on the skin and sometimes permanent injury.[12]

Advertising appeals to African Americans offer a telling contrast to the promotional pamphlets and trade cards distributed at large. Addressed implicitly to white women, the latter promoted preparations to cover up blemishes, bleach freckles, and whiten the skin, all the while proclaiming their products' naturalness. Advertisements do not necessarily or directly mirror popular attitudes, but in this case, they seem to have touched upon a common cultural practice. Women might purchase a skin whitener that covered and colored the skin and simultaneously disclaim its status *as* paint. For women of European descent, whitening could be absorbed within acceptable skin-care routines and assimilated into the ruling beauty ideal, the natural

Hagan's Magnolia Balm trade card, late nineteenth century, addressed to white consumers.

face of white genteel womanhood—although, as Jessie Benton Frémont testified, one glance at the hands could undo this careful effort to naturalize artifice. For African Americans, the fiction was impossible: Whitening cosmetics, touted as cures for "disabling" African features, reinforced a racialized aesthetic through a makeover that appeared anything but natural.

The idealization of the "natural" face occurred, ironically, within a middle class beginning to define itself through consumption. Other places in which private and public intertwined—the clothed body, the well-furnished parlor—were accepted, indeed celebrated, as sites of commodity culture. The face, however, was deemed outside fashion, a sign of true identity, even as it served a highly contrived self-presentation, in which artifice shaped the body to a fashionable silhouette and clothing was often exuberantly ornamental.[13]

It was women like Ellen Strong and the Bloom of Youth consumers who upended the conventional meaning of *paint* as an unnatural mask. They saw the face not as a transparent window into inner beauty, but as an image of their own making, an integral part of their own daily performances. Their perspective came to seem more credible and accurate in the latter half of the nineteenth century, when several long-term developments—new urban sites of consumption and display, a flourishing fashion economy, the spread of image-making technologies, and a nascent culture of celebrity—changed how Americans perceived the face.

Seeing and being seen took on greater cultural importance in the late-nineteenth-century city. Middle-class women enjoyed a new round of social activities: They strolled the streets, went shopping, attended matinees, and ate out. For those with little money to spend, "just looking" was a pleasant diversion. As historian William Leach shows, a new class of merchants prodded consumers to picture themselves in a world of consumer goods and stylish looks. While browsing wares for sale, women saw well-dressed manikins, gazed at themselves in plate glass windows and mirrors, and took note of each other's appearances.[14]

Beyond the city too, fashion sense flourished. Dressmakers, milliners, and seamstresses catered to an accelerating demand for stylish clothing. Women's magazines, fashion dolls, and paper patterns spread Parisian fashions to middle-class women throughout the United States. Working-class women sewed their own smart outfits, remodeled castoffs, or bought at secondhand shops. The lure of looking touched even country women. In an 1885 story by Zona Gale, one character described viewing the fashion plates hanging in the dressmaker's window: "It made a kind of nice thing to do on the way home from the grocery, hot forenoons—draw up there on the shady side . . . an' look at Lyddy's plates, an' choose—like you was goin' to get one." Protean, emphasizing the surface and the novel, fashion altered attitudes toward the body and self-presentation.[15]

It may be that earlier in the century, American women and men had only a hazy apprehension of their facial qualities. When itinerant painter James Guild offered a young girl a portrait in exchange for washing his shirt, it "looked more like a strangle[d] cat than it did like her," but he "told her it looked like her and she believed it." Diary entries and letters relied on well-worn and indefinite figures of speech to describe beauty—"a charming mingling of the rose & lily"—that could be visualized in any number of ways. Many people owned mirrors, but their quality was uneven. When Maria Lydig Daly stayed overnight in a room with a bad looking glass, she "looked so old and ugly that I felt distressed," and was relieved to return home to her familiar mirror. "How few of us have a perfect idea how we look, or who we resemble, or look like," photographer H. J. Rodgers observed, "we look differently in as many mirrors as we may choose to scrutinize." Portraits commissioned by wealthy Americans, painted by artists versed in a visual language that expressed beauty, character, and social role, tended to idealize and flatter. The less affluent hired itinerant painters to render their likenesses, but these portraits merely conveyed general facial features and hair style and used personal possessions—a tool, a book—to represent the sitter's individuality. When it came to the celebrated beauties of the period, art historian Abigail Solomon-Godeau notes, there was a "frequent dissonance between written accounts and the visual record." Diarist Emma Holmes was "dreadfully disappointed" when she finally met Mary Withers, the "far famed beauty." Withers had "by no means a beautiful complexion," complained Holmes; "it was ordinary and I expected an extraordinary one, from all the praises bestowed on it."[16]

Over the course of the nineteenth century, mirrors, fashion plates, printed engravings, and chromolithographs streamed into Americans' lives, but it was the advent of photography in 1839 that most changed how people knew their appearances. At first photographs were treated as articles of memory and contemplation, readily incorporated into the Victorian cult of sentimentality. But new techniques and formats quickly made photographs cheap and widely available. In the 1860s, the carte-de-visite craze struck middle-class Americans, who traded and collected each other's card-sized portraits. At the same time, the ferrotype or tintype became the "picture for the million." Farmers, artisans, and working women earning a modest income purchased miniature "gem" tintypes, a dozen for a dime or quarter. Thus the photograph rapidly found a place in family and social life—in parlor albums, on jewelry, and as postcards and calling cards.[17]

Americans went to the photography studio ready for a performance, as historian Alan Trachtenberg aptly describes it, "the making of one-self over into a social image." They appeared dressed in their Sunday clothes, laden with jewelry, primed to hold a pose or expression. Elite photographers Southworth and Hawes hired fashion advisers to guide female patrons "in arranging their dress and drapery"; for the ordinary studio, leaflets entitled "Pretty Faces" and the like instructed the photographer how to "answer all vexatious questions put to you by your sitters."[18]

What most vexed the public was that the photograph revealed the face and body with a degree of detail and precision never before seen. Its realism raised questions about the body and identity: Did photography capture only surface appearances, or did it represent the inner self? As the photograph became a popular commodity, it made beauty a more problematic category. What had once been a matter more for the imagination and the mirror was now externally fixed on the photographic plate. Believed to be factual, photographs measured the distance between idealized representations and real faces. Many photographers applauded this failure to flatter; others adopted painterly techniques of lighting and pose in the interest of offering a more penetrating—and pleasing—likeness.

From the sitters' perspective, however, the photograph pulled in another direction, toward a critical assessment of appearance itself. The pictorial truth could be quite painful, and patrons leaving the photographer's studio often looked dismayed. A Massachusetts woman recalled her experience before the camera: "After various sittings most unsatisfactory—one with the mouth too large, another with the expression too grave, a third presenting an affected style, with a kind of contraction very unnatural about the lips—I shook my head and turned disgusted away." In these "permanent mirrors," wrote an amateur photographer, "our self-love does not always permit us to look with pleasure."[19]

In response, sitters often demanded retouched or tinted pictures. Photographers ridiculed customers who would "not care to have their own faces enamelled" but insisted on a "highly-retouched fraud which represents them as marble." They developed techniques to apply colored powder, often ladies' rouge, to negatives and prints, so that "the coarse skin texture, the pimple and freckle blemishes were converted into fine, soft complexions." Artistic photographers delicately colored the entire picture—face, clothing, and background—to create the illusion of nature. But in the cheap photograph factories, employees rubbed just a blush of red pigment on the cheeks and gold flecks on the jewelry, with the image otherwise untouched. This convention was artifice that revealed itself—a bit of color to signify the living person.[20]

If retouching and tinting lessened the gap between self-image and the camera eye, so did cosmetics. American women who ordinarily shunned paint requested it at photographers' studios. "All kinds of powders and cosmetics were brought into play, until sitters did not think they were being properly treated if their faces and hair were not powdered until they looked like a ghastly mockery of the clown in a pantomime," photographer Henry Peach Robinson complained. At a cheap studio on the Bowery, where clerks and shopgirls came to be photographed on Sundays, the owner observed, "I have known colored ladies to sit for tintypes and they ask me why I didn't put a little more rouge on their cheeks." H. J. Rodgers's manual of photography reveals explicitly how image making intensified attention to the face and, for women, justified cosmetics use. Rodgers viewed male sitters simply as character "types"—such as the "rough," the gentleman, and the dandy—but believed that photography could capture each woman's unique beauty. His manual offered ample advice to women on clothing styles, colors, and how to compose expression. Despite his advocacy of nature and hygiene, Rodgers nonetheless concluded his book with page after page of cosmetics recipes.[21]

As new visual technologies began to standardize female appearance, those standards became increasingly defined by actresses and
professional beauties—no longer seen as women of questionable
morality, but rather as celebrities and stars. Although Americans had
been enchanted by such performers as Jenny Lind and Fanny Kemble
in the antebellum period, women achieved new prominence on the
stage after 1860. Many were players in serious drama, but the most visible and controversial performed in burlesques and variety shows that
combined sexual display with comic dialogue. Such stars as Adah
Menken and Lydia Thompson brought to the American theater a new
kind of performance that blurred the line between scripted roles and
stage personae based on their real lives. Their novel self-presentation
included bleached hair and even paint, inspiring the most daring
women to emulate them.[22]

Objects of a budding cult of celebrity, actresses and professional
beauties were viewed, talked about, and incorporated visually into
Americans' private lives. As early as the 1860s, observers noted the
rising "commercial value of the human face." Photographs of the
prominent flooded the market—not only generals, politicians, and ministers, but thespians, ballet dancers, and burlesque stars. Pictures of
actresses in and out of their stage roles appeared in urban shop windows, mail-order catalogues, and theater doorways. Middle-class
Americans often placed these images in their personal albums, often
on the same pages as photographs of family and friends.[23]

Making faces into "pictures for the public gaze" involved the frank
use of makeup commonly used in the theater. Actresses' photographs
display smooth and flawless skin, as well as the use of eyeliner and lip
pencil. By the 1880s, Lillie Langtry, Adelina Patti, and other performers appeared in cosmetics advertisements, in testimonials, and even as
product brand names. Makeup slowly began to cross from the stage
into everyday life. Women wore paints for amateur theatricals, coming-
out parties, and balls. Even women who ordinarily shunned powder
might coat their skin with liquid whiting to appear as statues in
tableaux vivants. Beauty manuals distinguished between daytime activ-

ity and the evening "play-world,"
when women might justifiably apply violet-tinted powder or beauty
cream tagged a "gas-light cosmetic." The spread of electric
lighting in cities after 1890, considered "fearfully trying to even the
best of skins," warranted rouge.
But even in daylight, as women
promenaded the streets, looked in
shop windows, socialized in public,
and scrutinized one another, a
number found reason to apply powder and paint.[24]

A fundamental and far-reaching
change was taking place: the
heightened importance of image
making and performance in everyday life. Photographic and stage
techniques of making up and pos-

Hunter's Invisible Face Powder trade card, featuring actress Lillie Langtry.

ing introduced external and standardized models of beauty that challenged the "natural" ideal. For some advice writers, social life itself
had become a performance that called for makeup, but only if used,
paradoxically, to enact the part of one's true, natural self. Thus a
woman whose pallor resulted from illness might legitimately apply
rouge. So could a young girl if "its use originates in an innocent desire
to please," but the "old campaigner," who reddened her cheeks to trick
a man into marriage, remained a "painted Jezebel." Although some
women adhered to these rules, others vested self-portrayal with a degree of choice, play, and pleasure. The idea that a woman could remake
her face—and that being natural was itself a pose—found its embodi-
ment in Julian Eltinge, a female impersonator. In the early twentieth
century Eltinge won acclaim playing fashionable and genteel debutantes onstage. So convincing was his portrayal that he issued a beauty

magazine and sold his own cosmetics line, offering "a chance for every woman to be as beautiful as Julian Eltinge"![25]

Women's growing interest in beauty products coincided with their new sense of identity as consumers. Women had long bought and bartered goods, but around 1900 a new, self-conscious notion of the woman consumer emerged. Women's magazines and advertisers inducted their female readers into a world of brand-name products and smart shopping, while department stores created a feminine paradise of abundance, pleasure, and service. Home economists and reformers, such as the National Consumers League, proposed a contrasting image—the rational consumer with a social conscience—but they, too, bolstered the view that consumption was integral to women's role.[26]

Many, however, were not yet ready to endorse the idea that women should buy their way to beauty. Cosmetics sales grew only incrementally between 1870 and 1900. Although they accelerated thereafter, as late as 1916, according to a trade estimate, only one in five Americans used toilet preparations of any sort, and per capita expenditures were a mere fifty cents. Many retailers remained nonplussed by beauty preparations. The mail-order Zion City General Store, whose "profits [were] used for God," excluded cosmetics entirely; another catalog company sandwiched its Sur-Pur Face Powder for "ladies of culture and refinement" inconspicuously between livestock remedies, patent medicines, and harnesses. Some retailers issued advertising pamphlets that juxtaposed brand-name cosmetics with beautifying recipes, identifying women simultaneously with home production and market consumption.[27]

Women's magazines and the women's pages of city newspapers, appearing after the 1890s, also took an ambiguous position on the traffic in beauty aids and advice. Except for skin creams and lotions, cosmetics were not widely advertised in national magazines, unlike convenience foods and soaps. Editorial advice pushed homemade preparations and discouraged the use of makeup. *Ladies' Home Journal* columnist Ruth Ashmore told "Anxious," for instance, that face powder roughened the skin but was acceptable if used "to take away the disagreeable gloss." She recommended girls improve their general health and use such homemade remedies as buttermilk or almond meal for the complexion. Such advice against the tide of commerce was, however, unable to stanch the flood of readers' queries about beauty aids and makeup. The *Baltimore Sun*, for instance, ran over a dozen letters each Sunday from women who wanted to rid their face of freckles, fill out their cheeks, or darken the eyebrows. Some could not afford to buy the products they desired and asked for a comparable formula to mix at home; others wanted a recipe to take to the drugstore, to be compounded and purchased there.[28]

There were other signs of the growing importance of beautifying in the consumer-goods market. Druggists continued to compound their own cold creams and lotions, but such large wholesale drug suppliers as W. H. Schiefellin and McKesson & Robbins offered dozens of brand-name cosmetics, foreign and domestic. By the turn of the century, one wholesaler sold fifty different brands of cream, as many American-made powders and skin preparations, and eleven brands of cosmetique. Retail druggists began to see profit in promoting beauty aids to the healthy as well as filling prescriptions for the sick. They embraced modern methods of selling, highlighting packaging, free samples, island displays, and show windows.[29]

Druggists remained the primary distributors of beauty preparations, but other retail outlets boosted cosmetics sales. For the affluent consumer, department stores brought beauty secrets into a new urban setting of publicity and spectacle. At first merchants played down these commodities, jumbling a small array of powders, lily whites, and beautifiers with fancy goods and sundries. The most prescient, however, believing that toiletries put women in a spending mood, started to place cosmetics front and center on the main selling floor. A Macy's executive proudly told perfume manufacturers in 1909 that department stores intentionally "lured" women "to the counters by playing on their senses of smell." At the lower end of the market, new chain drugstores and variety stores aggressively pushed bargain brands and private-

A sample envelope for
Tetlow's Gossamer, a popular
commercial face powder
whose sales pitch emphasized
innocent flirtation.

label cosmetics. Rural and small-town customers could buy beauty products from door-to-door and mail-order firms. As early as 1897 Sears offered its own line of cosmetics, including rouge, eyebrow pencil, and face powder, along with such brands as Harriet Hubbard Ayer, Pozzoni, and Tetlow.[30]

Cosmetics entrepreneurs also detected a budding demand among African Americans. Inventors began to patent hot irons and straightening tongs, while peddlers hawked hair growers, wigs, pressing oils, and complexion creams. One firm, based in the drugstore trade, had sold an ordinary ox-marrow pomade to white customers for years when "one day a young colored woman came in and purchased a dozen bottles." This triggered a "great discovery," "like finding a nugget of gold":

> We asked her: "What are you going to do with so much?" She replied, "It makes my hair long, soft and easy to comb, and I am getting it for my friends." We then said, "Tell us all about it and we will give you a dozen extra bottles." She then told of the merits of our pomade when applied to the hair of colored people.

The company began to canvass in black communities, started a word-of-mouth publicity campaign, and advertised extensively in black newspapers. Another established patent medicine company, Brooklyn-based E. Thomas Lyon, promoted the hair tonic Kaitheron to African Americans with a pamphlet called *What Colored People Say* and an *Afro-American Almanac.*[31]

Many firms selling to black women originated in such places as

Richmond, Louisville, and Memphis, cities of the upper South with sizable black commercial districts, growing numbers of African-American migrants, and nascent chemical and pharmaceutical manufacturing. In Richmond, for instance, Henry Schnurman developed Hartona in 1893, Thomas Beard Crane followed in 1898 with Wonderful Face Bleach, and Rilas Gathright manufactured a number of products under different names by 1900, including a "magnetic comb," O-zo-no hair preparations and deodorant, and Imperial Whitener. All of these companies developed a wide mail-order trade, and their ads could be found in black newspapers across the country.[32]

In the early years of the twentieth century, women who wore rouge and powder without shame sparked a new outburst of public notice and debate. Once "the painted face was the bold, brazen sign of the woman's character and calling," wrote a woman to the *Baltimore Sun* in 1912, but "now women and young girls of respectable society are seen on our streets and fashionable promenade with painted faces."[33] Painted women had escaped the seamy neighborhoods of vice, and urban Americans now found the once familiar sign of female iniquity harder to read.

The women most stigmatized by their use of makeup—prostitutes—were no longer so easily identified by it. Traditionally, women who became prostitutes abandoned their corsets, put on loose fitting robes, and made up their faces to advertise their trade. A reformed prostitute, telling her story of brothel life, however, said she had refused to apply makeup—"I had to draw a line somewhere"—rouge and eye paint being the most potent sign of her fall. A prostitute's appearance also depended on her place within an intricate vice economy and on the vagaries of urban policing. Streetwalkers wore makeup to attract the glances of likely customers, but some shunned it to avoid scrutiny from the cop on the beat. The "street girls" of Syracuse, a 1913 investigation found, "dress quietly, and use but little paint or powder." Even brothel dwellers, sheltered within a house, used different elements of contemporary fashion and style to signal their occupation and sense of group identity. Some wore short skirts and boots; others—usually high-priced courtesans—often imitated ladies of fashion and spent extravagantly on modistes, hairdressers, and perfume. Turn-of-the-century prostitutes wore kohl on their eyes when they posed for New Orleans photographer E. J. Bellocq, but a delivery boy in the Storyville brothels pinpointed a finer distinction between the worlds of vice and virtue: "Prostitutes wore night-time makeup at the wrong time of day."[34]

It was not only prostitutes whose appearances confused. Cosmetics had long been associated with "fast" and "sporting" women. Neither prostitutes nor performers, these women enjoyed the city's underworld as pleasure seekers, their bold dress and free-and-easy manners conspicuous in dance houses, concert halls, and cafés. At various moments in the nineteenth century, some women tested the limits of bourgeois propriety by wearing fashions that referenced this demimonde. Makeup was an especially plastic aesthetic form—easily heightened, toned down, or washed off to register one's place within different social circles. As more and more women entered into the expanding realm of urban commercial nightlife, they made elements of this racy public style their own.

But however indebted to the demimonde, this trend toward painting was part of a historic transformation in feminine appearance affecting women of different classes and cultural backgrounds. Saleswomen, factory hands, middle-class shoppers, and socialites all began to paint, although journalists and commentators pointed especially to society women and working girls as the chief offenders. "Society women now paint" even in "very select circles," read a New York *World* headline as early as 1890. Despite the "tradition that 'making up' is tabooed in the best New York society," stated the reporter, "it is the very best upper-crustdom that puts aside tradition and authority and bedizens itself as much as it pleases." Nodding to trendsetting French women who used visible makeup, some asserted their social leadership within the *haute monde* through cosmetic fashion.[35]

Assertive young working women were also known for their makeup use. Decked out in cheap but fashionable clothes and hats, they wore switches and "puffs" in their hair, powdered generously, and even rouged their cheeks. For many, being up-to-date included cosmetics, even though they were sometimes sent home for powdering excessively or harassed by men on the streets, who saw them as loose. "Tough girls"—white working-class women thought to be uninhibited and sexually active—especially embraced the theatrical qualities of cosmetics. Urban reformers commented on the "almost universal custom" at dance halls, where young working women stored powder puffs in their stocking tops, pulled them out and flourished them whenever they wished "to attract the attention of a young man."[36]

Women were using makeup to mark any number of differences, asserting worldliness against insularity and sexual desire against chastity. Moving into public life, they staked a claim to public attention, demanded that others look. This was not a fashion dictated by Parisian or other authorities, but a new mode of feminine self-presentation, a tiny yet resonant sign of a larger cultural contest over women's identity.

Still, painted women remained spectacles to a significant extent before World War I, conspicuous among the curiosities and commotion of urban life. "I have seen women going along the street with their cheeks aglow with paint, everyone twisting their necks and looking," one woman observed. Working women were sent home for appearing on the job with an "artificial complexion"; the manager of Macy's fired one rouged saleswoman in 1913 with the comment that "he was not running a theatrical troupe but a department store." Public authorities tried in vain to preserve the older ideal of womanly beauty. In 1915, a Kansas legislator proposed to make it a misdemeanor for women under the age of forty-four to wear cosmetics "for the purpose of creating a false impression." Several years later, policewomen in Newark collared teenage girls at the train stations, "overawed them by a display of their police badges, and forced them to wash rouge and powder from their faces." Juvenile courts granted parental requests to bar their delinquent daughters from making up. In these circumstances, paint still implied sexual enticement and trickery, a false face.[37]

Men in particular maintained these conventional views. Edward Bok, editor of the *Ladies' Home Journal,* observed in 1912 that men continued to see rouge as a mark of sex and sin: "The stigma has never been removed by men, and is not, in their minds, today." Letters to the *Baltimore Sun* from male readers confirm his observation. "Such decorating is the same as an invitation to a flirtation," one man stated flatly. "Every painted or flashily dressed woman is deemed by most strange men to be of questionable character." In an expanding consumer culture, these small goods posed yet another danger. One Evansville, Indiana, man sued for divorce, claiming his wife spent eighteen dollars monthly on cosmetics and perfume; another denied responsibility when his wife charged $1,500 for toiletries on their store account, saying she was "possessed of a passion for such luxuries." The old notion of cosmetics as witchcraft lay just below the surface.[38]

Among women, painting aroused a more ambivalent response. Edward Bok peevishly commented that respectable "women have done a curious thing" by now tolerating painted women they once had shunned. A class of young working women at New York's Cooper Union in 1914 debated the question of artificial beauty and resoundingly voted in favor of it.[39] But when the *Baltimore Sun* ran a contest asking "Should Women Paint?" women answered in the negative by over two to one. The female opponents of makeup essentially reiterated the charges made by men, but with greater urgency, for it was their respectability that painting called into question. Makeup certainly attracted attention, "but not the kind that a good woman wishes bestowed upon her," said one woman. "Maidenly dignity is underestimated 50 per cent by her penciled lashes and over-dyed cheeks and lips," which emboldened men to harass women, observed another. Women's motives for making up also came under scrutiny: When girls posed as mature women or matrons affected a youthful appearance, they both used subterfuge to ensnare men. Most writers agreed that makeup's artifice was ultimately self-deception. "Aids to beauty are only shams," wrote Jessie Barclay. "Everybody can detect them." A number echoed the nineteenth-century ideal that true beauty resulted from "right living and right thinking." As one letter writer proposed, "Why not be satis-fied with ourselves just as we are?"[40]

The champions of paint rejected excessive coloring but condoned the cautious imitation of nature. They too left unchallenged the as-sumption that women's virtue and beauty were intertwined, but argued from it that women's moral duty to be attractive justified moderate arti-fice. Women's intentions and authenticity, not makeup itself, deter-mined the harm or innocence of the painted face. As one of the Cooper Union debaters argued, "If you use cosmetics in a nice way they will not detract from your beauty or injure your character."[41]

Here were some very fine distinctions. The *Sun* contest winner, Nicketti McMullen, wrote about the difference between young women and old, contrasting the girl with naturally rosy cheeks who improperly "indulges in artificial aids," and the matron whose color fades with work and time and who legitimately "finds it necessary to rouge." "When painting reveals the application it is disgusting," wrote another entrant, but mimicking nature, enhancing the features, or even recall-ing a beauty that once existed was acceptable art. One writer went so far as to observe that rouging was an admission of ugliness, and thus enacted honesty, not deception![42]

A few turned away from the older moral aesthetic to reappraise the meaning of paint altogether. "We can't all be born beautiful," observed one woman, and cosmetic aids equalized opportunity in a world where beauty might affect women's fortunes. This had long been true of the marriage market, but now, as they entered the workplace in greater numbers, "women who start out to battle with the world alone will be more successful and demand more respect if they are attractive and well dressed." Thus some women started to uncouple paint and im-morality, but could not fully detach themselves from the notion that paint covered up a true self. "As beauty is only skin deep anyhow," wrote one, "cannot paint and powder, false hair and pads hide a true heart and chaste soul?"[43]

Changes in cosmetic products and applications reflected and rein-forced the growing use of beauty aids by respectable women, and hastened the transformation of paint into makeup. Lily whites, enamels, and vinegar rouge—the traditional white and red colorings in liquid or cream form—continued to be available but were in decline by 1900. As a movement for safer food and drugs arose in the Progressive era, popular outcry over lead, mercury, and other deadly ingredients in cosmetics grew louder, and many of the older "washes" and paints containing them began to disappear from the market.[44]

New face powders and application techniques competed with the older paints and began to supplant them. So-called "invisible" powder had been advertised since the 1860s by such manufacturers as Solon Palmer and Pozzoni. Pure white and bright red-pink remained the most widely available colors, but more natural-looking powders and dry rouges, developed by French perfumers and imitated by American manufacturers, slowly gained a foothold. Cosmetics firms promoted such new tints as "brunette" and "flesh" (cream and light beige shades), intended to harmonize with the complexion. Anthony Overton introduced High-Brown face powder to African Americans around 1900, spurring other companies to sell darker powder shades in the African-American market. Makeup techniques also evolved. Liquid whitener and rouge, usually applied with a sponge, were often quite visible and bright, giving the skin a masklike veneer. In the early twentieth century, such firms as Pond's and Pompeian publicized "vanishing cream" as a transparent base for face powder, which allowed skin tones and facial expression to surface.[45]

Beyond powder and rouge, women often improvised their makeup with preparations sold for other purposes. Cosmetique and mascaro, as it was called, were all-purpose dyes in pomade or cake form, which men applied to graying mustaches and hair along the temples, and women used to tint eyebrows and lashes. Paste rouge was applied to the lips as well as cheeks. Some women apparently adapted theatrical makeup for everyday use—not greasepaints, but lighter-weight, tinted powders, which they toned down and blended for the street, restaurants, or evening parties. When Max Factor opened a professional makeup studio for stage and screen actors in Los Angeles in 1909, ordinary women came in to purchase theatrical eye shadow and eyebrow pencil for their home use; Factor began to package these as everyday cosmetics. As women began to buy theatrical preparations, tinted powders, and dry rouge, the notion of paint as unnatural and makeup as mask increasingly gave way to the modern sense of makeup as an expression of self and personality.[46]

A scene of the new urban beauty culture. John Sloan, Hairdresser's Window, *1907.*

• • •

To paint or not to paint? Women pondered the question, with its charged implications for appropriate female behavior and appearance, as the commerce in beauty goods, information, and services swelled. Although some women remained embarrassed consumers or continued to use homemade products, for others, painting the face, once the symbol of the most disreputable form of commerce, was now simply one option among many. In the crescendo of talk and circulation of goods, a public commercial realm devoted to female beautifying had begun to take shape. In the nation's cities, journalist Anne O'Hagan commented, women in their pursuit of beauty could turn to "the Turkish baths, the manicure establishments—almost as thick upon the city street as the saloons; the massage places, the electro therapeutics, the 'don't worry' clubs . . . ; the dermatological institutes; the half of every drug store." It was a confusing world. More and more cosmetics were available on the market, but their production and marketing remained haphazard, a jumbling of goods that invited skepticism, if not outright censure. Patent cosmetics makers, perfumers, and druggists contended over the efficacy of their products; beauty doctors and complexion specialists competed for clients; columnists in magazines and newspapers offered conflicting advice. Still, as O'Hagan observed, slowly "something of a system is being evolved from the hodgepodge."[47] That system, created to a large extent by women themselves, was known as "beauty culture."

Beauty Culture

and Women's

Commerce

C osmetics today seem quintessential products of a consumer culture dominated by large corporations, national advertising, and widely circulated images of ideal beauty. The origins of American beauty culture lie elsewhere, however, in a spider's web of businesses—beauty parlors, druggists, department stores, patent cosmetic companies, perfumers, mail-order houses, and women's magazines that thrived at the turn of the century and formed the nascent infrastructure of the beauty industry. Few of these enterprises used the kinds of systematic marketing and sales campaigns so familiar to contemporary Americans. Nonetheless, the proliferation of products, services, and information about cosmetics and beauty definitively recast nineteenth-century attitudes toward female appearance.

Women played a key role in these developments. Indeed, the beauty industry may be the only business, at least until recent decades, in which American women achieved the highest levels of success, wealth, and authority. Such well-known figures as Helena Rubinstein and Elizabeth Arden, the remarkable African-American entrepreneurs Madam C. J. Walker and Annie Turnbo Malone, and post–World War II businesswomen Estee Lauder and Mary Kay Ash mark an ongoing tradition of female leadership. Although exceptional businesswomen, they are only the most visible signs of a much larger phenomenon. As beauty parlor owners, cosmetics entrepreneurs, and "complexion specialists," women charted a path to mass consumption outside the emergent system of national advertising and distribution. In so doing, they diminished Americans' suspicion of cosmetics by promoting beauty care as a set of practices at once physical, individual, social, and commercial. Their businesses transformed the personal *cultivation* of beauty—the original meaning of the expression "beauty culture"—into a *culture* of shared meanings and rituals.

Before the Civil War, women dressed their own hair or, if affluent, bade their maids or slaves to do so. Professional hairdressers, often men who visited the homes of the wealthy, were relatively few in number. Commercial beautifying was generally considered a "vulgarizing calling," a legacy of its ties to personal service and hands-on bodily care. This view changed as women's need for jobs grew more pressing in the late nineteenth century. Industry, immigration, and urban growth had transformed the American economy and society. Working-class women expected to support themselves or contribute to family income, but even middle-class women were thrown back on their own resources when their husbands died or failed in business. The vast majority of female wage earners toiled in factories, on farms, or in private homes as domestic workers, but growing numbers worked in clerical, retail, and service jobs. These included hairdressing, cosmetology, manicure, and cosmetics sales.[1]

Although commercial beauty culture mainly offered women low-wage work, it became one of a handful of occupations—along with dressmaking and millinery—to sustain female entrepreneurship and ownership. Ironically, the feminine stereotypes that rendered women unfit for the world of commerce validated their endeavors in the beauty business. Promoters proclaimed that "no profession is more suitable for women, or more pleasant, than that of helping others to become beautiful and youthful in appearance." Some, like Mary Williams, became salon proprietors. The daughter of slaves who had bought their freedom, Williams learned the hair trade after the Civil War and opened a shop in Columbus, Ohio, in 1872. Serving both white and black residents, Williams eventually ran the "leading hair-dressing establishment in the city," sold hair goods, and taught the trade to other African-American women.[2]

Women also became inventors, manufacturers, and distributors of beauty products. The full extent of their business activity remains unknown. Still, the U.S. Patent Office recorded the efforts of many women bent on achieving success selling cosmetics. They patented improved complexion creams, combs to straighten or curl hair, and clever devices to carry powder or dispense rouge. Most often women sought trademark protection for their products. From 1890 to 1924, they registered at least 450 trademarks for beauty preparations, the bulk of them after 1910. These confident inventors and manufacturers probably represent only a fraction of all the women who peddled their own formulas to neighbors or sold them in local salons. Many filed papers with the Patent Office years after they had put their product into use; only when they perceived a market for it, or faced imitators, did they choose to register the trademark.[3]

Beauty entrepreneurs came from all walks of life. Some of the more affluent had found themselves caught between women's new educational opportunities and ongoing sex discrimination in employment, especially in the sciences. Anna D. Adams aspired to be a surgeon, Marie Mott Gage a chemist. Adams abandoned her career in surgery when faced with the prejudice of male physicians, became a professor of chemistry, and eventually founded a chain of beauty parlors. Gage, who grew up in a family of doctors, studied chemistry at Vassar, but by the 1890s was writing beauty manuals and manufacturing products for the "scientific cultivation of physical beauty."[4]

A few women from wealthy or middle-class families turned to beauty culture in desperation, when circumstances forced them to support themselves. Harriet Hubbard Ayer, one of the first women to establish a large cosmetics manufacturing operation, was born into a prosperous Chicago family in 1849 and married the son of a wealthy iron dealer at age sixteen. For a time she lived the life of a society matron, but growing marital conflicts and her husband's business failure led Harriet to divorce him in 1886. As sole support of her children, she took a series of jobs, then moved to New York and began manufacturing a face cream named after Madame Recamier, a French beauty of the Napoleonic era. "Not a vulgar white wash" but "intended to replace the so-called blooms and enamels," Recamier cream proved a success. "Within a month," a contemporary account observed, "the house was filled from top to bottom with women trying to manufacture toiletries fast enough to meet the public demand." Ayer traded upon her elite connections to elicit rare endorsements from prominent society women and gain display space in department stores.[5]

Most women entrepreneurs, however, started out in less fortunate circumstances. They were farm daughters and domestic servants, immigrants and African Americans, ordinary, often poor women. They lived all over the country, in cities, small towns, and rural backwaters. From socially marginal origins, they risked little going into a business whose reputation remained dubious. Traces of their local or regional exploits exist only in old fliers, ads, and patent records. But even those who became most successful, who shaped the national development of the modern cosmetics industry, often started out poor and disadvantaged.

Florence Nightingale Graham was born around 1878, some time after her parents had emigrated from England to become tenant farmers in Canada. Little is known about her early life, except that Florence grew up in poverty and had a limited education. As a young woman, she took one low-paying job after another, in turn a dental assistant, cashier, and stenographer. Following her brother to New York City in 1908, Florence found work in Eleanor Adair's high-priced beauty salon, first as a receptionist and then as a "treatment girl" specializing in facials. To better serve the wealthy patrons, Graham taught herself to

Elizabeth Arden in the 1920s.

Helena Rubinstein in the 1920s. (Photograph by Hal Phyfe)

speak with proper diction and to project an image of upper-crust Protestant femininity. A year later, she joined cosmetologist Elizabeth Hubbard in opening a Fifth Avenue salon. Their partnership quickly dissolved and Graham bought the shop, decorated it lavishly for an elite clientele, and, improving on Hubbard's formulas, developed her own Venetian line of beauty preparations. When she reopened the salon, she took the name Elizabeth Arden, one she considered romantic and high class.[6]

In contrast, Helena Rubinstein had already achieved considerable success by the time she arrived in the United States. The facts of her early life, like Arden's, have been obscured in a haze of publicity notices. In the 1920s and 1930s, she claimed to have been born into a wealthy family of exporters, taken advanced scientific and medical training at prestigious European universities, and obtained her winning skin cream from the famed actress Modjeska. Her 1965 autobiography and other sources present a somewhat different picture. Born in 1871, Rubinstein came from a middling Jewish family, her father a wholesale food broker in Cracow. Helena's medical education ended after two years when her parents, apparently opposed to her fiancé, sent her to live with relatives in Australia. In the 1890s, she worked as a governess and perhaps as a waitress. The cream used in her family had been made by a Hungarian chemist and relative, Jacob Lykusky, who taught her the simple beauty techniques she ultimately capitalized upon: cold cream to cleanse the face, astringent to close the pores, and vanishing cream to moisturize and protect the skin. Her friends clamored for the cream, and Rubinstein began to sell it. Finally she opened a beauty shop in 1900, using money lent her by a woman she had befriended on the passage to Australia.[7]

Within two years Rubinstein had become a success. She moved to London in 1908, opened a salon in Paris in 1912, and when war erupted in Europe, relocated to New York and opened a salon off Fifth Avenue, not far from Elizabeth Arden. There the two rivals warred for leadership in the high-status beauty trade. Disdainfully referring to each other as "that woman," they refused to acknowledge how much they had in common—their troubled family life, economic insecurity, string of typical female jobs, their immigrant status, and not least, the acts of self-making they performed to become cosmetics entrepreneurs.

Annie Turnbo and Sarah Breedlove also found in the beauty trade an escape from poverty and marginalization, an outlet for entrepreneurial ambition. Born in 1869 and orphaned as a child, Annie Turnbo lived with her older siblings in Metropolis, Illinois, a small border town on the Ohio River. She received an education, taught Sunday school, and joined the temperance movement, but how she earned a living as a young woman is unknown. As a girl Turnbo learned plant lore by "gathering herbs with an old woman relative of mine . . . an herb doctor [whose] mixtures fascinated me." In the 1890s she began experimenting with preparations to help black women like herself care for their hair and scalp. Many of them needed remedies for such common problems as hair loss, breakage, and tetter, a common skin ailment, but women also considered lush, well-groomed hair a sign of beauty. By 1900 Turnbo had produced a hair treatment containing sage and egg rinses, common substances in the folk cosmetic tradition. In that year she and her sister moved to Lovejoy, Illinois, a river town inhabited only by African Americans. They began to manufacture the product Turnbo called Wonderful Hair Grower and canvassed door to door. Facing a skeptical black community, she recalled, "I went around in the buggy and made speeches, demonstrated the shampoo on myself, and talked about cleanliness and hygiene, until they realized I was right."[8]

Demand quickly outstripped the two sisters' ability to produce the hair grower, and Turnbo hired three young women as assistants. Urged by friends to expand the business, in 1902 she moved across the Mississippi to St. Louis, drawn by its vibrant black community, a robust drug and toiletries trade, and the Louisiana Purchase Exposition, then being planned. Once well established in St. Louis, Turnbo began to extend her market, first throughout the South, then nationally. In 1906, as competitors began to imitate her product, she proudly registered the trade name "Poro," a Mende (West African) term for a devotional soci-

Annie Turnbo Malone.

*Madam C. J. Walker,
circa 1914.*

ety. When she married Aaron Malone in 1914, Annie Turnbo Malone's
Poro was a thriving enterprise.

Sarah Breedlove, or Madam C. J. Walker as she became known,
also entered the hair-care business in these years. Her early life bore
some similarities to Malone's, her chief rival. Born to former slaves in
Delta, Louisiana, in 1867, she was orphaned as a child and moved in
with her older sister. In 1882, at age fourteen, she married laborer
Moses McWilliams. Over the next few years, she gave birth to her
daughter Lelia, then her husband died in an accident. Moving to St.
Louis in 1888, Sarah did housework and laundering, raised her daughter, and joined the African Methodist Episcopal church and several
charitable societies. She also briefly became a Poro agent.[9]

When her hair began to thin and fall out, Sarah experimented with
formulas containing sulphur, capsicum, and other stimulants, and began to sell her own remedy. She too called her product Wonderful Hair

Grower, which may have been one of the reasons Malone registered the Poro trade name. Although each woman claimed to have invented hair-care systems for African Americans, they probably modified existing formulas and improved heating combs already on the market, adjusting them for the condition and texture of black women's hair. Their technique for pressing hair, using a light oil and wide-tooth steel comb heated on a stove, put much less strain on the scalp than earlier methods using round tongs or "pullers." By straightening each strand, this "hot comb" process created the desired look of long, styled hair.[10]

McWilliams moved to Denver in 1905 and began to sell in earnest. "I made house-to-house canvasses among people of my race," she recalled, "and after awhile I got going pretty well." She married newspaperman Charles J. Walker, who helped her start an advertising campaign and mail-order business. Over the next few years, Madam Walker extended her business to the South and Midwest and in 1910 settled the company in Indianapolis, which she considered a favorable spot both for African Americans and for national distribution. Although she incorporated the company in 1911, the major decisions and the profits remained in her own hands.[11]

In another period, Arden, Rubinstein, Malone, and Walker might have lived and labored in obscurity, a fate shared by most women. At the turn of the century, however, women's need for employment in a growing commercial and service economy joined with new cultural perceptions about appearance making and self-display, to foster women's enterprises in beauty culture. Finding ways to overcome the economic barriers and social impediments women faced, these four shrewdly took the measure of their times—and the market—to build business empires.

Like those who started other consumer-oriented businesses, beauty entrepreneurs grappled with common problems of ensuring distribution, creating brand recognition, and increasing demand. Sex discrimination intensified the host of challenges they faced. Women had less access than men to credit and education in business methods. They were generally barred from professional training in pharmacy, which was necessary to run drugstores and was the path men usually took into toiletries manufacturing. These obstacles had profound consequences for women's businesses. Although information about these early enterprises is limited, most remained small-scale affairs: a one-woman manufacturing operation based in a kitchen or a sideline to salon services, requiring little capital investment.[12]

In some of the larger companies, women controlled promotion and marketing as the firm's public face, but husbands or brothers held key positions in finance and manufacturing, where they oversaw both money and workers. When Elizabeth Arden expanded from salon services to product sales in 1918, she attended largely to her exclusive salons while her husband supervised production and distribution of the cosmetics line. In other cases, men played lesser or adversarial roles. Although Charles Walker initially helped his wife establish her hairgrower business, it was Madam Walker who ambitiously expanded the enterprise into the national market. Women often struggled with husbands or relatives for control of their companies. The marriages of Walker and Malone ended in divorce over business conflicts; Harriet Hubbard Ayer's ex-husband and daughter charged her with mismanagement, committed her to an asylum, and assumed control of the company. The Woman's Cooperative Toilet Company found it necessary to explain to a prospective sales agent in 1891, "We are not men doing business under assumed ladies' names," and derided this "*mania* of our men imitators."[13]

Gaining access to distribution networks and retail outlets especially plagued women entrepreneurs. Competition for shelf space in department stores favored the more prestigious male perfumers, considered skilled craftsmen. Druggists relied on large wholesale supply companies, which tended to carry established brands and hired men as traveling sales agents. African-American entrepreneurs faced these problems and more. With few black-owned groceries, general stores, and pharmacies, they needed to convince white retailers to stock their products. The success of cosmetics manufacturer Anthony Overton was unusual. Overton remembered calling on the trade for the first time— "several white merchants refused to even look at our samples"—but with enormous persistence he eventually broke through the color line in drug and variety stores. Only after Malone and Walker had created demand through other means were their goods accepted onto drugstore shelves.[14]

In response to these difficulties, beauty culturists redefined and even pioneered techniques in distribution, sales, and marketing that would later become commonplace in the business world. Working outside the conventional wholesale-retail system of trade, they parlayed salon- and home-based enterprises into mail-order and door-to-door peddling operations. These were already familiar methods of selling that had, by the late nineteenth century, reached into small towns and rural areas of the country and brought an array of consumer goods into American households. In the cosmetics field, the California Perfume Company (later renamed Avon) became most famous for this sales strategy. Book salesman David Hall McConnell founded the company in 1886 when he discovered that the sample bottles of perfume he gave away were more popular than the books he sold. He turned over daily operations to a Vermont woman, Mrs. P. F. E. Albee, who developed a plan to recruit women to sell perfumes and toiletries in their neighborhoods. By 1903, there were about 10,000 such house-to-house "depot agents" across the country.[15]

Many women entrepreneurs successfully imitated California Perfume's sales strategy in the 1890s and early 1900s. In magazines and circulars, they advertised for clerks, sewing women, domestic servants, and women "doing hard, muscular work" who might prefer the ease and refinement of selling cosmetics. When a Miss Prim inquired about a genteel and private occupation, Bertha Benz described her plan "for giving paying employment to ladies everywhere." She offered Prim a branch office covering her county in North Carolina, from which she could sell the "Famous Tula Water for the Complexion." The work, she said, consisted "of filling agents' orders of mailing circulars answering letters of inquiry etc which you can do quietly in your own house without renting an office for this purpose."[16]

House-to-house canvassing and mail order permitted businesswomen with little capital or credit to expand their manufacturing operations. They reduced their risk and gained cash flow by defining sales agents as resellers, requiring them to purchase the goods, rather than take them on consignment or sell on a salary basis. Mail-order cosmetics firms kept relatively little inventory, manufacturing as orders came in. Madam Walker's business from the first "operated on a cash with order basis and very little capital has ever been necessary for its operation," observed an Internal Revenue Service agent, puzzling over Walker's haphazard bookkeeping. Starting out in 1905, she had managed, in a mere thirteen years, to build a business with thousands of sales agents and annual gross sales of $275,000, a staggering success.[17]

Beauty culturists developed "systems" and "methods," signature skin- and hair-care programs that facilitated, and subtly redefined, these distribution networks. Gone were miscellaneous creams and lotions, replaced by specialized and coordinated products and step-by-step techniques. Skin-care systems required cosmeticians to apply an array of cleansing and "nourishing" creams and to massage the face with wrinkle rollers, muscle beaters, or other devices; customers were encouraged to follow the program at home. Each product performed a single function, but together they became a therapeutic "treatment line" in a regular beauty ritual. Unlike powder or paint applied temporarily to the surface of the skin, such methods promised to assist nature and secure a lifetime of beauty.[18]

Systems were frequently taught through beauty schools and correspondence courses, replacing casual apprenticeships with formal training and certification in hairdressing and beauty culture. The first academy of hairdressing appeared in 1890, and over the next two decades beauty schools sprang up across the country, many of them founded by women. Among the earliest was Madame Le Fevre's school of dermatology, which trained fifty-seven women in one year to fulfill

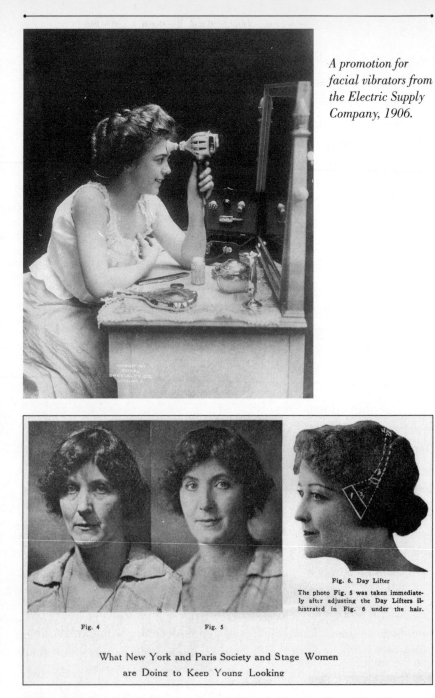

A promotion for facial vibrators from the Electric Supply Company, 1906.

Fig. 6. Day Lifter

The photo Fig. 5 was taken immediately after adjusting the Day Lifters illustrated in Fig. 6 under the hair.

Fig. 4   Fig. 5

What New York and Paris Society and Stage Women are Doing to Keep Young Looking

A "face lift" device from Susanna Cocroft. Detail, "Success Face Lifters" pamphlet.

"her desire to establish competent women in business in cities and towns where she is not represented."[19]

A number of entrepreneurs developed franchise operations in conjunction with beauty schools. These enabled certified beauticians to own salons, advertise their services as "system" shops, and capitalize upon the entrepreneur's name and reputation. Innovative beauty culturist Martha Matilda Harper, based in Rochester, New York, began to license her "Harper Method" in 1890 and eventually had more than 300 franchised salons. The Marinello Company, founded by Ruth Maurer, opened its first beauty school in 1904 and became one of the dominant organizations in the business, training white and black women and setting up franchises around the country. The Poro and Walker systems, and later Sara Spencer Washington's Apex, attracted thousands of black hairdressers as well, some of whom made the transition to proprietor. Although unrecognized by business historians, women entre-

From the Poro Hair and Beauty Culture Handbook, *1922.*

PORO COLLEGE

A Poro Graduating Class

PORO Agencies are now conducted by enthusiastic Agents in every state in the United States, and in Africa, Cuba, the Bahamas, Central America, Nova Scotia, and Canada. The opportunity of the PORO Agent to render genuine service is boundless.

PORO profits bring economic independence.

Madam C. J. Walker and others in an open touring car.

preneurs were in the vanguard of modern franchising methods that would take off more generally after World War II.[20]

Other women pioneered in the direct sales methods known today as multilevel marketing or "pyramid" organization. In addition to beauty services and product sales, agent-operators earned money and other rewards by recruiting women into their organization and training them in their specific beauty method. Entrepreneurial black women made this strategy highly successful. Malone and Walker traveled into every region of the country to teach women how to treat hair and sell products—remarkable journeys in this period of intensifying segregation and violence against black Americans. Their recruits trained others in turn, widening the circle of distribution. Sales agents fanned out to areas otherwise isolated from the consumer market. Walker's traveling representatives were instructed to "thoroly canvass Virginia, North and South Carolina," and the Sea Islands, because "there are more Negroes and more money there than in all other states combined." Like many direct-sales firms today, Malone rewarded agents not only with cash but with other incentives, bestowing diamond rings, low-cost mortgages, and public accolades for recruiting new agents, for becoming top sellers, and even for demonstrating thrift and charity. Led by compelling, larger-than-life personalities, these companies were early examples of what Nicole Biggart calls "charismatic capitalism," institutions that combined the profit motive with the qualities of a social or even religious movement.[21]

Women in the beauty business faced a specific cultural dilemma as they promoted the consumption of cosmetics: How were they to champion products that to a large extent still signified female immorality, goods whose use consumers often denied? If beauty was a "duty," as the prescriptive literature proclaimed, its achievement remained hedged about by women's embarrassment and anxiety about maintaining their good name. When she went into the beauty business in 1888, Mrs. Gervaise Graham observed, "Ladies went veiled to the Beauty Doctor, for fear of being ridiculed for their vanity." Similarly Harriet Hubbard Ayer recalled "how amused I was to get orders for a simple emollient cream, with the request that it should be sent in a plain wrapper."[22]

Men in the patent cosmetics and drugstore trade used two distinct appeals to induce women to buy beauty preparations. Patent cosmetics advertisements, like those for medicinal elixirs, featured sensational copy, dramatic before-and-after pictures, and promises of magical transformation. By 1900, retail and manufacturing druggists wished to separate themselves from such ballyhoo yet wondered how to handle women consumers—perceived as irrational and impulsive—in the growing market for cosmetics. With typical condescension, Chicago druggist B. S. Cooban described the problem, given cosmetics' "miscellaneous character" and the exacting requirements of "the 'dear creatures' who are our chief patrons":

Miracles are not only expected but demanded. To meet these demands and keep the girls, both old and young, in line, requires a great variety of stock, and the exercise of considerable judgement and tact in recommending articles for individual needs. And such needs! Did you ever take especial notice of the beauty troubles and tales of woe that women give you? How they *will* "roast" some powder or lotion![23]

Promoting cosmetic wares as staple goods and toilet necessities, Cooban and other druggists advertised their intrinsic qualities, celebrated low prices, and provided instructions for use. Nonplussed by beauty and by women, they offered the dry, indulgent humor of the man behind the counter, the laconic language of "good enough," and matter-of-fact descriptions of their miscellaneous goods.

Women entrepreneurs hawked cosmetics in a different key. They called themselves beauty experts who identified with women's wants and desires, and often cited their own bodily trials and tribulations as the reason they had become manufacturers. Necessity was indeed the mother of invention. One turn-of-the-century beauty culturist, known as Madame Yale, often said that she had wanted to be a general physician until she had the "personal experience of the worst forms of female disease." She healed herself, so she claimed, then decided to devote "her life-work to the benefit of her Sister Women" by developing a complete program of physical and beauty culture. Yale reminded clients that, as a "woman precisely like yourself," she knew "more about and underst[ood] better the secrets of woman's ills than all the male doctors and so-called 'professors' in the world." Some advertisements simply telegraphed women's ownership—as in a wrinkle eradicator by "B & P Co. (Two Women)"—female identification conferring instant legitimacy. Claiming authority through shared experience created a powerful link between producers and consumers, indeed, blurred the line between them.[24]

Women's anomalous place in the business world dictated this commercial strategy. After all, beauty expertise was deemed a natural form of female knowledge that women were expected to possess. Some businesswomen even hid their active experimentation with formulas and chemicals behind divine revelation. Madam C. J. Walker claimed she "had a dream" in which "a big black man appeared to me and told me what to mix up for my hair" and prophesied that she would beautify and uplift the race. French immigrant Marie Juliette Pinault, who had little else in common with Walker, also named a dream the inspiration for her products.[25]

These businesswomen shrewdly understood that their own personalities were business assets, integral to their sales strategies. They carefully crafted their self-images, creating distinct versions of femininity that resonated with the particular aspirations and social experiences of those they targeted as consumers. White beauty culturists often shed their names, hometowns, and social backgrounds to create personae as beauty experts. In a business dedicated to illusion and transformation, they were self-made. Madame Yale was, in fact, Maude Mayberg, who lied about receiving a degree from Wellesley College and whose other claims about formal training in chemistry, physical culture, and art are dubious. Poverty had "induced" Ida Lee Secrest "to take up the business," and, carrying some cosmetics recipes given her by an uncle, she fled Chanute, Kansas, for New York City. There she became "cosmetic artiste" Madame Edith Velaro, literally her own creation, whose "eyebrows were artificial, her lashes dyed, her complexion made up, her eyes brightened and made to look large by one of her preparations."[26]

Elizabeth Arden and Helena Rubinstein fashioned contrasting public personalities on which to base their cosmetics marketing. Arden, as a 1938 *Fortune* profile correctly observed, was "an alias concealing many things"—a chain of salons, a manufacturer, a sales corps, and, not least, Florence Nightingale Graham herself as she curried favor with elite society. "Arden pink" was her signature, coloring her apparel, salon interiors, and cosmetics packaging. Promotional letters under her name imitated her whispery, intimate speaking voice to create poetic pictures of youthful loveliness, considered models of "writing in woman's own language" in the advertising industry. Often described as a dithering, smiling figure, Arden undoubtedly exasperated the male executives around her. According to several reports, she was "fond of asking male advice on money and business, and almost invariably disregard[ed] it." This criticism reflects less upon Arden's "unbusinesslike manner" than on the control she exerted over her image and the company. Pink femininity concealed Arden's acts as an exacting and tough manager who broke a threatened strike, fended off complaints from the Food and Drug Administration, and remained the sole stockholder of her company, despite several marriages and buyout offers.[27]

Rubinstein also adopted a high-society image but invoked elements of the New Woman. In her view, the beauty specialist was a professional woman, "who is human in her sympathies, and will express these sympathies thru [sic] science." Typically photographed in a lab coat or striking dress and jewelry, she presented a dramatic figure of modernity—exotic, urbane, and scientific. Reporters often commented that Rubinstein, a Polish Jew, was "not a talker"—her speech was heavily accented—but also stressed her worldliness and sophistication: "a woman without a country who is at home in any country." Characteristically, she took an inclusive view of beauty culture, welcoming "stenographers, clerks, and even little office girls" into her salon and acknowledging the variety of skin types in a nation of immigrants. Unlike Arden, who only flirted with the suffrage movement when it was fashionable, Rubinstein became a long-term supporter of women's equal rights.[28]

If white beauty culturists sloughed off their origins to perform the American myth of self-making and individual mobility, black entrepreneurs tended to embed their biographies within the story of African-American women's collective advancement. Madam Walker identified closely with the struggles and dignity of poor women even as she sought entrance into the ranks of the black economic and social elite. She had remade herself in certain ways, hiring a tutor in standard English and carefully fashioning a refined and elegant appearance. Still, she persistently tied her business to the fortunes of the unschooled and poor women whose life experiences she had shared. In 1912, she burst into public awareness when she attempted to address the National Negro Business League at its annual meeting. Booker T. Washington repeatedly refused to recognize her, apparently not wanting to endorse such a disreputable calling. Finally Walker rushed up to the podium, exclaiming "surely you are not going to shut the door in my face," and launched into an impassioned speech. "I am a woman that came from the cotton fields of the South; I was promoted from there to the wash-tub . . . then I was promoted to the cook kitchen," she said emphatically, "and from there I promoted myself into the business of manufacturing hair goods and preparations." Walker proved her mettle, and Washington welcomed her back the following year, when as a featured speaker she pointedly declaimed, "I am not ashamed of my past; I am not ashamed of my humble beginning. Don't think because you have to go down in the wash-tub that you are any less a lady!"[29]

The projection of personality and expertise was central to the sales strategies women entrepreneurs adopted. Many of them advertised their beauty culture systems in local newspapers, distributed trade cards, and sent pamphlets through the mail. Advertising, however, did not dominate their marketing efforts. Beauty culturists placed relatively few advertisements, for example, in the national women's magazines then gaining popularity. Perhaps the cost of ad space was prohibitive. Then, too, some women's magazines banned ads for "quack" beauty cures, and none carried advertising from black-owned companies. At the same time, businesswomen's orientation to localism—apparent in their salons and door-to-door operations—may have disposed them against the type of advertising campaigns mounted by soap companies, packaged goods producers, and other manufacturers. Instead, beauty entrepreneurs concentrated on women's aesthetic and cultural practices, weaving their trade into the fabric of women's everyday lives. Addressing a heterogeneous public split along racial, class, and regional lines, they devised new forms of female interaction to create a sociable commerce in beautifying.

White businesswomen in the late nineteenth century exploited popular notions of womanly bonds, ironically promoting a consumer sorority around beauty in an era when class and ethnic differences deeply divided white women. Appealing to customers as "friends" and "sisters," manufacturer Flora Jones endorsed a view of commerce as simply "woman helping woman." This language advanced the distribution and marketing of beauty culture. Door-to-door canvassers, who construed their work as *calling* or neighborly visiting, stepped into the gap between reluctant cosmetics consumers and distant companies. At least one male manufacturer believed that the growing public acceptance of beauty aids after 1880 resulted in large part from the efforts of women who "solicit the business from the housewives of their various localities." Some mail-order firms encouraged women to form purchasing clubs for discounts and premiums. They believed that friends who shared catalogs, discussed products, and wrote up orders together made cosmetics more acceptable to one another. When women requested toiletries in plain wrappers, one perfume company pleaded, "do not feel ashamed to let your friends know you use it, but recommend it to them also."[30]

Even mail order, seemingly the most impersonal form of exchange, was refurbished as a hub of intimate correspondence, sisterly service, and trusted counsel. Madame Yale urged mail-order customers to write and "tell me all, everything—just as you would talk if we were sitting in my parlor face to face." A 1915 advertisement encouraged readers to "write Madame Rubinstein for an appointment or for advice and she will answer you personally." Handwritten, confidential promotional letters masked the commercial relations in which they were produced. To handle the volume of "private" correspondence, large manufacturers designed complexion analysis charts for women to identify their facial defects and employed armies of clerks to prescribe personalized corrective programs.[31]

These business methods may be seen in the letters of beauty cultur-

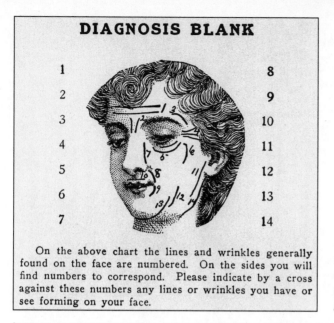

DIAGNOSIS BLANK

1	8
2	9
3	10
4	11
5	12
6	13
7	14

On the above chart the lines and wrinkles generally found on the face are numbered. On the sides you will find numbers to correspond. Please indicate by a cross against these numbers any lines or wrinkles you have or see forming on your face.

From a Susanna Cocroft brochure, circa 1912.

ist Susanna Cocroft to Ethel Vining, the wife of a Longmeadow, Massachusetts, businessman. Vining paid eighteen dollars to Cocroft in 1913 for a mail-order course that promised weight loss and improved appearance. Cocroft asked Vining for a "kodak picture, showing the lines of your figure," noting "I like to keep my pupil's face before me as I dictate her lesson." Every few weeks, Cocroft sent her a form letter—personalized with references to Vining's case—with instructions for dieting and exercise and leaflets advertising her toilet preparations. Vining, in turn, dutifully sent in reports detailing her weight and measurements. "If you could realize how eagerly I scan your report," said Cocroft, "I am watching your progress." Three weeks later, however, the relationship had begun to turn sour. "There is something wrong with the way you are doing your work," she complained. "You are not reducing as rapidly as you should, Mrs. Vining." Casting the situation in terms of personal inadequacy and betrayal, Cocroft blamed Vining for the failure of her course.[32]

Many white beauty culturists tried to turn grooming habits into

The genteel manicure parlor, from Mrs. Mary E. Cobb, "How to be Your Own Manicure" pamphlet.

bourgeois social rituals. Such terms as beauty *parlor* and *salon* invoked the rooms where public met private. For Madame Caroline, profits from her face beautifier seemed incidental to securing her place in the round of social visiting: "When orders are not received, or some of Mme. Caroline's fair patrons do not call as usual, then she knows they are either ill or not alive." A trip to the beauty salon fit into the urban pleasures women newly enjoyed, along with shopping, promenading, and taking in a matinee. One elegant Chicago salon urged "parties of ladies who are in town for a day" to visit for beauty treatments, lunch, and rest, and promised they would "go forth blooming and beautiful, ready for any social duties." In the 1910s, Marinello advised its beauticians to sponsor tea parties and fashion shows in their salons or at women's homes, prefiguring the successful sales strategy of Mary Kay Cosmetics.[33]

Public demonstrations made hidden beauty practices visible, easing women's embarrassment and ignorance about cosmetics use. Adopting a stylized patter as they worked on their own faces, beauty culturists taught their systems of cleansing, face massage, and cosmetic application. To advertise her "World Renowned Face Bleach," Madame Ruppert in 1889 invited the public to witness an exhibition of women at different stages of the treatment. Madame Yale traveled the country in the 1890s, giving public lectures to women on "The Religion of Beauty, the Sin of Ugliness." With her pink complexion and mass of blond hair, Yale proclaimed herself to be a middle-aged woman who looked and felt twenty years younger. She wore a tunic without corset or stays, demonstrated beauty exercises, and appeared in *tableaux vivants* as Diana and Helen of Troy to the enthusiastic acclaim of her followers, whom the press deemed the "Yale cult."[34]

Although drawing upon the conventions of middle-class life, beauty culturists cast a wide net for consumers. Before the advent of market research, there is little way to know who actually purchased their preparations. However, beauty culture targeted not only native-born, affluent white women but other women aspiring to middle-class respectability. Madame Ruppert, for instance, advertised her face bleach in the *American Jewess,* an English-language magazine for Jewish women of German and central European background. Articles praised the New Jewish Woman, who adhered to tradition but fit into modern American life. Ruppert's face bleach, with its promise to lighten and "refine" the skin, reinforced the magazine's assimilationist message. Similarly, beauty culturists placed an occasional notice in *Die Deutsche Hausfrau,* a German-language "home journal" addressed to rural and small-town immigrant housewives. "Are worry wrinkles starting and your features beginning to look disfigured?" asked Helen Sanborn, who offered the magazine's readers a "free coupon" for advice on skin care.[35]

In order to promote cosmetics to a diverse public, beauty culturists created a palatable ideal, mixing older and newer outlooks on feminine beauty that could be translated readily into the terms of the market. In salons, lecture halls, clubs, magazines, and advertising, they fostered a paradoxical female world of discipline and indulgence, therapy and luxury. Like most middle-class Americans, they believed the face was a window into the soul. "Is your complexion *clear?*—Does it express the clearness of your life?" asked Susanna Cocroft. "Are there discolorations or blemishes in the skin,—which symbolize imperfections within?" At the same time, they parried the idea that self-decoration registered female vanity and deceit. Reversing the Victorian logic that made appearance a function of character, they claimed that beautifying was a "moral necessity" that honored God's handiwork and nature's laws. "The day has passed forever for self-beautifying to be considered a confession of weakness," asserted Madame Yale. Women could fulfill the old adage, "beauty a duty," yet give in to the new siren song of consumption. As Susanna Cocroft urged, "Don't be ashamed of your desire for beauty."[36]

That desire could even include rouge, mascara, and lipstick. As they stressed the permanent improvement of appearance characteristic of beauty culture, businesswomen nevertheless rehabilitated the "painted woman." Madame Yale offered "temporary beautifiers" to ladies "too indolent to cultivate natural beauty," as well as "actresses and all those whose inclinations or pursuits render 'make-up' necessary." This shift in language—from paint to makeup—indicated that face coloring too could be considered an essential finishing touch in women's daily beauty ritual. "In this busy, *critical* world," observed Madame Thompson, "we need all the *help* we can command."[37]

Just as they grafted their trade onto womanly bonds and bourgeois social rituals, so beauty entrepreneurs capitalized on changes in women's lives, their new roles in that "busy, *critical* world." The beauty business emerged during the ferment of the late-nineteenth-century women's movement. In a period that both celebrated and feared white women's entrance into the public world of the workplace, college, and politics, businesswomen struggled to etch those large social changes on the face and body. Some firms advocated a form of feminism oriented to women's economic independence, linking it to their efforts to train and employ women in the beauty trade. Observing that "all the women of the twentieth century are workers," Marinello explicitly supported women's suffrage and employment opportunities. Madame Yale argued that "the progress of women" included "efforts in aiding them to make the most of their appearance and retain their youth." She wanted beauty culturists represented in the Woman's Building at the 1893 Chicago World's Fair, but the reform-minded Lady Organizers thought otherwise. Objecting to rouge and powder as "not things we wish to dwell on or emphasize," they prohibited displays from women in cosmetics manufacturing. Yale had the last word, however, issuing fraudulent notices that her preparations had been awarded the fair's top honors.[38]

Typically, businesswomen affirmed the feminist critique of women's enforced delicacy and weakness, without the accompanying politics of the women's movement. In their view, beauty was "more powerful than the ballot." The pale, frail lady and the corpulent dowager, physical types circumscribing women's freedom, would give way to a new model of modern femininity: "A living, breathing, animated, infectious personality of flesh and blood . . . a hearty play-fellow; a good comrade, who rides, walks, rows, golfs and wouldn't be guilty of fainting for a kingdom," as Yale defined her. "Miss Cocroft has made a new woman of me," a testimonial declared, but Cocroft herself denied that the New Woman fundamentally challenged society's gender arrangements. "The women of today, yesterday, and tomorrow are the same, but our horizons are broadening," she said. "And this will not make us mannish. We can be as sweet and dear and lovable in the street as in the home." Thus beauty culturists offered women the possibility of claiming the mantle of "advanced *fin de siècle* woman" simply by changing their grooming habits.[39]

These techniques of promotion and sales served white beauty culturists' aim of fashioning a distinctive feminine market out of a varied population of women. In the 1910s, however, one segment of the salon trade—that oriented to fashionable, wealthy white women—developed into large-scale cosmetics manufacturing. Arden and Rubinstein spearheaded the effort to convert elite beauty culture into a modern industry. This "class" segment of the cosmetics trade capitalized upon distinctions of wealth and status. Having expanded their salon opera-

Helena Rubinstein with workers preparing flowers and herbs for cosmetics, around 1925.

tions into large cities and affluent beach resorts, Arden and Rubinstein turned to high-volume product sales. In 1917 Rubinstein established the manufacturing arm of her company, and Arden followed suit in 1918. Both confronted the paradoxical problem of the class market for cosmetics: how to preserve an aura of exclusivity, wealth, and high fashion *and* sell to all who had the dollars to buy. Already identified with elite women, Arden and Rubinstein designed marketing campaigns to reinforce the prestige of their systems, urging women to emulate and vicariously join high society by purchasing costly cosmetics. Both companies began to advertise in such status-conscious magazines as *Town and Country* and *Vogue*. They approached only specialty shops and higher-priced department stores, often extending to a single retailer in a city or town exclusive rights to sell the line. By the early 1920s, beauty culturists Dorothy Gray, Marie Earle, and Kathleen

Mary Quinlan had all established manufacturing and marketing operations to sell specialty cosmetics. The creation of expensive "treatment lines" promoted through exclusive salons and sales venues—a segment of the trade built by white women—had become a major route into the modern cosmetics industry.[40]

Commercial beauty culture moved in a different direction for African-American women, taking an increasingly collective and political turn. Walker, Malone, and other black entrepreneurs had much in common with white beauty culturists, for instance, their use of systems, promotion of women's economic opportunities, and belief in the social significance of appearance. They too worked within ongoing cultural traditions and capitalized upon women's patterns of sociability. But race profoundly divided white and black beauty culturists. From the first, the cosmetics industry developed along parallel but largely segregated tracks. The "ethnic market," as it is euphemistically called today, involved separate distribution networks and advertising strategies, even when white-owned firms tried to extend their sales into it. Racial stereotypes provided the features against which dominant white beauty ideals were defined and marketed. All the white beauty culturists who manufactured face bleach, such as Madame Ruppert, reinforced those stereotypes as they sold an image of fair-skinned, genteel beauty.

The many black women who entered beauty culture responded to these matters in different ways. Some conveyed a frank message of emulation, that African Americans would benefit by, and be more attractive with, lighter skin and straighter hair. Like white beauty culturists and black men in cosmetics manufacturing, they marketed face bleaches and light powders. The leading firms owned by black women took another path, however. Walker and Malone refused to sell skin bleaches and never spoke of hair straightening as an aspect of their beauty systems. Rejecting any hint of contributing to black self-denial and emulation, they argued instead that improved appearance would

reveal to all the inner worth of black women, especially those who, la-
boring as domestics or farmhands, were most demeaned and ill-treated.
In their vision, beauty culture was a vindication of black womanhood, a
way to achieve personal dignity and collective advancement. Most important, they embedded the beauty trade in the daily life of black communities linked by kin, neighbors, churches, and schools. In so doing,
they created a singular form of beauty culture in which profit making
was intertwined with larger ethical and political purposes. Many
African-American women responded enthusiastically to these ideals.
As one admiring customer put it, "We's here to help one another and
feel each other['s] care."[41]

Hair grooming had long brought black women together to socialize
while engaging in the time-consuming rituals of washing, combing, and
plaiting, the tactile pleasures of working with hair mingling with the diversion of visiting and chatting. Teacher and one-time Poro agent
Mamie Fields recalled the "official hair wrapper" in every Southern
neighborhood, the talk and "fun working on each other's heads." Word
of hair growers and shampoos made by African-American women
spread rapidly. Women convinced each other to try these new products,
buying boxes of glossine and hair grower for relatives and friends,
practicing the art of hairdressing on each other. Like many women,
Elizabeth Clark placed an order with Madam Walker "not for my self"
but "for a friend of mine." For these businesses, word of mouth was the
finest form of advertising.[42]

Commercial affiliations followed from family ties and women's
friendships. Lubertha Carson applied to be the agent for Landrum,
South Carolina, writing that "all my friends ask me to take the trade so
that they can get the treatment from me." Women took great pride in
"making an agent"—teaching the beauty system to a trainee and presenting her with her first sales kit and diploma. Grace Clayton instructed her sister Page for six weeks and then wrote Madam Walker, "I
am shore she is all right now and ready to recive your papers." Mattie
Stephens "is quite a promising agent and will do well in her Section,"
wrote her sponsor; "there is no other agents at this place and there are

quite a few Colored people there." To sell in most places, the Walker Company instructed, "All you have to do is to get around among the people, in other words be a mixer." Indeed, newcomers to a community had difficulty entering the trade. Belinda Bailey "did not take up your work," she wrote Walker, because "i am a Stranger around Heare i Believe i Better waite untell i get Better quanted with the People it is hard for me to catch on to the ways of them."[43]

Beauty culture spread rapidly in part because it promised direct, practical rewards—the means to earn a living. For African-American women, finding steady and dignified work was a tremendous challenge. The rigidly sex- and race-segmented labor market allowed them only a handful of occupations, and most struggled to earn a living as domestic servants, washerwomen, and field hands. In a time when Southern black domestic workers earned only one or two dollars a week, the Walker Company claimed its agents could "easily make from three to five dollars a day." Actual earnings are difficult to determine: Although some women gained only a small clientele, top saleswomen pulled in as much as $100 a week. The most successful hairdressers moved out of their kitchens to open storefront beauty shops. One agent credibly contended that Walker had enabled "hundreds of colored women to make an honest and profitable living where they make as much in one week as a month's salary would bring from any other position that a colored woman can secure."[44]

Hair work also offered flexible hours and part-time employment for women who had other jobs or family responsibilities. While her brother fought in Europe in 1918, Annie Bell cared for his child; unable to "work out" as a maid she became a Walker agent. A small-town telephone operator in Arkansas sold Walker products as a profitable sideline, "to supply some few ladys who have used your goods before." The trade also attracted women with little education, physical ailments, and limited job prospects. Ethel Cornish, forced by illness to leave her factory job, went to a free course offered by Walker and became an agent: "I received my comb and preperation a month ago and have nine costomers at present all of them seem to be satisfied." A deaf woman who had trouble finding work enthused, "I am wild to start the treatment and would much rather have your art of hair growing than any other position."[45]

Beauty culture unleashed tremendous entrepreneurial energy among women used to suppressing their ambitions. As they traveled throughout the country, Walker and Malone galvanized city women and farm-dwellers alike. "I told you when you were in Des Moines that your talk inspired me so that I was determined to see what good I could do in this world and for my people," wrote Beatrice Crank to Walker after opening a beauty parlor. Maggie Branch of Chuluota, Florida, could canvass only a few hours a day but had quickly acquired six customers. "I am Still Working right on I am confident this wonderfull remedy will sell like hot cakes," she wrote Madam Walker. Sallie Adams competed for one of the prizes given out at the annual Walker convention and wrote, "I am both day and night with my hair work."[46]

Even educated and professional women who once scorned hair work now seized the chance to earn a higher income. Melinda Burleigh, a teacher in Portsmouth, Virginia, started out selling Walker products as a sideline but quickly expanded into full-time work. She trained women to become hairdressers, solicited customers in nearby counties, and became manager of a distribution depot. "I have given up teaching," she wrote. Some college-educated women set up their own beauty systems. Ezella Mathis Carter, a Spelman College alumna, had been a teacher and school principal in rural Georgia before entering the beauty trade; Sara Spencer Washington's family goaded her to teach, but instead she founded the Apex Hair and News Company, which became one of the largest black-owned businesses in the 1920s and 1930s.[47]

Walker and Malone worked with the leading institutions of African-American life to expand their companies. Despite early opposition from some ministers, who believed hair pressing was neither natural nor godly, churches became key places for promoting hair systems and distributing goods. Walker and Malone lectured to Baptist and African Methodist Episcopal congregations across the country and donated goods for church fairs and fundraisers. They often addressed consumers in a religious idiom: Malone's "evangels of Poro" spread "the gospel of 'better personal appearance,'" while Walker instructed agents selling to a new prospect to "imagine yourself a missionary and convert him." Sales agents and customers alike answered in kind, praying for God's blessings and closing their letters alternatively "yours for success" and "yours in Christ." Churches often became the staging ground for campaigns into new markets. F. B. Ransom, Walker's general manager, wrote a sales representative on her way to Chicago that "there are some two or three large churches on the west side and quite a community of colored people." He noted, "You could do a big business over there."[48]

African-American beauty culturists eagerly addressed women's clubs, lodge halls, and colleges. Walker actively took part in the National Association of Colored Women and spoke at its convention on several occasions; in 1918, she appealed "for club women to get closer in touch with our women in the factory." She also sought permission to install beauty parlors in women's dormitories at black colleges. Booker T. Washington refused to allow a salon at Tuskegee, but Roger Williams University, Guadalupe College, and the Arkansas Baptist College, among others, all agreed to the arrangement.[49]

Advocating Christian principles in business, both Walker and Malone dedicated themselves to black social welfare and community building, including industrial education, recreational programs, and charitable giving. Malone built Poro College to be "more than a mere business enterprise," nothing less than an institution "consecrated to the uplift of humanity—Race women in particular." Opened in 1918, it not only housed Poro's factory and offices, but offered theater, music, athletics, lectures, chapel services, and art murals. Reaching out to young women in need of training and jobs, Malone gave them—and black St. Louis—a wider view of culture.[50]

In many cities and towns, agent-operators formed clubs to embody the ideal of the "business family group," encouraging trade while serving the community. As Walker put it, clubs would "solidify the commercial, civic and racial interests of our women." Dozens of Poro and Walker clubs formed in the 1910s and 1920s, and smaller firms followed suit. Agent-operator clubs protected companies from people posing as official agents or adulterating trademarked products, a problem afflicting the large firms from the beginning. At the same time, they combined two common forms of working-class affiliation, the mutual aid society and the social club. Members mingled, shared beauty tips, enjoyed outings and entertainments, gained insurance benefits, and raised money for churches and charity. Beauty salons—known for their spirited conversation between beauticians and clients—became neighborhood centers for sharing information and organizing. Annie Turnbo Malone stressed that "every PORO Agent should be an active force for good" and rewarded agents' service to the community as well as their sales prowess.[51]

For many working-class black women, beauty culture strengthened their involvement in community affairs and even carried them into political activism. Two hundred Walker agents attended their first national convention in 1917, and heard Madam Walker speak on "Women's Duty to Women." Walker had long financed efforts for African-American uplift, but she increasingly supported the more militant politics of the National Equal Rights League and the International League of Darker Peoples. "We must not let our love of our country, our patriotic loyalty, cause us to abate one whit in our protest against wrong and injustice," she declared to the delegates. As American soldiers marched abroad, the convention sent a petition to President Woodrow Wilson, protesting mob violence and lynchings at home in the wake of the St. Louis riot.[52]

Black women entered the market for hair-care and beauty products at a particular historical juncture. New visions of economic self-sufficiency, personal autonomy, and social participation, spreading throughout African-American communities, arose to combat the deepening privations and assaults of everyday life. In this context, commercial beauty culture was something much more than an isolated act of consumption or vanity. In the hands of African-American women entrepreneurs, it became an economic and aesthetic form that spoke to black women's collective experiences and aspirations.

"The cosmetic business is interesting among modern industries in its opportunities for women," Helena Rubinstein observed. "Here they have found a field that is their own province—working for women with women, and giving that which only women can give—an intimate understanding of feminine needs and feminine desires."[53] More accurately, it was Rubinstein, Arden, Walker, and many other beauty culturists who defined those needs and desires. These businesswomen fashioned, in effect, a consumer market for beauty largely outside dominant distribution networks and the emerging organizations of national advertising and marketing. Linking the growth of commerce to job creation and training, entwining cosmetics purchases and beauty services, many of these enterprises braided together women's identities as consumers and workers. In this way they brought groups of women into the growing consumer culture who had previously had only a tenuous connection to it. Poor, working-class, and black women, largely ignored by national advertisers and magazines, joined the affluent in the market for beauty.

Rubinstein and the other women entrepreneurs established a tradition of beauty culture, which claimed women would find a lifetime of beauty by adopting daily rituals of skin and hair care that required coordinated products and techniques. Rubinstein never achieved her dream that society would quit viewing beauty culture as a "frivolous or wasteful expenditure of time"—a view that had much to do with lasting stereotypes of women.[54] By drawing upon female sociability and customs, however, women entrepreneurs made formerly hidden and even unacceptable beauty practices public, pleasurable, and normal. In this way, they contributed substantially to modern definitions of femininity, to the growing emphasis on making and monitoring appearance, and to the centrality of commerce and consumption in women's lives.

By promoting the idea of improving nature, women entrepreneurs validated beauty culture for a broad range of women. "Women may be divided into two classes, those who have good complexions and those who have not," Madame Yale observed with her usual aplomb, capsizing a social structure based on wealth, occupation, and ethnicity.[55] In the female democracy of manufactured beauty, all could improve their looks—and those who did not had only themselves to blame!

These ideas, of course, circulated in the service of profit. Whatever Madame Yale's assertions, women's commerce recognized the profound cultural differences among women. The businesswomen who addressed those differences, whether appealing to poor black women or wealthy society matrons, understood how much social origins, income, and prejudice weighed upon women who sought to remake themselves through appearance. Indeed, they had built their businesses on that very understanding.

The Rise of
the Mass Market

Women's growing acceptance of beautifying blossomed into a mass market for cosmetics after World War I. From expensive skin creams to dime-store makeup, new goods tumbled into the marketplace. Between 1909 and 1929 the number of American perfume and cosmetics manufacturers nearly doubled, and the factory value of their products rose tenfold, from $14.2 million to nearly $141 million. In 1929, sociologist Robert Lynd estimated, Americans were spending $700 million annually for cosmetics and beauty services. In a very short time, cosmetics had become an affordable indulgence for American women across the socioeconomic spectrum.[1]

From the 1890s through the 1910s, a local, service-oriented beauty culture dominated by women had played the leading role in creating beauty consumers. During the same period, however, an emergent class of managers and professionals were developing new methods that would come to dominate American business. They devised a national system of mass production, distribution, marketing, and advertising that transformed local patterns of buying and selling and fostered a culture of consumption. By 1920, new cosmetics firms, led primarily by men, embraced these methods to create a mass market and sell beauty products to all women. But if the mass market overwhelmed the older tradition of women's beauty culture, it simultaneously required a new ensemble of businesswomen—advertisers, beauty experts, brokers, and tastemakers—to "cash in on women's sphere." The "business exploitation of femininity," as *Fortune* called it, intensified women's connection to beautifying, albeit in unexpected ways.[2]

Fundamental changes occurred in the beauty business during the early twentieth century. The miscellaneous wares manufactured by patent-cosmetics firms, perfumers, and local druggists increasingly lacked appeal to consumers. Jars of private-label cold cream and ballyhooed complexion remedies seemed old-fashioned and ineffective when compared to beauty culture, which offered women a comprehensive program of beautifying and encouraged their steady purchase of goods. Many earlier manufacturers did not anticipate the growing demand for cosmetics among all classes of women, and they stumbled trying to produce goods for national sale.

Perfumers, who saw themselves as skilled artists, especially disliked the prospect of selling to the masses. In 1909 they resisted opening the door of their trade association to companies making "tooth powders, massage creams and a series of goods that are advertised largely, with which we have little or no sympathy." At the same time, French firms offered sharp competition with high-quality powders and cosmetics superior to most American brands. Coty, Rigaud, and Bourjois hired New York agents after 1900 and then developed American subsidiaries that traded on the reputation of Paris for fashion and elegance. Richard Hudnut's was one of the few companies that successfully shifted from making high-priced perfumes to selling a mass-market brand. Most familiar American perfumeries of the nineteenth century simply disappeared.[3]

Meanwhile, growing pressure from consumers, reformers, and the government for safe products put patent cosmetic manufacturers on the defensive. The *Ladies' Home Journal* had long banished ads for patent remedies and toiletries from its pages. The 1906 Food and Drug Act excluded most cosmetics from government regulation, but prohibited cosmetic mislabeling, banned the use of such harmful ingredients as lead, and required proof of extravagant therapeutic claims. These regulatory measures pushed many marginal manufacturers to modify their formulas and rewrite their sales pitch, or go out of business.[4]

A few older companies joined with a new generation of entrepreneurs to build the modern cosmetics industry. They envisioned a mass market of beauty consumers, in which large-scale production, national distribution, and advertising would make cosmetics affordable and indispensable to all women. Pond's, for example, started out as a patent-remedy company in 1846, when Theron Pond invented an all-purpose antiseptic to heal nosebleeds, cure "women's complaints," and restore sunburned or diseased skin—a typical self-help elixir. After the Civil War, the company added soap and toiletries as a sideline to the sale of Pond's Extract. An advertising survey in 1891—an early instance of market research—identified a growing demand for skin-care preparations, and Pond's began to reposition itself as a beauty business. By 1914, the original Extract was no longer advertised. Jars of cold cream and vanishing cream became the pillars of the company.[5]

A handful of enterprising pharmacists turned private formulas dispensed locally into trademarked goods sold in the national market. Although such top sellers of the 1910s and 1920s as Hinds' Honey and Almond Cream and Ingram's Milkweed Cream have faded from view, others remain familiar brand names. Baltimore druggist George Bunting concocted a remedy to soothe sunburn and "knock eczema" in 1914; he sold Noxzema at Maryland's beaches for years before hiring a New York advertising firm to promote it nationally as an inexpensive cleansing and moisturizing cream. The largest cosmetics firms before World War II sold such basic creams and lotions, staple items found in most bathroom cabinets.[6]

The riskier business of selling rouge, lipstick, and other forms of makeup—products still controversial among consumers—attracted a motley group of small-time druggists, import agents, hair dealers, and venturesome entrepreneurs. By the 1920s, men with little cosmetic expertise saw easy money in selling beauty and hustled into the trade. Advertising pitchman Claude Hopkins founded a successful firm not by inventing new products—he hired a private manufacturer to make a generic skin-care line—but by convincing aging actress and "Eternal Flapper" Edna Wallace Hopper to lend her name to the brand.[7] Among the cosmetics entrepreneurs who developed the mass market, however, more typical were Carl Weeks and Max Factor, one now obscure, the other a household name.

Carl Weeks, born into a Midwestern homesteading family in 1876, worked in a pharmacy as a youth. He was a drugstore owner and unsuccessful manufacturer of patent medicines when he began to experiment with a formula for long-wearing face powder. In 1910 he successfully produced an adhesive mixture of dry cold cream and talc but had no idea how to promote the powder. For five years, he recalled, it "lay around the factory, gradually being used up by the girls." Eventually Midwestern druggists began to stock the product, and Weeks established the Armand Company in 1915. He promptly hired the prominent New York firm N. W. Ayer to develop a national advertising campaign. Ayer associated the Iowa-made powder with French elegance, packing it in a tiny hatbox that looked "as though it had just left the shop of a chic Parisian milliner." As Weeks put it, "the package was wrapped up in ideas." Weeks poured his own energies into developing and maintaining a secure distribution network among retail druggists, who comprised 95 percent of his business. A believer in personalizing dealer relations, he lavishly supplied free samples, designed window displays, and issued breezy newsletters full of pep talks and sales advice. From a $5,000 concern in 1912, Weeks parlayed face powder into a $2.5 million business by 1927. Within a few years, however, Depression-era price-cutting and women's changing taste, from heavy to sheer powders, led Armand into a steep, irreversible decline.[8]

In the same period, Max Factor transformed his theatrical makeup line into a mass-market brand. Factor, a Russian Jew born in 1877, had emigrated to the United States in 1904, not, his son observed, "the practically penniless immigrant," but already a successful wigmaker and cosmetician. After four years in St. Louis, he moved to Los Angeles in 1908 and quickly established a barbershop, wig business, and makeup studio. The movie industry had settled in southern California, and Factor's studio served both stage and screen performers. Although he sold traditional stage makeup, he invented a "flexible greasepaint" in 1914 for use in films, which could be applied thinly and looked more natural in movie lighting and close-up shots.[9]

From the beginning, Factor made a few nontheatrical cosmetics that he sold only in his shop—three shades of face powder and two shades of rouge little different from those of other manufacturers. Spurred by local demand, in 1920 he introduced Society Makeup, a cosmetic line for everyday use. But for the most part, Factor, an immigrant and craftsman devoted to the theatrical trade, left the actual development of the mass market to his Americanized children and a company specializing in new product promotions. They cultivated druggists along the Pacific coast, then expanded into Eastern and Midwestern cities, using the same techniques as Carl Weeks. As Factor's eldest son, Davis, explained, they would "go to the drug stores week after week, [would] keep the merchandise displayed on the counters, even trim their windows if they have to and . . . show the druggist how to sell cosmetics." It was not until 1927 that Max Factor achieved national distribution; a year later, Factor's first advertisements ran in mass-circulation movie and romance magazines.[10]

Born only a year apart, the face powder king of Iowa and makeup artist to Hollywood stars could hardly have been more different. Yet their biographies illuminate several key issues in the growth of the cosmetics mass market. In particular, they highlight the decisive turn of the cosmetics industry toward national advertising and media-based marketing in the 1920s.

The various brands of powder, cream, and rouge were more alike than different, so far as their ingredients and formulas were concerned. If an advertiser focused only on cosmetics' intrinsic qualities, copywriter Dorothy Dignam observed, there were "few built-in copy appeals to attract women buyers." Of course there were inventions that distinguished certain brands: Factor's Pan-Cake foundation, a screen makeup modified for everyday use, was a highly praised innovation. Most manufacturers at this time, however, including Weeks and Factor, tinkered with stock formulas, making small alterations in the balance of ingredients, tints, and perfumes. Cold cream, for example, was the basis for specialized preparations containing a host of unusual ingredients—turtle oil, vitamins, hormones, even radium—to bleach, firm, or "nourish" the skin. (As critics of the cosmetics industry never tired of complaining, these additives were often bogus, sometimes hazardous, or in quantities too small to have any noticeable effect.)[11]

A look at the industry explains the similarities. Cosmetics production was still a relatively small-scale affair in the early decades of the twentieth century. Factories required a modest number of workers and used batch methods of production; nationwide, toiletries companies employed fewer than 9,000 workers in 1925. A routine practice in the cosmetics industry was the use of private-label manufacturers, who created standard products for a number of companies, which then packaged and sold them under their own brand names. Department stores and mail-order operations had long used this arrangement for "house brand" skin-care preparations. The growing popularity of cosmetics, especially makeup, led many start-up companies to contract with private-label firms. Manufacturing rouge, lipstick, and mascara required special equipment and expertise, and only the largest companies made them in their own plants. A few private-label manufacturers successfully went into brand-name marketing themselves; two of the most popular cosmetics of the 1920s and early 1930s, Tre-Jur compacts and Outdoor Girl powder, originated in this way. Most private-label houses, however, served the cosmetics industry behind the scenes, an arrangement that ensured the similar composition of many preparations.[12]

Packaging face cream in a Chicago factory in the 1920s.

At the same time, cosmetics firms flooded the market with products packaged to appear new and different. By 1930 women could choose from a bewildering array of three thousand face powders and several hundred rouges. A handful of leading brands controlled about 40 percent of cosmetics sales, which left much room for hundreds of companies to jockey for a share of sales. In this volatile trade, most of the entrepreneurs who developed the top makeup brands of the 1920s (in contrast to skin-care products) had only a short burst of success. In addition to Max Factor, the only pre–World War II American companies producing makeup that grew into large, long-lived corporations were Maybelline and Revlon, founded in 1914 and 1932 respectively. Significantly, both had started out as specialty firms that honed in on a niche of the market—Maybelline producing mascara, Revlon nail polish—and their explosive growth as general cosmetics firms occurred only after 1945.[13]

With so many products on the market, companies competed fiercely for shelf space in stores. Unlike the early women beauty culturists, mass-market manufacturers—mainly men—moved comfortably within the regular system of wholesale and retail distribution. That system was changing, however, as new drug syndicates, five-and-tens, and chain stores challenged independent pharmacies and department stores. Retailers embraced the new merchandising techniques at the point of purchase. "The toilet goods counter and all that it can be made to suggest is, to thousands of women, the very nearest they can ever come to romance," stated one promoter. "The qualities of change and excitement to be found there will do more to induce a buying urge than any intrinsic value of the goods themselves." Cosmetics companies courted retailers with an array of "dealer helps," from window trims and counter cards to display trays and free samples. For O. N. Falk & Son, a small-town Wisconsin druggist, the trickle of such offers from cosmetics firms turned into a flood by the 1920s.[14]

But retailers were not simply conduits for manufacturers' goods. Independent shopkeepers demanded special deals on merchandise; chain stores promoted their own "house" lines; and both cut manufacturers' suggested prices. Weeks and Factor's sons were typical of cosmetics manufacturers who made tremendous efforts in dealer relations. For them, consumer culture was less a world of glamour and fantasy than a protracted and prosaic skirmish over gaining sales outlets, differentiating products, pushing stock, and maintaining prices.

Their chief weapon in the war for profits became advertising. Modern advertising had developed in the late nineteenth century, serving manufacturers' efforts to increase consumer demand, gain leverage over retailers, and regularize production. Before the 1910s, however, national advertising played a small role in the sale of cosmetics. Perfumeries and patent cosmetics firms advertised their wares on trade cards, posters, sample envelopes, sheet music, and broadsides, but much of the trade was local and word of mouth. Magazine advertising was quite limited. A few firms sold creams and powders in women's magazines, but rarely did an ad for rouge or eye makeup appear. Unlike toilet soaps, presented in full-page, lavish designs in the 1880s and 1890s, most cosmetics ads were set in small type and remained in the back pages of magazines.[15]

By World War I, however, advertising agencies boldly began to proclaim, "Extensive Use of Cosmetics Due to Advertising." French exporters and large American manufacturers of skin-care products were among the first to develop major national ad campaigns. Smaller domestic firms, especially those selling makeup, followed after 1918, and beauty ads filled the popular media. Advertising expenditures in the thirty largest mass-circulation magazines mushroomed from $1.3 million in 1915 to $16 million fifteen years later. During the 1920s, toiletries placed third among all classes of goods advertised in magazines generally, second in women's magazines, and fifth in newspapers. In four popular women's magazines studied in 1929, about 20 percent of advertising space was devoted to cosmetics.[16]

When radio broadcasting began in the late 1920s, the cosmetics industry hastened to sponsor programs and purchase commercial spots. Between 1927 and 1930, the investment of cosmetics and toiletries firms in advertising on the radio networks climbed remarkably, from $300,000 to $3.2 million annually. The French company Bourjois successfully introduced a perfume called Evening in Paris on the radio, airing the music and sounds of Parisian nightlife. In 1931, Lady Esther became the first cosmetics firm to allot almost all its advertising budget to the airwaves; promoted as a Depression-era product cheaper than its competition, Lady Esther saw sales increase 400 percent within a year of its first broadcast.[17]

Ad placements in national magazines varied considerably in the 1920s and 1930s, and show a distinct but not rigid pattern of marketing to specific groups of consumers. Salon-based firms like Arden and Rubinstein publicized their exclusive lines in a handful of major women's magazines and more elite publications like *Town and Country* and *Vogue.* Many mass-market companies also ran ads in *Vogue,* less to address society women than to announce their serious intentions to the trade. Such large mass marketers as Pond's covered the wide field of women's magazines and general periodicals. In contrast, Maybelline placed ads promoting mascara, still a controversial type of makeup, in numerous movie and confession magazines, Sunday newspaper supplements, and specialized journals, such as *Theater*. Whatever strategy companies followed to position their products, advertising required a significant outlay. In only one month in 1926, Maybelline spent $4,000, Arden $20,775, and Pond's nearly $60,000 in major national magazines.[18]

Businesswomen were at a disadvantage in the new market for cosmetics, with its increased competition for consumers, commitment to costly national advertising, drug- and department-store distribution, and greater need for capital. "Production on a small scale is now practically prohibitive," Rubinstein observed, but this had been the way women had traditionally entered the business. Beauty culture's original strength—its localism and service orientation—proved a weakness in this changing climate. Although for many women a trip to the beauty parlor had become a weekly habit, the salon no longer provided the springboard into cosmetics manufacturing and sales. Women dominated the ranks of hairdressers and beauticians, to be sure, but skin treatments and makeup composed a declining percentage of beauty parlor profits. After World War I, the craze for hair bobbing and permanent waves, along with growing pressures for training and certification, made hair styling the central work of the beauty parlor. When consumers wanted cosmetics, they turned to department stores and drugstores, which were more likely to carry the nationally advertised brands of large manufacturers.[19]

The compass of women's activity and power in the cosmetics industry thus narrowed after 1920. The beauty culture tradition continued in the profitable "class" segment of the industry pioneered by Arden and Rubinstein, but few women managed to establish successful massmarket firms. Edna Murphey Albert expanded a door-to-door operation selling homemade deodorant into the Odorono Company. Princess Pat, one of the most successful makeup lines in the 1920s, was the brainchild of husband-and-wife team M. Martin Gordon and Frances Patricia Berry: He supervised the manufacturing process, while she managed promotion and sales, lecturing on cosmetics and eventually broadcasting as "Beauty Editor of the Air." Beauty culturist Madame Berthé, maker of Zip depilatory, allied with a larger manufacturer to enter the mass market.[20]

These women were more the exception than the rule. "Of the many firms once owned and operated by women," observed fashion writer Catharine Oglesby in 1935, "the great majority have passed over into the hands of large companies controlled by men who are directors in large holding companies." Dorothy Gray, who had established her New York salon in 1916, sold her high-priced skin-care line in 1926 to Lehn and Fink, an established drug supplier and manufacturer of such staple goods as Lysol disinfectant and Pebeco toothpaste. Marie Earle, Ruth Maurer of Marinello, Edna Albert, Peggy Sage, and Kathleen Mary Quinlan also sold their companies in the 1920s, although the latter two continued as stockholders and directors. Even Helena Rubinstein succumbed in 1928 to a large offer for her American manufacturing operation from Lehman Brothers, the investment firm. But when Lehman tried to turn the Rubinstein label—sold in specialty shops and department stores—into a cheap variety-store line, an enraged Madame Rubinstein protested. She pressured Lehman to return the company to her by writing women stockholders that men did not understand feminine beauty needs. After the stock market crash, she bought back enough stock—at a substantially reduced price—to regain control of the company.[21]

Elizabeth Arden retained continuous ownership of her company—alone among the leading white beauty culturists—but she recognized the sea change taking place. Turn-of-the-century beauty culture had emphasized a discipline of skin care that would supposedly lead to lasting beauty, but it was the growing emphasis on rouge, lipstick, and mascara that increasingly spurred the industry's development. The "'temporary' beauty business," as Arden disdainfully called the trade in makeup, had won. "The great days of the salons are over," she sadly concluded in 1937.[22]

The African-American beauty industry is usually perceived to have been segregated from these developments, and in many ways it was. Black-owned firms addressed black women almost exclusively, and they did so in African-American magazines and newspapers, not mass-circulation publications. Nor did African Americans appear in national magazines or advertising, except as demeaning stereotypes, such as Aunt Jemima, or as the butt of racist jokes. Nevertheless, as the cosmetics industry expanded the market among white women through national advertising and mass marketing, a parallel set of developments occurred in the African-American beauty trade. In many respects, black and white entrepreneurs followed similar paths in capitalizing upon the desire for beauty.

Even as women pioneered an African-American beauty culture, many black patent medicine makers, druggists, barbers, and peddlers entered the cosmetics trade. Working on a small scale, one pharmacist recalled, black entrepreneurs "usually made up enough goods to supply their customers and distributed the same from the ordinary hand bag." Relatively few in number, drugstores nevertheless developed more rapidly than other black-owned retail outlets, largely because they were patronized by African-American physicians. Like their white counterparts, some black pharmacists went into manufacturing hair tonics and skin creams for local patrons, then expanded into regional and national distribution. By the 1910s, the demand had grown so great that scores of would-be entrepreneurs—from porters to teachers—rushed to profit from the new opportunities. Although hair products remained dominant, skin creams, powder, and even makeup appeared on the market.[23]

Some black businessmen used beauty culture methods, developing their own hair systems, beauty schools, and correspondence courses. Others launched cosmetics businesses with a vision of consumer culture closer to that of the predominantly white mass market. Anthony Overton paved the way with High-Brown preparations. Born in Louisiana in 1864, the son of slaves, Overton earned a law degree in 1888, then worked variously as a judge, Pullman porter, peddler, and proprietor of an Oklahoma general store. In 1898, he founded the Overton-Hygienic Company to manufacture baking powder, then added preserves and extracts. Within a few years, he began to make High-Brown Face Powder, designed "to harmonize with the color and skin texture of the women of our race." With the discovery that women "used more face powder than baking powder," Overton's cosmetics business took off, especially in the South and Midwest. Overton was a "race man," hiring only black salesmen and office clerks. "Having abiding faith in our own people," he once said, "we have conducted our business strictly as a Negro enterprise." In the early 1900s, Overton used door-to-door agents to sell products, and he approached black colleges and other institutions to carry his goods. But Overton also aggressively sought mainstream channels of distribution. In 1911 he moved his manufacturing plant to Chicago, a hub for distribution and transportation, hired five full-time traveling salesmen, persuaded large jobbers to carry the High-Brown line, and gained access to variety stores and neighborhood drugstores. He also underwrote a magazine for black women called the *Half-Century,* published from 1916 to 1922, which carried full-page ads for Overton-Hygienic products. Overton's success, the head of the National Negro Business League observed, "made it easier for other toilet products to reach the retail trade through regular channels."[24]

Overton may have been the inspiration for a group of Chicago-based black investors, who formed the Kashmir Chemical Company and launched Nile Queen cosmetics in 1918. Among them was Claude Barnett, a pioneering publicist and journalist. A graduate of Tuskegee, Barnett had worked for mail-order magnate Richard Warren Sears and for the U.S. Post Office. Deeply committed to Booker T. Washington's vision of black economic development, he also appreciated modern methods of marketing. He set up his own advertising agency in 1916 and created a mail-order operation to sell portraits of well-known African Americans. In 1919 Barnett founded the Associated Negro Press, the first press service for black newspapers. He distributed ANP news releases in exchange for advertising space, which he sold to other advertisers or used to promote Nile Queen. The cosmetics ads were strikingly elegant and fashion conscious, reflecting Barnett's familiarity with commercial design and advertising appeals. In this way, Barnett simultaneously shaped public opinion and fostered a consumer culture among African Americans.[25]

With the tremendous growth of the African-American cosmetics market, white-owned companies eyed the field with greater interest. Increasingly aware of black purchasing power, some white druggists and chain-store managers displayed cosmetics specifically for African Americans and included the black community in store promotions, although these were often segregated. In Fort Gibson, Oklahoma, when a drugstore held a gala week of free entertainment, food, and product samples, "the negro population was not forgotten," reported *Colgate Shavings* in 1923: "More than $200 worth of prizes were given to the colored population at the same time, and twenty-five gallons of ice cream were delivered to negro churches."[26]

Some mass-market firms that had sold primarily to white consumers began to solicit black patronage. Boncilla Laboratories created a popular fad in the early 1920s with a clay cleansing mask; mainly advertising in mass-circulation romance and movie magazines, Boncilla also placed ads in the Pittsburgh *Courier,* a leading black newspaper. Such long-established companies as American Products, a mail-order firm, and J. E. McBrady, a wholesale supplier, also courted African Americans. In 1922 American Products included a High Brown tint in its Zanol line of face powders, "made especially for dark complexioned people, something entirely new in face powders and already in popular demand." As the Second City's black population grew around World War I, Chicago-based McBrady started a complete line of "Specialties for Brown Skin People," sold only through agents and advertised with appeals to race pride.[27]

Most important were the white start-up entrepreneurs who built huge businesses manufacturing hair and skin preparations especially for African Americans. In the mid-1920s a black political journal, the *Messenger,* concluded that "probably the largest number of manufacturers of such commodities are white men."[28] Relying heavily on newspaper advertising campaigns, they made such trade names as Golden Brown, Nadinola, and Golden Peacock familiar to black women.

Plough Chemical Company was the most aggressive and successful of these. Sixteen-year-old Abe Plough started in the drug trade in 1908 in Memphis, a center for drug manufacturing in the South. Press histories of the company tell how Plough took a $125 loan from his father, peddled "healing oil" and blood tonics, and built one of the largest pharmaceutical houses in the United States. African Americans remembered the story differently. "Many Negroes like to think that the Plough fortune is founded upon the generous support which colored people gave to his early efforts," the Associated Negro Press reported sardonically in 1951. "Plough used to go about driving an old crippled white horse to a buggy, selling hair straightener, pomades, perfumes, etc."[29]

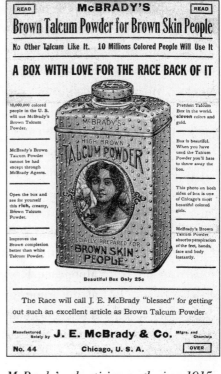

McBrady's advertising card, circa 1915.

In 1914 Plough bought a drugstore on Beale Street, the commercial hub of black Memphis, where he promoted a bleach cream to African Americans. He sold his Black and White cosmetics line through drugstores, not agents, and priced it below the Walker and Poro brands. By World War I, Plough had become the largest advertiser in black newspapers, able to pressure publishers for free publicity and reduced rates on ads. Plough "made a fortune out of advertising in Negro newspapers," one black business leader recalled. In the 1920s Plough invested his profits from cosmetics in the drug trade, purchasing St. Joseph's Aspirin, and he began advertising Black and White beauty preparations to white women in national publications. These ads replaced the explicit racial message of the ads directed at black consumers with a general promise of light, clear skin, like other mass-market advertising. In a similar way, Plough "whitened" his company's public face, erasing its origins in the black cosmetics trade as it became a pharmaceutical giant.[30]

African-American cosmetics manufacturers tried to counter this competition by forming a trade association in 1917, which over the next decade discussed how to force "unscrupulous white concerns off the market." Cooperation proved difficult. Although the call for racial solidarity was an influential commercial strategy, the African-American press, precariously dependent on advertising revenue, resisted pressure to reject white-owned companies' dollars. To sidestep the problem, some white companies, like McBrady's and Golden Brown, simply masqueraded as "race businesses" to gain consumers' trust; as Walker's general manager F. B. Ransom warned, they were "operated by colored but actually financed by white capital." Moreover, black manufacturers could not compete with mass-market tactics: White businessmen like Plough gave drug and chain stores special deals, offered lower prices, and effectively undercut African-American firms.[31]

Black businesswomen made various attempts to adapt to the new conditions of marketing and selling. Because national mass-circulation magazines excluded African-American companies, Madam C. J. Walker and Annie Turnbo Malone purchased advertising in scores of black newspapers, farm journals, and religious periodicals to cobble together coverage coast to coast. Although both continued to rely on agent-operators, the Walker Company also sought drugstore distribution, even when Walker agents balked and demanded "proper protection" from retail competition. Adding to her complement of hairdressing products, Walker inaugurated a line of face powders and skin-care cosmetics in 1919, responding to "the demands of the times and the requests of our many agents"; Malone, the more conservative of the two women, followed suit in 1922. While hair grooming involved longstanding traditions upon which African-American beauty culture capitalized, the introduction of powder and paint indicated a turn toward a more modern sensibility.[32]

Walker held fast to her earliest commitments, however. She included in her cosmetics line a witch hazel jelly for the hands of "those who work in the open and women who put their hands in hot water." Even more significant was her refusal to manufacture skin bleach. After Walker's death in 1919, the company was run by general manager F. B. Ransom. Although he retained the agent-operator system, he came to depend increasingly on drugstore distribution, newspaper advertising, and complexion product sales. Most indicative of the changing tenor was the introduction of the skin bleach Tan-Off. Sales of the original hair grower declined sharply in the 1920s and early 1930s, while Tan-Off sold briskly, "our best seller in some sections," the *Walker News* reported.[33]

Poro suffered in 1927 when Annie Malone and her husband Aaron divorced and fought for control of the business. When a St. Louis court put Poro into receivership and a white man in charge, black public opinion rallied to the woman entrepreneur. "Madam Malone's fight becomes the Race's fight," said one newspaper. Annie Malone eventually won, but at great cost, with Poro in ruins. In 1929, according to Claude Barnett, Poro did only $475,000 in sales, while Plough, in contrast, sold $5 million in products to African Americans, about 40 percent of the company's total sales in cosmetics and drugs.[34]

The Great Depression sealed the fate of many black women's businesses. Hair work remained an important source of employment for black women, ranking sixth in nonagricultural jobs in 1930. National agent-operator systems did not disappear, as Sara Spencer Washington's success with Apex in the 1930s demonstrates. Beauty shops too endured as vibrant sources of economic, social, and even political strength in black communities. But the grand vision of beauty culture had been battered by the economic crisis, aggressive white competitors, and black businessmen who embraced mass-market advertising and sales strategies. As Barnett observed, organizations that mingled business and philanthropy could not compete with the single-minded pursuit of profit.[35]

The consumer culture that emerged in the 1920s, with its emphasis on advertising and media-based marketing, is today so integral to American life that it appears an inevitable, almost natural development. Cosmetics, consumption, and femininity seem part of a seamless fabric. In this formative period, however, mass-market firms actively searched for ways to package their goods that would legitimize cosmetic products and practices still questionable in the eyes of many Americans. Gaining insight into women consumers, and channeling their apparent needs and desires into sales, remained a perplexing problem for many of the men who now ran the cosmetics industry.

Compounding the difficulty was their self-consciousness as men in the business of feminine beauty. "We know each other as men and have learned to respect each other as men," toasted the Manufacturing Perfumers Association in 1907. Salesmen and drummers spoke a gung-ho, hail-fellow language that filled cosmetic trade journals. "The merchant who orders the full line is hitting on all four cylinders of the TRE-JUR Sales Engine," read a trade advertisement for women's powder compacts. Carl Weeks constantly appealed to masculine pride and camaraderie, exhorting salesmen and druggists not to be "yellow bellies" in the commercial arena. He hired clean-living salesmen—never women—and insisted they abstain from liquor, gambling, and smoking. Druggists responded enthusiastically: "Each letter, and each bit of advertising you send us, seems so 'chummy,' that it *never* goes into file X without being read."[36]

These businessmen were undoubtedly aware of and eager to erase the taint of effeminacy and homosexuality that marked men who beautified women. Although the history of gay men in beauty work remains to be written, we know that the image of the male hairdresser, who had

*Max Factor, Sr., with
actress Alice White in
a 1920s publicity
photo. (Copyright
Procter and Gamble)*

served wealthy female clients in the eighteenth and nineteenth centuries, was often that of the dandy or fop. What may have been an acceptable personal relationship between male cosmetician and female
client became more problematic when presented in mass media—in
the movies, where censorship boards and studio guidelines tried to ex-
punge images of gay men, and in advertising. The handful of male
beauty experts in the mass market usually represented themselves as
professional men of science or the stage. Max Factor, noted a newspaper article, "refus[ed] absolutely to wear the mannerisms of dandified
beauty specialists." Photographs of Factor show him simultaneously as
makeup artist, chemist, and father figure. Although short in height, he
often appeared to be standing over compliant actresses who deferred to
his know-how. Early publicity interviews with Factor presented him as
a successful immigrant who spoke pidgin English with a Yiddish in-
flection: "Grease paint is not for street. Yong girl might use powder, a

little—mebbe." By the 1930s, company publicists polished his image into that of an articulate lab-coated expert, even as, according to one source, they urged the real Factor not to speak in public. When he died, his son Frank took his name, so that authoritative advice could continue to come from Max Factor.[37]

Factor was an exception. The challenge of selling an intimate, feminine item to women more commonly led cosmetics firms to simulate a female world of beautifying. Carl Weeks often wrote Armand promotional leaflets that druggists distributed with samples or mailed to their best customers. Weeks would visualize women before composing the copy. He thought of himself sitting in "a dimly lit room" with "silken drapes," and, he reported, "got one of the sweet sisters in my mind's eye and wrote [a] letter to her." Sometimes he wrote *as* a woman, in the first-person, telling a tale of how switching to Armand brought romance and happiness. One draft, however, drew groans from many women on his staff, playing as it did on the stereotype that women would do anything to catch a man. Although some found it "catchy" and "modern," others attacked the idea as "so trite—so overworked in advertising." Calling it "hooey," one secretary asserted, "If I got this in the mail I'd put it in the waste paper basket along with 'True Stories.' " Weeks knew how to speak to his fellow salesmen but stumbled when he addressed women consumers.[38]

Cosmetics companies frequently hired or created female beauty experts identified with the brand. Although this practice was common in the marketing of consumer goods—exemplified by the fictive Betty Crocker—the genuine tradition of female leadership in beauty culture lent authority to mass-market cosmetics companies. Many brands had their version of Madam Jeannette, "Specialiste en Beauté" for Pompeian preparations, or Jeanne Armand, who signed replies to consumers' inquiries. Radio multiplied the presence of such mass-market experts, whose beauty talks, sponsored by cosmetics firms, spread "the methods in beauty science which up to this time have been largely limited to the rich women." "Lady Esther Serenade," for instance, featured musical numbers interspersed with advice from Lady Esther herself—or rather a radio actor playing the beauty adviser. The "sugary band and a woman with a sickening voice," advertising pioneer Helen Woodward ruefully observed, was "radio's best example of success."[39]

Some firms simply fabricated a complete illusion of the woman-owned business. Around 1920, a group of Lowell investors with no experience in the beauty trade hired Woodward to develop a cosmetics company called Primrose House. Although manufacturing a complete cosmetics line for the mass market was prohibitively expensive, she determined that a salon-based skin-treatment line could be started for much less, about $60,000. Woodward hired a private-label manufacturer to make fifty standard products, wrote ad copy publicizing them as the beauty secrets of a woman diplomat, and created an exclusive salon featuring trained nurses to give facial massages. Finally Woodward engaged Mrs. Gouverneur Morris as a beauty specialist, capitalizing not on her cosmetics expertise—she had none—but on her prominent name in high society. "All this was done before a single ounce of cold cream was manufactured," Woodward recalled. The company started out well, but conflicts between the male investors and women managers soon erupted. According to Woodward, the men failed to appreciate how costly an aura of feminine exclusivity could be. They ousted the women and placed the company under new management in 1926, but preserved the ambience of women's beauty culture and remained active into the 1930s.[40]

The white male owners of the Golden Brown Beauty Company went even further, performing not only in drag but in blackface. Hessig-Ellis, a wholesale drug company in Memphis, registered the Golden Brown trade name and set up a "dummy" organization that employed thirty-five black workers and sold only to black consumers. Advertisements celebrated Madam Mamie Hightower, supposedly the company's founder and leader. One ad sketched Hightower's "meteoric rise" from a "mere nobody" to owner of a Beale Street salon, and finally to "beauty culturist of international repute" and "Race Benefactress." The Hightower story was an elaborate invention, probably produced by

Hessig-Ellis's white advertising manager, Harold Gilbert, who also served as Golden Brown's vice president. Mamie was, in fact, the obscure wife of Zack Hightower, a porter for Hessig-Ellis; she may have been a home-based "hair presser" but never owned a beauty parlor in Memphis. The ruse seems to have worked. Although Claude Barnett and others knew the truth, black newspapers publicly lauded Hightower, urging that her "good work go steadily on." Indeed, when a report surfaced in 1929 that Golden Brown was sending racist advertising circulars to white druggists containing references to superstitious "darkies," the *New York Age* expressed puzzlement, concluding that Hightower's company had been taken over by whites.[41]

Ironically, even as women were displaced from ownership of cosmetics firms, manufacturers and advertisers increasingly turned to them for their leadership and knowledge of beauty matters. This was a striking development, since women had little authority—except as consumers—in the mass market at large. In advertising agencies, women made up only a small percentage of professional staff. The magazines and newspapers that circulated the images and ideals of consumer culture were owned and published by men; on the mastheads of the major women's magazines, male editors outnumbered women two to one. In the beauty industry, by contrast, there were significant numbers of professional women working in advertising, marketing, sales, and media. Mainly white, middle-class, and college-educated, they filled a particular role as tastemakers and cultural brokers of the new mass cosmetics industry, mediating between male manufacturers and women consumers.[42]

According to copywriter Dorothy Dignam, men wrote the earliest ads for toiletries but "when face powder began to come out in shades and creams could 'beautify overnight' and perfumes were all moonlight-and-roses men got fed up and women began to compose the selling prose." Women were disproportionately assigned beauty accounts in advertising agencies. Such pathbreakers as Helen Woodward, Helen Landsdowne Resor, Edith Lewis, and Dignam, among others, developed major national campaigns, while many others worked on beauty advertising in local agencies, department stores, cosmetics firms, and mail-order houses.[43]

At the J. Walter Thompson Company, which specialized in advertising to female consumers, women wrote all the copy for the firm's beauty accounts. Helen Landsdowne, one of the first women in advertising, became a guiding figure there. She briefly worked for a Cincinnati toilet-goods manufacturer, but quickly moved on to advertising in the early 1900s. Stanley Resor, later the head of J. Walter Thompson, hired her as a copywriter; they transferred together to New York in 1911 and married in 1917. An ardent feminist—said to have led a Thompson contingent in New York's mass suffrage parades—Helen Landsdowne Resor brought many professional women into the company. Believing that women would advance further in a single-sex environment, she created separate editorial departments for women and men. "The women were terrifically powerful," one executive confirmed.[44]

Most were college graduates who had worked in business, as publicists, writers, merchandisers, product testers, or market researchers. Others were active in social reform and the suffrage movement, including several publicists newly jobless after women won the right to vote. Ruth Waldo had worked for the Russell Sage Foundation and the Charity Organization Society before joining the firm in 1915. "When Waldo went back to tell the Social Work people, they were scandalized," recalled one of her coworkers. "You see, they thought it was fine to be helping people, but not to work to make money." She added: "Miss Waldo felt a bit that way herself."[45]

This first generation of advertising women advanced, with some ambivalence, a "woman's viewpoint" in consumer culture, an outlook more influential in the marketing of cosmetics and toiletries than in that of any other consumer products except food and fashion. As a more self-conscious notion of the woman consumer took hold, it became axiomatic among mass-market manufacturers and advertisers that "if you are selling to women, nothing succeeds like a woman's viewpoint." Advertising appeals "must be made with knowledge of the habits of women, their methods of reasoning, and their prejudices," commented Resor. On cosmetics, food, and fashion accounts, Thompson copywriter Frances Maule explained, "a woman naturally falls into the vocabulary—those little phrases and intimate ways of talking that strike a housewife as ringing true." Women "have a tradition and specialized association from which men are completely cut off," Aminta Casseres agreed.[46]

The contradictions of the woman's viewpoint were apparent to the professionals who espoused it. It repackaged age-old stereotypes about women as impulsive and emotional, driven by "inarticulate longings" and easily swayed by flowery French phrases, snobbery, and romantic imagery. And it implied that women secured their jobs and succeeded in advertising, not through professional training and achievement, but by virtue of their womanly empathy. Some chafed at a sales pitch based on sex differences, but many, eager to take advantage of new job opportunities, invoked their special female insight into consumer motivation. Occasionally they would reveal that their womanly empathy was more tactical than natural, as when Dorothy Dignam caricatured her method of composing beauty advertisements: "If it's face powder, I pretend I'm covered with dreadful freckles, and I've just found the only thing in the world that will hide 'em from the cruel world. And then I write my copy about the cosmetics." News stories about Dignam often called her "girlish" but documented her shrewdness and professionalism.[47]

Adopting this approach to selling advanced the professional standing of white women throughout the cosmetics industry. They staffed cosmetics firms, department store merchandising offices, and the women's departments of daily newspapers. They became beauty editors, "service personalities," market researchers, publicity directors, and freelance writers specializing in beauty. Circulating from one post to another, they amplified the promotional efforts of the new mass-market commerce in beauty products and strengthened its institutional base.[48] Such niches of professional employment and influence within the new consumer economy were nonexistent for African Americans. Although black women wrote beauty columns, edited the occasional women's magazine, and appeared as company mouthpieces, their work in the beauty business remained segregated from and invisible in the mass market. For a tier of white professional and business women, however, mass-market cosmetics opened new opportunities.

In search of an effective way to address women, advertisers turned to beauty culture for a usable commercial language. Treatment lines, complexion analysis, beauty systems, demonstrations, empathy: These central elements of beauty culture were readily transferred to the mass market. Ad agencies, based in New York and other cities, particularly understood the vitality of salon-based beauty culture and its appeal to women throughout the country. Millions of women had no access to beauty parlors for skin care and could not afford the high-priced preparations of Elizabeth Arden or Dorothy Gray, but were familiar with the principles of beauty culture from the women's pages or from friends. Advertisers capitalized upon this interest, touting the democratization of beauty. "From advertising," N. W. Ayer proudly proclaimed, all women everywhere "are learning the secrets of great beauty specialists." Although advertisers increasingly favored images over words, cosmetics ads were often filled with text: Market researchers found that "women will read as many as 900 words of small, closely set type *straight through*, if it is about beauty."[49]

Helen Landsdowne Resor borrowed beauty culture techniques to transform the mundane use of Pond's cold cream into a daily beauty ritual. As early as 1906, the company's long-time ad agency, J. Walter Thompson, had associated Pond's Extract Soap with beauty specialist Grace Truman-Hoyt, headlining the "New Beauty Culture" in advertisements. Resor, however, conceived of Pond's staple cold cream and vanishing cream as a "system," and in 1916 began an ad campaign that featured the two products together as a single beauty treatment for all women. "Every normal skin needs two creams," ads proclaimed, cold cream to cleanse the face in the evening, vanishing cream to protect the skin and provide a base for face powder during the day. Vanishing cream was relatively new to the market, and the ads gave detailed instructions and urged women to adopt both products. Sales of the creams tripled between 1916 and 1920: Beauty culture had become the springboard for Pond's rebirth as a mass-market cosmetics company.[50]

Woodbury's complexion soap underwent a similar metamorphosis. It had been developed in the 1880s as a cure for skin diseases and advertised "on a very cheap patent medicine basis, featuring symptoms of the worst kind and illustrations of neckless heads." After 1915, the Thompson agency redefined Woodbury's as a beauty aid for all women, with ads promising "a skin you love to touch"—the famous and, for the time, slightly racy slogan written by Resor. Again, copywriters promoted beauty culture methods to sell a mass-market product. Calling it the "Woodbury Treatment," ads explained how to cleanse the skin with Woodbury soap and hot water, massage the face, then close the pores with cold water or ice, all skin-care techniques long used by beauty culturists. Adapting the demonstrator's running commentary on skin problems and cures, other ads targeted a series of disorders such as "conspicuous nose pores," solving each one with the Woodbury treatment. The campaign transformed an unpleasantly stinging soap into a wildly popular beauty aid.[51]

The power of cosmetics advertising derived not only from the potent imagery, evocative language, and personal appeals of the ads themselves, but from the ways they circulated among American women. The turn to national advertising in the 1920s fostered increasingly dense ties among cosmetics manufacturers, advertisers, retailers, periodicals, and mass media—"synergies," in the parlance of today's corporate leaders. While manufacturers, merchants, and magazines had been cooperating to promote consumption since the 1890s, their systematic collaboration to sell cosmetics was new. It multiplied the impact of cosmetics advertising, further legitimating women's pursuit of beauty and binding that pursuit to the purchase of goods.

The "big six" women's magazines—*Ladies' Home Journal, Mc-Call's, Delineator, Woman's Home Companion, Pictorial Review,* and *Good Housekeeping*—appeared on the scene between 1885 and 1910, before the flowering of the mass-market cosmetics industry. Starting as dress-pattern and farm publications, they gradually became all-purpose journals for middle-class women. Their editorials, fiction, and a parade of fashions and household comforts deliberately enticed readers into the new consumer economy of brand-name, mass-produced goods. By 1900, magazine layout itself reinforced the consumerist message. Editors broke up the text of stories and articles, forcing readers to turn to the back pages where most of the advertising was placed, and they began to coordinate advertising and editorial material, placing food ads next to cooking columns, for example.[52]

At first women's magazines saw little potential revenue from cosmetics firms and did not apply these techniques to cosmetics promotion. When the *Delineator* polled its readers in 1904 about the brands they purchased to guide its choice of advertisers, the survey listed only face powder, soap, complexion cream, perfume, and dentifrice in the toiletries category. Despite readers' frequent queries about beauty, women's magazines remained reluctant advisers. Their concern with respectability and purity—in women and in goods—heightened their suspicion of cosmetics. "We fought shy of any beauty page for a long time," explained the editor of the *Ladies' Home Journal.* "Almost every one who writes the beauty page has an axe to grind." The magazine devoted less than one percent of each issue to beauty in the 1920s, and home journals oriented to small-town and rural housewives, such as *Modern Priscilla,* still less. Even as they ran more and more cosmetics ads, such women's magazines continued to issue paeans to inner, natural beauty.[53]

In their shadow, however, newspapers and cheap magazines offered outlets for beauty news. Women's pages, tabloids, and Sunday magazine inserts covered beauty extensively for urban readers, and syndicates like King Features made beauty columns available throughout the country by the early 1920s. In a 1929 survey of women's pages in small-city newspapers, 60 percent featured at least some beauty articles, most of them syndicated features. Movie and romance magazines, aimed especially at working-class and young women, regularly included articles on beauty and contained ads for mass-market and mail-order cosmetics. *Motion Picture* introduced a beauty hints column in 1916 at the same time that cosmetics ads began to feature screen stars. Such pulp magazines as *Beauty* and *Beautiful Womanhood* (from the publisher of *True Story*, Bernarr Macfadden) also appeared on newsstands.[54]

As cosmetics became a leading source of advertising revenue, the major women's magazines increasingly bound beauty to the marketplace. Regular beauty columns were standard fare by the 1930s, and editors eagerly extended "editorial cooperation" to the largest cosmetics firms. Wooing potential advertisers, the *Woman's Home Companion* claimed it "presold" cosmetics in editorial pages that "discuss products, stimulate wants, [and] prepare the market for brand-selling." Another magazine similarly touted its short stories and articles for their subliminal messages about toiletries. "The fascination of subtle perfumes," it declared, "is a frequent lure of the heroine of fiction." Magazine editors placed cosmetics ads next to relevant beauty articles, did "special work with local dealers," and offered, as Helen Woodward put it, "large gobs of free editorial space." Woodward, for her part, explained how trading on the niceties of women's etiquette softened the hard edges of business competition. She gained free publicity from women's magazines by taking the beauty editor to lunch and sending her free goods, which usually guaranteed a favorable notice. "We always dealt directly with her and spoke as though we weren't advertisers at all," Woodward remarked.[55]

The line between dispensing general beauty advice and hawking specific products blurred more and more. Advertisers mimicked the design and substance of magazine beauty features, clouding the reader's ability to distinguish between advertising and editorial content. J. Walter Thompson copywriters called it the "beauty editorial style," featuring a "light and intimate tone" with exhaustive facts and details. Marinello ads imitated confession-magazine fiction, with stories of heroines who win back straying boyfriends by a timely trip to the beauty salon.[56]

Initially beauty editors refrained from puffing brands in their columns and instead mailed leaflets with product information, prepared by the magazines, to readers upon request. These proved extremely popular: *Ladies' Home Journal* beauty editor Louise Paine Benjamin reported that a single beauty column in 1936 generated 40,000 letters asking for leaflets. By this time, however, the scruples of other editors had begun to disappear. Bernice Peck's column in *Mademoiselle*, a magazine oriented to college and young career women, frankly touted cosmetics by name. Some beauty editors and writers appeared in magazine ads, broadcast radio shows, and sold the use of their names to companies. When syndicated beauty columnist Antoinette Donnelly agreed to put her name on a cold cream soap, the trade press applauded, noting that consumers "have acquired a confidence in her judgment through years of familiarity with her writings." Although beauty writer Nell Vinick claimed her show on Gimbel's radio station offered talks "of a non-commercial nature, the stress being laid on the idea of service," her appearance advertised the New York store's cosmetics department.[57]

Magazines and advertisers also collaborated on early market research. When J. Walter Thompson conducted an investigation of the toiletries market for Pond's in 1923, *McCall's* Service Department mailed eighteen hundred questionnaires to women readers, and Hazel Rawson Cades, beauty editor of the *Woman's Home Companion*, opened her readers' mail to the ad agency. *Harper's Bazaar* introduced a Debutante Department in 1928 to gain market information for advertisers; it surveyed three thousand well-to-do young women, rewarding each with a grab bag of cosmetic gifts. Similarly, in the mid-thirties, the *Delineator*'s Beauty Institute called upon eight hundred readers to be "beauty consultants" for product development and marketing purposes.[58]

Many cosmetics firms combined national advertising with elaborate point-of-purchase promotions. The "tie-in," as it was called, was to the mass-market cosmetics industry what "system" had been to beauty culture: It spurred consumer demand by coordinating the efforts of manufacturers, advertisers, and retailers—parties who had distinct interests but remained mutually dependent. Cosmetic tie-ins usually ex-

MARY PICKFORD
1917 "POMPEIAN BEAUTY" PANEL
To get large, beautiful calendar, use
coupon on back page.

In one of the earliest advertising campaigns featuring movie stars, Mary Pickford promoted Pompeian beauty preparations.

ploited popular fads and fancies, from the suntanning craze to the 1922 discovery of Tutankhamen's tomb. "Everything Egyptian is now getting a billion dollars' worth of publicity," bragged the LeBlume Import Company, touting its Ramses line of powders and perfumes. The most successful tie-ins involved the stage and screen, which had already done much to popularize the look of makeup. Motion picture press books suggested that local exhibitors and retailers could link movies and toiletries by holding beauty contests, divulging the heroine's beauty secrets, placing movie stills in drugstores, and making up manikins to look like actresses. Edna Wallace Hopper even demonstrated her line in matinees "for women only," in which the "entire intimate performance [was] exquisitely shown in a boudoir bath."[59]

Max Factor—makeup artist to the stars—particularly exploited the movie tie-in. All advertisements prominently featured screen stars, their testimonials secured in an arrangement with the major studios that required them to endorse Max Factor. The company apparently did not seek personal appearances from actresses, who, Davis Factor complained, were often late, temperamental, and "always caused us lots of grief." Instead, company representatives draped the glamorous image of the movies around their products. At movie matinees, they set up stands in theater lobbies, made up women onstage, raffled cosmetic kits, and distributed complexion analysis cards with the names of local drugstores. On one occasion, Factor

Still from the 1924 movie Men, *used in drugstore tie-ins.*

sponsored a gala on the Venice (California) pier, with cosmetic give-aways, makeup contests, and special consultation booths, all adver-tised with "big cards over the whole town and streamers on loads of the Pacific Electric cars."[60]

Product demonstrations, long used within beauty culture, were em-braced by mass marketers, not only to sell specific brands but to accli-mate women to systematic cosmetics use. In department stores, demonstrators set up tables piled with merchandise, applied creams and lotions to their own faces, and kept up a steady patter of instruc-tions and promises. Often demonstrators chose a likely mark from the crowd. At a 1921 beauty show in Atlantic City, Aubrey Sisters repre-sentatives "selected middle-aged or elderly women with fairly smooth, unwrinkled faces, but poor complexions; made them up with creams, 'Beautifier' and rouge and really quite transformed them."[61]

As Helena Rubinstein and Elizabeth Arden expanded from salon services to product sales, they converted the demonstrator into a sales

"*YOU can ride, swim, dance or pre-spire and your Peachglow complexion remains unimpaired.*"
—*New York World.*

The demonstration as seen by a New York World *cartoonist. From* Toilet Requisites, *1928.*

Opposite: *This flapper promoted a powder compact in a shoe buckle, for use at dance halls and nightclubs. From* Toilet Requisites, *1927.*

representative who toured exclusive shops and department stores throughout the country, demonstrating cosmetics, training saleswomen, and generating publicity. Carl Weeks complimented Arden's representatives for "educating women to using a complete line of merchandise." Mass-market manufacturers and drug syndicates soon adopted the method. As early as 1917, the United Drug Company, which distributed Rexall products, dispatched demonstrators to small-town drugstores. For twenty-five dollars a week, "the well trained Beauty Specialist does more than merely stay in the store and wait on people," the firm announced; "she gives demonstrations and free facial massages by appointments in the home."[62]

By the early twenties, department stores and drugstores regularly sponsored "beauty marts" and "beauty weeks" filled with lectures, makeup sessions, and free samples. The arrival of New York cosmetics

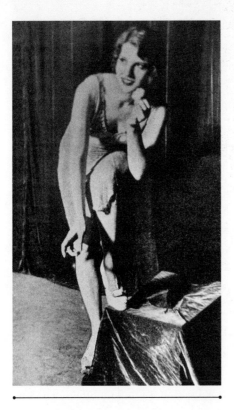

experts was a heralded event. The Owl drugstore in Los Angeles in 1922 featured fifty manufacturers' booths, a perfume fountain, and a stage where movie stars and fashion models appeared. "One of the big front windows was devoted to the art of 'Making Up,' a live model going through the process," commented a journalist, "and this proved to be such an attraction that demonstrations could only be held for fifteen-minute periods. The Police Department placed a detail of three men in front of the store; and yet at times it was impossible to get by."[63]

In addition to tie-ins with advertisers and retailers, cosmetics firms joined with garment manufacturers, merchandising stylists, and women's magazines to rationalize the fashion trades and, as one promoter put it, "reduce the element of speculation in style merchandising." Style bureaus, fashion merchandising clinics, and associations like the "Breath of the Avenue" and the Fashion Group reported on trends in art, color, design, and popular culture. Cosmetology educator Florence Wall advocated "co-operative promotion by beauty culturists with milliners, fashion designers, and textile manufacturers."[64]

Package design exemplified the turn to a fashion appeal. Before the 1910s manufacturers had used stock jars, plain pasteboard cartons, and standard labels made by printers or box makers. Competition from Paris, where artistic package design flourished, spurred American manufacturers like Weeks to consult art museums and hire artists to create distinctive boxes and bottles. Abandoning beauty culture's plain containers for striking colors and modernist motifs, Marinello packed a beauty cream in a translucent pink set-back skyscraper. The most important innovation in cosmetics packaging was portability, which turned powder compacts and lipstick cartridges into fashion accessories. Designed to be flourished in public, compacts flashed silver and enamel finishes, imitated golf balls and cigarette cases, and were even turned into belt and shoe buckles.[65]

"No two things are more closely allied" than a woman's "fashions and her cosmetics," stated *Vogue*'s beauty editor, but this was a strategic alliance, not an eternal truth. In the nineteenth century, beauty culture had touted timeless principles of enhancing appearance, and makeup was fashion mainly to the fast social elite and daring working-class women. In the 1920s and 1930s, manufacturers and consumers alike increasingly perceived the face as a style, subject to fashion trends and fads. In recognition of this development, the leading cosmetics trade journal changed its name in 1937 from *Toilet Requisites* to *Beauty Fashion*.[66]

Tying complexion to ever-changing fashion offered companies a powerful rationale for introducing new products. Although some skin-care companies resisted the call, many manufacturers jumped on the style bandwagon. In 1929 Carl Weeks introduced Symphonie face powder in one translucent shade, and touted its suitability for all (white) women's complexions. Although such a product offered little basis for a fashion appeal, that was precisely the tack Weeks took. That year the *Ladies' Home Journal* grandly proclaimed the "return to feminine charm," as a fluid and elegant silhouette deposed the boyish flapper look. To manufacturers, the *Journal* promoted this "Charm Decade" as a rich merchandising and advertising opportunity. Buying into the *Journal*'s fanfare, Weeks tied Symphonie to the new style with the theme, "New Clothes by Paris—New Complexion by Armand." When the fashion-based advertising, developed by Dorothy Dignam, was shown to Armand salesmen, "the boys were literally stunned"; industry commentators called it a "radical departure from ordinary merchandising policies."[67]

Although Weeks adopted a big advertising campaign, the fashion appeal, and the tie-in—all central to the new promotion of manufactured beauty—Symphonie was a striking failure. Dealers and customers were confused by the advertising, their eyes captivated more by the stylish clothes and attractive models than by the product itself. "We are not selling fashions," Weeks complained about the dominance of the image in the ad. "We are introducing a new idea—the copy is what tells women about it." Meanwhile, women who tried Symphonie disliked the powder's heaviness and rejected Weeks's assurances that a single shade fitted all skins. Symphonie demonstrated, to Weeks's despair, that modern marketing methods could not overcome the product's limitations.[68]

Weeks's experience was hardly unique. In those years, the cosmetics industry was highly volatile,

Armand advertisement, 1930.

with companies rapidly rising and declining, new products appearing and disappearing. The industry had staked its fortunes on modern advertising and marketing methods, as did many consumer-goods businesses in the 1920s and 1930s, but as Weeks learned, success was by no means certain. The industry acknowledged as much through an unusual commercial practice known as the "hidden" or "closed" demonstrator. Hired and trained by a cosmetics firm, the hidden demonstrator masqueraded as a regular saleswoman but actually induced customers to buy her employer's products. A related practice was known as "push money" or "p.m.'s," in which saleswomen employed by the store received a commission from the manufacturer for pushing its line. Such saleswomen were often paid openly on the job, but in cases where the retailer objected, they were paid "confidential" or "secret push money" at their homes. The premium amounted to as much as 10 percent of the sale.[69]

The use of hidden demonstrators was a widespread phenomenon peculiar to the cosmetics business among American consumer-goods industries. According to a 1923 study, several dozen toilet-goods manufacturers used hidden demonstrators or push money. Although cosmetics firms argued that hidden demonstrators relieved stores of significant labor costs and sold entire lines of goods at full retail prices, many retailers resisted the practice. Wanting control over its workforce, stock, and pricing, Macy's stopped using demonstrators altogether in 1928; other companies barred aggressive selling and required saleswomen to sell any product requested by customers.[70]

The use of hidden demonstrators continued into the 1940s, despite passage of legislation to curtail the practice. In the highly competitive cosmetics field, demonstrators provided an edge. "With most of the larger stores having from five to twenty demonstrators," an Armand salesman complained in 1929, "we can only hope to get a minimum amount of business." Throughout the 1920s Carl Weeks had opposed this "most debauching practice in modern merchandising," but even he gave in. As Armand sales declined during the Depression, he approached stores with push money and sought to place an "exclusive girl [who] will be high powered and should do us some good."[71]

That hidden demonstrators existed at all, however, is also testimony to the established tradition of beauty culture and to the significance of women's everyday beauty rituals. In employing demonstrators, manufacturers acknowledged that the cosmetics business required more than fantasy images of glamour and romance. It required communicating cosmetic information, educating consumers, providing services, and fostering women's sociability. "If a salesgirl began her talk as indirectly as some cosmetic copy," one demonstrator observed in 1933, "she would sell nothing." Like the relationship between beautician and client, or door-to-door agent and neighbor, the demonstrator mingled the intimate and the commercial. In a period when many women did not use cosmetics, demonstrators explained how to apply creams and makeup, urged women to buy related products or entire cosmetics lines, and persuaded them to try new preparations. They also steered patrons away from poor products and circulated hearsay about dangerous wares. "The demonstrators rather generally disparage liquid polish—in all lines—as a fundamentally unsatisfactory article," wrote a market researcher at a Brooklyn department store in 1921, which was probably an accurate assessment at that time. Some lied about competitors' brands, saying that Max Factor manufactured only theatrical makeup unsuitable for everyday use, or that Armand powder contained lead. Market researchers at the time marveled at the influence of the hidden demonstrator. "A woman may know a product more or less thru the advertising," explained one, "but a sales person can easily 'queer' a sale, or make it as the case may be." Secretly selling behind the counter, another commented about her customers, "you can talk them into almost anything."[72]

Producing a mass market for cosmetics involved a complicated mixture of borrowings and invention, images and interactions. In the process, women entrepreneurs were increasingly sidelined, retaining a presence mainly in the high-priced salon and African-American trade, but less able to compete in a mass market driven by national advertising, media, and distribution. Ironically the men who controlled the industry appropriated the methods of beauty culturists, engaged in female impersonation, and hired a new ensemble of business and professional women to translate beauty into business. Through close collaboration with magazine publishers, mass media, advertisers, and retailers, they threaded the new mass commerce in cosmetics into women's reading, shopping, theatergoing, and housework—the web of women's daily habits and social rounds.

Promoting the
Made-Up Woman

The fashionable ideal has changed many times in recent decades, but the 1920s marked the moment when mass-produced images distinctly and powerfully began to influence female self-conceptions and beauty rituals. Glamorous screen stars, chic Parisiennes, aristocratic beauties, and breezy flappers all became familiar faces. Intended to dictate women's buying choices, these images derived their power from conscious design, visual resonance, and widespread circulation. They seemingly addressed all consumers, including, on occasion, women of disparate ethnic backgrounds. But the mass market's democratic vision of beauty denied African Americans entry. And while black and white manufacturers often mirrored each other in their business strategies, the images they created, and the ways women responded to them, diverged along racial lines.

White women were the audience for national advertising that tied beautifying to broad cultural concerns over female sexual mores and social roles. Like beauty culturists, mass marketers initially summoned women to proclaim their liberation from the fetters of the past by using cosmetics. In their effort to create beauty consumers out of a diverse populace, advertisers drew upon an array of existing images representing modern womanhood—primarily socialites, actresses, coeds, sportswomen, smartly dressed wives, and an occasional working woman or politician. But the range of these images, never all-encompassing, quickly narrowed and became more conventional. Having challenged an earlier regime of female respectability and moralism, advertisers came to advance what would become key tenets of normative femininity in the twentieth century. Ironically, a period that began with cosmetics signaling women's freedom and individuality ended in binding feminine identity to manufactured beauty, self-portrayal to acts of consumption.

The new mass-market cosmetics industry celebrated itself as both cause and consequence of women's modernity and emancipation. Victorian codes of morality and taste had constrained women in the nineteenth century, but now the "movement for personal freedom" licensed the systematic cultivation of beauty. One trade journal applauded Americans' dawning realization "that there is no sane connection between morals and cosmetics." Cosmetics were "merely symbols of the social revolution that has gone on; the spiritual and mental forces that women have used to break away from conventions and to forward the cause of women's freedom," explained beauty writer Nell Vinick.[1]

These views had an appeal in the wake of campaigns for women's suffrage, higher education, and professional opportunities. Working-class women, long present in the labor force, had become newly visible within American society; so had middle-class wives who combined earning a wage and raising a family. While scientists debated whether women and men differed in intelligence and abilities, sexual theorists, feminists, and the avant garde acclaimed women's release from Victorian repression and espoused female self-expression and personal fulfillment. A variety of popular images pictured this "New Woman," from the mannish reformer, professional woman, and earnest labor activist, to the free-spirited outdoor girl and sexually assertive flapper.[2]

Yet for all the talk of social revolution and women's freedom, magazines and newspapers of the 1920s reveal few attempts to generate alternative conceptions of beauty linked to American women's new economic and political roles. The cosmetics industry abjured depicting women in the public realm traditionally occupied by men—the workplace, meeting hall, and polling booth. Occasionally businesswomen and secretaries who "make their own way in the world" and needed to protect their "face value" were addressed. Some cosmetics firms advertised in the professional journals of educators, artists, and performers. In *Normal Instructor*, Armand advised teachers to guard against "schoolroom dust, and drying, aging 'chalk film.' " But such appeals were relatively few. The working women most in evidence were actresses, depicted not as hardworking professionals but as glamorous beauties.[3]

Some well-intentioned advertisers struggled to envision a New Woman that challenged popular clichés. For a number of women at J. Walter Thompson, both market research and feminism argued against stereotyping female consumers. Frances Maule, Thompson copywriter and a veteran of the women's movement, criticized advertisers for relying too much on "the good old conventional 'angel-idiot' conception of women" and urged them to remember the "old suffrage slogan—that 'Women Are People.' " She emphasized: "It is just as impossible to pick out a single feminine type and call it 'woman,' as it is to pick out a single masculine type and call it 'man.' " Maule identified four categories of female consumers, each responding to different appeals: housewives concerned with a well-stocked and well-run home, society women oriented to fashion and leisure, club women interested in the politics of consumption, and working women, "an ever-increasing class with an entirely different set of needs."[4]

This more nuanced view of women consumers occasionally surfaced in Thompson's cosmetics advertising. A beauty contest sponsored by Woodbury's dared to "disregard the conventional boundaries" and welcomed "every type of American women," including grandmothers and women workers. A series for Pond's in 1923, probably written by Maule, focused on women who "tax their skins." One ad pictured a working woman at a dance with the headline, "They were wrong when they said, 'She will lose her charm.'" Its copy reassured women who traded their home life for the "rush and worry of business" that femininity and professional success were compatible.[5]

Pond's famous testimonial campaign reveals the limits of these efforts. In the early 1920s, Pond's had lost sales to Elizabeth Arden and Helena Rubinstein. "Pond's Creams through their very popularity were losing caste," one market researcher reported; "women thought the higher priced creams must be better." To change public perceptions, Thompson's female copywriters seized upon an old, if threadbare, advertising technique to spotlight and applaud women of accomplishment.[6]

Alva Belmont appeared in Pond's first testimonial, her cooperation secured through Frances Maule's circle of feminist friends. Belmont was a well-known society woman who had championed suffrage and bankrolled the National Women's Party. "Mrs. Belmont not only has given lavishly to women's causes from her colossal fortune, has been and is a tremendous worker," the Pond's ad stated, "but also is particularly interested in woman's special problem of how to keep her force and her charm throughout her whole life." Belmont agreed to the celebrity interview but refused to allow her photograph to appear. In its place was a picture of her library, an incongruous image for the sale of a beauty preparation. Following Belmont were several other women active in the world of politics, although more in its social rounds than governing circles. Alice Roosevelt Longworth, Washington hostess and daughter of Theodore Roosevelt, and Mary McConnell Borah, wife of Senator William E. Borah, both endorsed Pond's. Said Borah, "The Woman who cares about the dignity of her appearance—in the political life of Washington, on the plains of Idaho—looks to the smoothness, the firmness of her skin."[7]

This singular effort to showcase distinguished and newsworthy women was undermined from the start, however, by the need to project an "image of status and prestige" in order to improve Pond's rank relative to expensive treatment lines. Increasingly the ad agency turned to European aristocrats and American socialites whose celebrity derived simply from their wealth and standing. As staffers exploited their personal connections to

An Interview with Mrs. O.H.P. Belmont
on the care of the skin

"A woman who neglects her personal appearance loses half her influence. The wise care of one's body constructs the frame encircling our mentality, the ability of which insures the success of one's life. I advise a daily use of Pond's Two Creams."

Alva E. Belmont —

T was in the beautiful great hall of Beacon Towers on Sand's Point, Port Washington, Long Island, that I first talked with Mrs. O. H. P. Belmont.

I was excited and eager for the interview because I knew that Mrs. Belmont not only has given lavishly to women's causes from her colossal fortune, has been and is a tremendous worker, but also is particularly interested in woman's special problem of how to keep her force and her charm throughout her whole life.

From all this I expected to meet a very commanding woman the day I visited Beacon Towers. But Mrs. Belmont, on the contrary, is quiet and gracious and sweet. She could not have been a more charming hostess.

She herself opened the grilled iron door and I stepped into the big hall with its impressive mural paintings of the life of Joan of Arc and its wide doors opening straight onto Long Island Sound.

Here, I felt instantly, is the spirit of beauty strengthened by sincerity.

After we had admired the glorious view she showed me the pictures of her two sons, and of her grandson, who will some day be one of England's dukes, and—very proudly—the latest snapshot of her very young Ladyship, a small great grand-daughter.

"How fine textured and fresh her skin is," I thought. "And she has just acknowledged herself a great grand-mother!"

Begs Women not to Neglect Themselves

"NOW," she was saying, smilingly, "I suppose you want me to tell you what I think is the relation between a woman's success and her personal appearance."

"Yes," I admitted. "Just how important do you think personal appearance is?"

"It is vital. That is just as true for the woman at home or in business as for those who are socially prominent.

"A person may have great intelligence and yet make a very bad impression if her appearance is careless. So we do ourselves a great injustice if we do not give our bodies great care. It is very wise in every way to cultivate the knowledge of how to keep ourselves presentable and young."

"Don't you know," she said, "how often the woman with an unattractive face fails in the most reasonable undertaking? Nothing is so distressing. Neglect of one's personal attractions generally comes from ignorance and as I am greatly interested in the success of women in every possible way, I urge them not to neglect themselves."

The library of Mrs. O. H. P. Belmont at Beacon Towers on Long Island Sound, where this interview was signed. Mrs. Belmont, President of the National Woman's Party, is known all over America for her active services in securing the suffrage for women. Mrs. Belmont is also interested in better conditions for women, is strong for the abolition of child labor, and for the improvement of Children's Homes.

On the artistic side, she is a trained architect, and her three magnificent residences—Villa Isoletta in France, the famous Marble House at Newport, and the imposing country home Beacon Towers on Long Island are the products of time not devoted to politics and business. After years of the burden of great public and private interests, she has marvelously kept her freshness.

Pond's Two Creams
used by the women who must keep their charm, their beauty, their influence
EVERY SKIN NEEDS THESE TWO CREAMS

Frenchwomen say, Cleanse and Protect

"YOU spend a part of each year in France," I said. "Are Frenchwomen more beautiful than American women?"

"Certainly not, but American women can learn from them. It comes naturally to them to care for their appearance from youth until they are eighty years old!—and they never lose their influence with society or the individual."

"Do Frenchwomen use creams much?" I asked Mrs. Belmont.

"In France," she said, "they have had this knowledge for generations. They have always used cleansing creams and protecting creams, knowing that water is not enough and that the face cannot stand much strain and exposure."

"Then you think women should use two creams?"

"I know they should. That is why I advise the daily use of Pond's Two Creams, so that women can keep their charm and influence as long as they need them—and that is always," she smiled.

Use this Famous Method

GIVE your skin these two indispensables to lasting skin loveliness—the kind of cleansing that restores each night your skin's essential suppleness, and the freshening that, besides protecting, brings each time the beauty of fresh smooth skin under your powder.

For years the laboratories of Pond's were devoted to the development of two preparations that were to meet these two vital needs. Finally two distinctly different face creams were perfected—Pond's Cold Cream and Pond's Vanishing Cream.

Every night—with the finger tips or a piece of moistened cotton, apply Pond's Cold Cream freely. The very fine oil in it is able to penetrate every pore of your skin. Leave a on a minute. Then remove it with a soft cloth. Dirt and excess oil, the rouge and powder you have used during the day, are taken off your skin and out of the pores. Feel how your face is relaxed. *Do this twice.* Now finish with ice rubbed over your face or a dash of cold water. Your skin looks fresh and is beautifully supple again. If your skin is very dry, pat on more cream, especially where wrinkles come first—around the eyes, the nose, the corners of your mouth—and leave it on over night.

After every cleansing, before you powder, and always before you go out—smooth on Pond's Vanishing Cream very evenly —just enough for your skin to absorb. Now if you wish, rouge—powder. How smooth and velvety your face feels to your hand. Nothing can roughen it. When you get up in the morning, after a dash of cold water, this cream will keep your skin fresh and untired for hours. And it will stay evenly powdered.

Use this method regularly. Soon your face will be permanently fresher, smoother and you can count on the charm of a fresh, young skin for years longer than would otherwise be possible. Begin now. Buy both Pond's Creams tonight in jars or tubes at any drug store or department store. The Pond's Extract Company.

Compare the visual impact of these 1924 advertisements for Pond's.

Mrs. Reginald Vanderbilt

"YOUTHFULNESS *is the real pot of gold at the end of every woman's rainbow! Pond's Two Creams are a wonderful help to this coveted end.*"

Gloria M Vanderbilt

MRS. REGINALD C. VANDERBILT
in a black velvet gown by Vionnet. As Miss Gloria Morgan she spent her girlhood abroad. Since her marriage she has become a distinguished leader in the exclusive society of New York and Newport

MY FIRST GLIMPSE of Mrs. Reginald Vanderbilt brought a little catch to my throat. I had heard she was very lovely—this young woman, barely twenty-one, two years married to the son of one of America's oldest, wealthiest, most distinguished families, and mother of an exquisite baby girl. But I was unprepared for beauty so compelling, so unique.

"It's partly because she's so tall," I said to my companion, "and so slender. Did you *ever* see such grace?"

Mrs. Vanderbilt is "*brune*" but with a difference. Her hair seems black until the sunlight breaks its shadows into shimmering bronze. In the depths of her dark eyes burn the fires of golden topazes. And in the snows of her delicate skin blooms the rose of her full-blown lips, ruby-red and strangely beautiful.

In spite of her extreme youth Mrs. Vanderbilt carries an air. She might have been born to the purple. For she has the poise and the *cachet* of the woman who has lived her girlhood in the most distinguished society of Europe.

ALL these impressions flashed upon me. As Mrs. Vanderbilt moved toward me with a singing grace, I recalled what I had heard men say, "She dances—oh, divinely!"

"What a *bouquet* she lends that gown," I murmured. "The Parisian couturier who designed it must have thrilled to see its black velvet next arms and shoulders of such dazzling whiteness."

"But the contrast is in the color alone," said someone in our group. "When it comes to texture, there's little to choose between chiffon velvet and Mrs. Vanderbilt's skin."

Mrs. Vanderbilt spoke in a voice whose low modulations and finished diction come from fluency in three languages besides her own.

"It ought to be a good skin," she was saying. "I take good care of it."

"Of course," my friend rejoined. "No doubt you devote hours of every day to keeping it exquisite."

"On the contrary," cried Mrs. Vanderbilt, "only a few minutes—far less time than many of my friends. It's not the *time* that counts. It's the *method!*"

"Do tell us what your method is," we queried.

"Two Creams," said Mrs. Vanderbilt. "One to cleanse the skin and keep it fresh and firm. The other to protect and give it that 'velvety' finish you've just spoken of. I've used Pond's Two Creams for a long time and have never found any better."

IT is this approval, given by the women of Society who *must* keep their youth and beauty—for Mrs. Vanderbilt is only one of many—that is the final proof of the sterling worth of Pond's Two Creams.

The first step in following the Pond's method of skin care is a deep, thorough cleansing with Pond's Cold Cream. Smooth it lavishly over your face, neck, arms and hands. Let it stay on a few moments so that its pure oils may sink deep down into the pores and soften the dust, soot, hardened excess oil, powder and rouge that choke them.

Wipe all the cream off and note the dirt it brings with it. Repeat the process. And now, to close the pores, dash your skin with cold water, or rub it lightly with a bit of ice.

This daily Pond's cleansing should follow any prolonged time spent out of doors. If your skin is inclined to be either very dry or too oily, you should use Pond's Cold Cream twice or more. And to overcome the dryness that forms lines and wrinkles, leave some of the cream on all night.

The second step in the Pond's Method of caring for the skin is a soft finish and protection with Pond's Vanishing Cream. Fluff just a light film over the skin of your face and hands. It will vanish—for Pond's Vanishing Cream is greaseless.

NOTICE now, how even the surface of your skin looks. The Vanishing Cream has leveled off all roughnesses. It gives you a lustre, too, a soft bright, clear tone.

And how much more smoothly your rouge and powder blend and how well they stay over this delicate foundation of Vanishing Cream. You need have no more fear of nose-shine, now.

You should always use Pond's Vanishing Cream before you powder, and with particular care before you go out. For it protects your skin so that wind, dust, sun and soot cannot rob it of its natural oils, its bloom of youth.

Follow the lead of Mrs. Reginald Vanderbilt. Buy your own Pond's Creams. Find out for yourself that what she says is wholly true—"They constitute as simple, as effectual a method of caring for the skin as has yet been discovered." You may have the Cold Cream in extra large jars now. And both creams in the smaller jars you are familiar with. The Pond's Extract Company.

EVERY SKIN NEEDS THESE TWO CREAMS

FREE OFFER—Mail this coupon and we will send you free tubes of these two creams and an attractive little folder telling how to use them.

sign up the rich and famous, obtaining endorsements became something of a sport within the agency. When Queen Marie of Romania acquiesced, a Thompson executive rejoiced that "the securing of this testimonial was an achievement which astounded the advertising world." The distinguished women also played the game, bidding up the price of their names. Quickly the campaign, with its parade of royals and debutantes, degenerated into parody. "Alice Roosevelt on Pond's was so insincere," complained one staffer, "I got the impression that she had no respect for the product." Lady Margot Asquith's unbecoming photograph, another griped, belied the ad's headline "Woman's Instinct to Make Herself Attractive." More and more the agency turned to young, beautiful women. Thompson's market research found that consumers preferred Princess Marie de Bourbon among the endorsers because "she is young and pretty and the photographs were romantic and sentimental." Pictures of feminine beauty had trumped advertising copy that extolled women's accomplishments.[8]

The Pond's campaign suggests how fragile and circumscribed were efforts to imagine an alternative feminine appeal in beauty advertising. The limited presence of women in the advertising industry certainly played a part. But more important, the women who wrote cosmetics advertisements, even those who identified as feminists, found themselves caught in contradictory impulses. They recognized the variety of women's experiences in modern society and celebrated women's achievements. Caring for one's appearance, they could claim, was part of a larger commitment to women's social participation, self-expression, and dignity. But this view, a subtle and difficult argument to make, easily succumbed to the simpler notion of beauty as an end in itself. As advertising campaigns became conventionalized, the weak bond between female beauty and accomplishment dissolved.

If alternative visions of women's beauty were not in evidence, the mass-market industry did challenge some codes of feminine appearance that had seemed fixed and unshakable in the nineteenth century. Formerly distinct images of mother and daughter, leisured lady and wage earner, the decent and disreputable, now began to blur. In 1909, for instance, a Pompeian skin cream ad sentimentally depicted a venerable mother revered by her adult daughter, whose assurance, "You're All Right," referred not only to the mother's clear complexion but to her disposition. Fourteen years later, Pompeian portrayed a very different scene, of the modern mom inspected and approved by her family. "You're getting younger every day!" observed the daughter, and indeed, the 1923 mother had exactly the same face as her child. "Thanks to cosmetics," an industry analyst exulted, "the mother of today is more the big sister and enjoys and appreciates the pleasures of her daughters."[9]

Also transformed was the image of the painted woman, as alluring actresses wearing mascara and lipstick supplanted immoral kohl-eyed Jezebels. Theda Bara and other screen stars glamorized a painted look

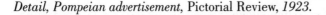

Detail, Pompeian advertisement, Pictorial Review, *1923.*

"Mother, you're looking younger every day!"

Viola Dana, Beautiful Photoplay Star, recommends Maybelline

"EYES THAT CHARM"

Maybelline

WILL BEAUTIFY YOUR EYES INSTANTL

A touch of MAYBELLINE works beauty wonders. Sca
eyebrows and lashes are made to appear naturally dark, long and lu
urious. All the hidden loveliness of your eyes—their brilliance, dep
and expression—is instantly revealed. The difference is remarkab
Girls and women everywhere, even the most beautiful actresses of t
stage and screen, now realize that MAYBELLINE is the
most important aid to beauty and use it regularly.
MAYBELLINE is unlike other preparations, it is
absolutely harmless, greaseless, and delightful
to use. Does not spread and smear on the face
or stiffen the lashes. We guarantee that you
will be perfectly delighted with results. Each
dainty box contains mirror and brush. Two shades:
Black and Brown. 75c AT YOUR DEALER'S
or direct from us, postpaid. Accept only genuine
MAYBELLINE and your satisfaction is assured.
Tear out this ad NOW as a reminder.

Maybelline Co., 4750-74 Sheridan Road, Chicago

Maybelline advertisement in
Pictorial Review, *1923.*

once associated with prostitution. Such firms as Maybelline increasingly turned to the movies for images that countered the prudish values of middle-class respectability. Close-up photographs of the female face, eyes darkened with makeup, projected a provocative but no longer sinful eroticism.[10]

Released from the Victorian underworld, painted women now paraded through advertisers' imaginary worlds. Scenes depicted them swimming, sunbathing, dancing, and motoring—pictures of healthy, athletic, and fun-loving womanhood. Paint no longer disqualified respectable women from romance or marriage. On the contrary, cosmetics figured prominently in everyday tableaux of love and rejection, triumph and humiliation. As copywriter Edith Lewis explained, successful beauty advertising created "situations that bring strongly before the reader's imagination the social disadvantages of a bad complexion, the social incentives for a good one."[11]

Indeed, cosmetics ads endlessly reminded women that they were on display, especially conspicuous in a world peopled by spectators and voyeurs: "Do you wonder, when you meet a casual friend, whether your nose is shiny? Do you anxiously consult store windows and vanity cases at every opportunity?" Even the most intimate moments—dressing in the boudoir, a kiss between lovers—were made visible to the magazine reader. Mirrors, movie cameras, and spectators placed in the ads underscored the idea that the eye constantly appraised women's appearance. Women were thus urged to transform the spectacle of themselves into self-conscious performances. "The woman in the

Strangers' eyes, keen and critical —
can you meet them proudly - confidently - without fear ?

From a Woodbury's Soap advertisement, Ladies' Home Journal, *1922.*

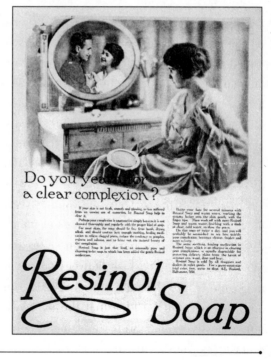

Resinol Soap advertisement in The Etude, *1918.*

home, the woman in business, in society, must make up for the part she is to play in life," said beauty writer Virginia Lee. Armand advertisements concurred: "The great moments of your life are 'close-ups.' "[12]

Challenging the older view of paint as a mask of deceit, the beauty industry promoted makeup as a tool for women to explore and portray their individuality in the modern world. As one cosmetic artist declared, "creative make-up will be the guide during the pilgrimage to the Holy Land of personality." Along similar lines, Armand's 1929 campaign, "Find Yourself," offered to lead women to self-understanding by analyzing their appearance. The company distributed 250,000 copies of a booklet developed by a popular psychologist and a beauty expert. "The questions and answers will discover the real you—not as you think you are—but as others see you," stated one ad.[13]

Makeup promised personal transformation, a pledge that sounded deeply in American culture—from conversion experiences and temperance oaths to the appeals of medicine men and faith healers. Beauty culturists had proclaimed the mutual transformation of external appearance and inner well-being. "Before-and-after" imagery appeared frequently in their works, as well as in the handbills and trade cards of patent cosmetics makers. But the mass-market cosmetics industry went one better, altering the terms of the physiognomic equation: In the coloring and contouring of facial surfaces, a woman could not only change her looks but remake herself and her life chances. When in 1936 *Mademoiselle* showed an ordinary reader, nurse Barbara Phillips, how to improve her appearance and featured her as the "Made Over Girl," the metamorphosis known as the *makeover* was born.[14]

The makeover offered a pliable advertising concept to cosmetics firms at both the high and low ends of the market. In the 1910s Arden, Rubinstein, and others in the elite salon trade had advised their clients to emulate the fashionable Parisienne's visible *maquillage* and so distinguish themselves from the *bourgeoise* who still scorned or concealed makeup. By 1919 importers and large domestic manufacturers were urging ordinary American women to imitate the lifestyles of the elite by buying powder and rouge. In cosmetics ads, compacts materialized at

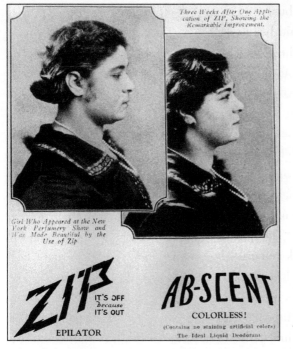

Zip advertisement, from Toilet Requisites, *1928.*

Saratoga Springs, the Paris Opera, and the races at Ascot. One observed, "Not all the users of La Dorine can be members of smart clubs but they are all eager to enjoy as much of the dainty refinement of the fashionable world as they can."[15]

Many mass-market firms advertised makeup as a leveler that broke down earlier class distinctions marking feminine appearance. "You can select ten ordinary girls from a factory and by the skillful use of such preparations as Kiija and proper toilet articles . . . you can in a short time make them as attractive and good-looking as most any ten wealthy society girls," a product brochure claimed. "It is not so much a matter of beauty with different classes of girls as it is how they are fixed up." A similar story appeared in a 1924 trade advertisement for Zip depilatory: A dark-skinned woman, with the appearance of an eastern or southern European immigrant, achieved social acceptance in America by ridding herself of superfluous hair.[16]

Beauty may have been considered the birthright of only wealthy or fortunate women in the nineteenth century, but cosmetics advertising sold the idea that an attractive appearance was an accomplishment all could easily achieve. Mail-order and tabloid-style ads promised cheap, instant beauty to working women unable to afford the time and money leisured women spent on beauty culture. "Quickly remake the complexion." End freckles and wrinkles "with the ease that an eraser rubs off a pencil smudge." "Now everyone can have" beauty clay, "formerly only available to the rich." The scrapbook of copywriter Ruth Lamb, who later left advertising to become an outspoken advocate of cosmetics regulation, was filled with such claims. "Yesterday's plain women are today smart-looking!" stated an Armand ad. " 'I am not good-looking,' they say, 'but I can look interesting!' "[17]

Cosmetics advertising qualified its utopian promises by containing personal realization within categories of physical beauty. "Individuality is the keynote," Marinello announced, yet urged women to "develop your beauty type to its full charm." In the "Find Yourself" advertising campaign, Armand helpfully provided a guide to "thirty-two quite distinct types of women" based on facial appearance. Sheba, Cleopatra, Cherie, and Lorelei all had different versions of "It," as popular writer Elinor Glyn called the magnetic personality. But female individuality clearly had its limits: Except for hair style and color, the women's faces were virtually indistinguishable.[18]

In Western literature and painting, the coloring of women's hair, eyes, and complexion traditionally signified distinct female character types— the pale, flaxen-haired innocent, the dark, sensual "oriental," the tubercular "celestial beauty" with a "crimson hectic flush" on her cheeks.[19] Late-nineteenth–century cosmetics firms advertised their wares to reluctant Americans specifically through exotic images of American Indian, Egyptian, Turkish, and Japanese enchantresses as well as European belles. Reproductions of "Little Egypt," whose dancing caused a furor at the 1893 Columbian Exposition, sold rouge and makeup, while Cleopatra

Detail, Armand advertisement, 1929.

An "exotic type" in a turn-of-the-century trade card. Murray and Lanham's Florida Water.

was virtually a cult figure. At the same time, theatrical makeup practices codified a variety of ethnic character types; one manual explained how to appear Italian by applying dark, moist rouge and olive powder. Even the names of theatrical makeup used ethnic signifiers, such as Stein's Mexicola rouge and Hess's Indianola paste.[20]

Modern marketing strategies built on these older iconographic conventions. Beauty types offered a formula for classifying products, consumers, and information. With eye and hair color or skin tone as guides, manufacturers developed complementary color palettes, designed coordinated makeup kits, and gave advice on appropriate cosmetics to consumers. Max Factor, for instance, promised an individual beauty diagnosis to each consumer, then instructed retailers how to make "personal" recommendations based on hair and skin types.[21]

The identification of facial types also offered a means of perceiving and classifying the dizzying array of complexions in a nation of immigrants. Armand's Sheba, Cleopatra, and other "alluring types" were euphemisms for ethnicity, identities defined as exotic looks. Addressing white women with olive or tawny complexions, one Armand ad suggested that "a dark skin may be your greatest attraction—you may be hiding it with a light powder."[22] Some companies advertised directly to ethnic communities, using the foreign language press, posters in immigrant neighborhoods, and local promotions. Carl Weeks marketed his goods among eastern and southern European immigrants, advertising, for exam-

ple, in the *Jewish Daily Forward.* Max Factor promoted Society makeup
to Latinas in Southern California with ads in the Spanish-language paper,
La Opinion. One in 1928, featuring the actors Lupe Velez and Ramon
Navarro, advertised a "dance of the Stars." "Come as you like," it invited,
"in street clothes, the clothes of your dreams, or traditional Mexican or
Hispanic garb." Velez also appeared in Factor's English language ads;
she had achieved stardom in Mexico and the United States, typecast as
the dark-haired Spanish beauty, tempestuous and passionate. Women
were even encouraged to play with their looks; ethnicity, defined as style,
could, like makeup, be easily applied and washed off. Factor's color harmony charts included makeup instructions for "Spanish types." The
wrong lipstick and rouge could ruin a brunette's beauty, an Armand ad
stated, but "make her lips like pomegranates, her skin like pale ivory—
she's Oriental, different and striking."[23]

Defining the face of America in light of its mixed population absorbed the cosmetics industry. "It is quite possible here in the United
States to join a Nordic skin to Italian hair and eyes, to color an English
skin with a warmth of Spanish, Jewish, or Russian blood," stated advice writer Helen Macfadden. "That's America, where for three hundred years we have been blending all the recognized types and
producing the most fascinating new ones!" A makeup artist agreed:
"Your face . . . is the story of the blending and merging of many peoples into one people."[24]

The melting pot of beauty types in advertising accepted Eastern European, Italian, and even Latina women, but excluded African Americans. Underlying the celebration of ethnic variety was the belief that the
true American face was still a white face. Mass marketers consciously
avoided black imagery in beauty advertising; in 1936, when Armand
changed its trademarked silhouette of a woman's head from "solid black"
to light gray, one trade journal believed it would "win new popularity for
Armand beauty products among the white women of the South."[25]

Bleach creams continued to be marketed to white women well into the
twentieth century; J. Walter Thompson compiled a list of 232 of them for
sale in 1930. Advertisers used traditional appeals to gentility, social

Nadine advertisement, 1924.

climbing, and Anglo-Saxon superiority. Dorothy Dignam's ads for
Nadinola skin bleach and Nadine
face powder, appearing in mass-
circulation women's magazines,
resurrected the Old South. Dignam later noted, "This line made
in the South was largely sold to
the Negro market; the advertising
was a planned attempt to capture
the white market also. I was never
told!" Her paean to "the beauty
secret of Southern women," featuring plantations, magnolia blos-
soms, and hoop-skirted belles,
erased any hint of Nadinola's
black clientele. Although usually
rendered obliquely, racial prejudice was an explicit talking point
for manufacturer Albert F. Wood: "A white person objects to a swarthy
brown-hued or mulatto-like skin, therefore if staying much out of doors
use regularly Satin Skin Vanishing Greaseless Cream to keep the skin
normally white."[26]

Nevertheless, many white women began to consider a tan acceptable
as sports and outdoor recreation grew popular. By the mid-1920s, suntanning had turned into a craze. This widespread desire for dark and
darker skin challenged the cosmetics industry's basic assumption—that
good skin was light skin—and many firms were slow to respond to the
vogue. Although a few produced "sunburn" tints in the early 1920s, it
was not until the end of the decade that tanning lotions and darker face
powders were generally available. By 1929, the industry insisted that
women "must buy everything from hat to shoes to match the shade of tan
she has just purchased."[27]

Allusions to "health, Palm Beach or Deauville" were used to sell tanning products, but the sales pitch often slipped into the language of race. "Lily white complexion is 'passé,'" claimed Tre-Jur, and the trade press buzzed with news of "Nubian hues," "Indian-hued maidens," and "dusky skins." Dark skin as fashion, however, only reinforced perceptions of racial difference. The "right shade of tan has become so smart," a beauty expert advised, but once autumn arrived, "it is high time we returned to our natural selves" by bleaching the skin. If the "idea of a complete change of complexion" reflected women's innate desire for novelty and style, said another, "underneath their tawny exteriors the roses and lilies bloomed undisturbed."[28]

The mass-market cosmetics industry recognized the heterogeneity of white American women and dismissed the profound differences among them with the reassurance that assimilation was largely a matter of aesthetics. White women, along with Tre-Jur, could confidently declare that lily white complexion was "passé"—that skin tone was a matter of fashion, that a dark complexion was one choice among many—as long as the boundary between black and white was secure. It took the African-American press to expose the easy coexistence of the tanning aesthetic and white supremacy. At an Asbury Park resort, "Life-guards, burnt so dark that they were eligible for the jim-crow car, were the envy, particularly of the women," the *Messenger* pointedly commented. "In the meantime the Negroes were huddled into a corner of the beach between two buildings that shut off the view like the blinders on a horse."[29]

The painted face had suddenly become a sign of the times. By the 1930s, how-to manuals and product inserts gave detailed instructions on contouring and coloring with new foundation creams, lipstick, and eye shadow. Women could easily learn the "Hollywood trick of dramatizing, heightening, and accenting" facial features, wrote one beauty expert. What had once been denounced as paint was now celebrated as *glamour*, "one of the thrill words of this decade." As a makeup artist proclaimed, "We can literally manufacture" facial glamour "right out of

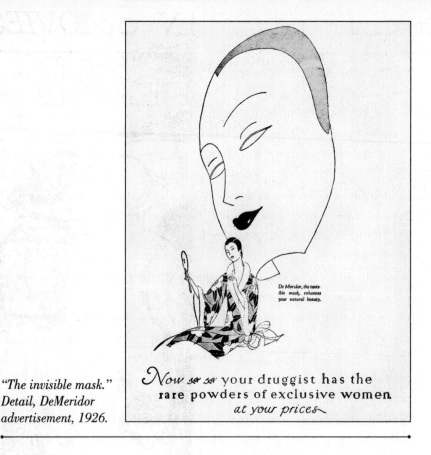

Dr Meridor, the invisible mask, enhances your natural beauty.

Now ᴍ ᴍ your druggist has the
rare powders of exclusive women
at your prices

"*The invisible mask.*"
Detail, DeMeridor
advertisement, 1926.

the paint-pot." At the same time, the painted woman continued to haunt cosmetics producers and promoters. If no longer the mark of the prostitute, too much makeup still implied female coarseness, promiscuity, and low social standing. Advice writers repeated the mantra that makeup should "make you look *naturally* more attractive—not artificial, nor obviously painted." Fearing a backlash, the trade press even tried to galvanize store clerks to advise customers not to use too much face powder—an effort that quickly failed.[30]

To make the mask invisible involved not just creating a natural look, but training the eye to perceive makeup as a natural feature of women's faces. The *Hollywood Mirror* contrasted the glamour of Garbo unfavorably to the charm of Janet Gaynor, a woman-next-door who

Cartoonist's view of natural beauty, Toilet Requisites, *1928.*

New Beauty Secret
made her look
more Natural!

HER name is a secret. But her story isn't. She's wealthy .. well-educated. *Yet men once questioned her good taste.* They said her painted lips were artificial-looking .. unnatural. Luckily, she found the one lipstick that gives natural-looking color .. without a trace of paint!

Detail, Tangee advertisement, in Ladies' Home Journal, *1933.*

needed "no artificial aid to hold a man's attention." It stressed that "cleanliness, correct cosmetics used with reserve, keeping one's hair well groomed . . . are the fundamentals." Even Max Factor, whose makeup was most closely associated with Hollywood glamour, described the "magic of make-up" to be an illusionism that made it "impossible for anyone to detect [where] the Make-Up begins or ends." But looking natural, like looking glamorous, now required a box full of beauty devices: foundation or vanishing cream, powder, rouge, lipstick, and for some, eyebrow pencil, mascara and eye shadow.[31]

The use of lipstick proved especially troubling. Considered the most artificial cosmetic in everyday use, it connoted the come-on, a sexually assertive, public pose that trifled with bourgeois conventions. Against the eye's perception, the industry declared lipstick natural. Beauty editor Dorothy Cocks did not object to "having your lip paste show, provided it shows an effort on your part to have it match the natural tone of your own coloring." Tangee actually looked orange in the tube but harmonized with lip color when applied; advertisements invited consumers to "make up your LIPS for KISSES!" and featured women with bright bow lips and dots of rouge, yet insisted the lipstick "can't make you look painted . . . it isn't paint." One ad pronounced a woman "innocent yet men talked"; her lipstick marked her as cheap and vulgar until she tried Tangee. Tying lipstick to sex, advertisers and advice writers acknowledged female eros yet guided it safely toward heterosexual romance and marriage. Vivid red lips impeded the fulfillment of those natural desires, a beauty writer warned: "You cannot afford to make yourself ridiculous if you have started for success, or you want to attract a REAL man."[32]

Applying makeup in public was also highly charged because it exposed the artifice behind the illusion, the backstage of women's performance. Advice columns and beauty manuals often editorialized against public primping in the 1920s. Powdering in restaurants or shops "stamps you as having poor breeding," noted one authority. Some manufacturers tried to calm women's fears about making a spectacle of themselves; Colgate offered a thin watchcase compact that "nestles into your hand so inconspicuously that you can use it anywhere without being noticed." Gradually beauty experts became more equivocal, and then stopped objecting to makeup "repairs" and "face-fixing" altogether. As *Vogue* proclaimed, putting on lipstick had become one of the "gestures of the twentieth century."[33]

Once makeup became widely accepted, advertisers and beauty experts regulated its use by trafficking in subtle distinctions. Coloring the eyelids and beading lashes were fun in the evening but bad taste in daylight; acceptable for adults but not for girls under eighteen; lovely on the dance floor but not in the office. "If you *must* be exotic, wait till after dark," instructed columnist Bernice Peck. Writers advised women not to wear movie makeup on the street—too colorful and showy—and warned against runny mascara and lipstick that came off on men's collars and on napkins. Delineating appropriate makeup based on time of day, activity, age, and circumstances became a commonplace of beauty reporting, crucial to the cycle of fashion, products, and news that propels women's magazines today.[34]

Advertisers set out to change the way women viewed their external appearance. To do so, they drew on new perceptions of the inner self beholden to psychology and psychiatry. In the 1930s, an explicitly therapeutic language began to pervade cosmetics promotions. It was not simply that makeup could "make us look and feel more self-possessed, poised, and efficient," as one beauty editor put it. Rather, women's mental health and feminine development depended on continually embracing new looks and beauty products. When any woman "begins to regard her appearance in her own mind as a fixed, unalterable quantity—that same moment, some vital, shining part of her is extinguished forever," said *Vogue's Book of Beauty* in 1933. A woman who fails to update her looks, it went on, "destroys those potential personalities that psychologists tell us are lurking behind our ordinary selves." Psychoanalytic terms began to course through the trade press. Those "who are conscious of their poor appearance" suffered from an inferiority complex, one psychiatrist judged. But help was literally at hand, industry spokesman Everett McDonough promised, for "many a neurotic case has been cured with the deft application of a lipstick."[35]

As an advertising medium that stressed storytelling over visual information, radio was particularly suited to communicate a message focused on the psychology of beauty. In a 1930 commercial for Ingram's Milkweed Cream, for instance, beauty expert "Frances Ingram" read a letter from a saleswoman passed over for promotion in a large Detroit department store. Criticized for lacking efficiency and personality, she resigned from her job: "It's the unfairest thing I ever heard of. But since listening to you, I've been wondering if maybe my appearance affected my chance of promotion." Ingram briskly observed that in this "age of self-development," women must cultivate their health and "internal cleanliness," acquire a "radiant, attractive, and likeable" personality, and attend to external appearance. "When a woman has a bad complexion, people notice it immediately, and they have to get past it before they really like that person," she diagnosed. "I believe that the dullness of your complexion may have reacted on your subconscious in such a way that your confidence in yourself has become impaired."[36]

The appeal to naturalism and psychology effaced differences among women, and it reinforced the notion that all women share identical desires. The great variety of female lives and looks were increasingly distilled into pure images of women who revealed nothing but their beauty. Elizabeth Arden's famous ad of a beautiful, anonymous head wrapped in a towel offered a quasi-religious motif—the laying on

USE
Elizabeth Arden's
Preparations

under her personal direction
And be assured of the clear loveliness of your skin

• • •

*W*HEN you use Elizabeth Arden's Preparations according to the methods carefully
evolved by Miss Arden herself, the health and clear
beauty of your skin are as assured as if you were
working under Miss Arden's personal supervision.

Every Preparation has been personally planned by
Miss Arden for a definite purpose — for a particular
type of skin. Every treatment has first of all been perfected, step by step, by Miss Arden's own swift, skillful
fingers. To secure the very best results be sure that you
use every cream, lotion or tonic exactly as intended.
Cleanse with *Venetian Cleansing Cream*, whose
melting purity penetrates every least little pore. Wake
up your sleepy tissues, give them new zest with *Skin
Tonic*, or if they are unusually sluggish, brace and
invigorate them with *Special Astringent*. Smooth away
every tiny roughness with *Velva Cream*. Fill out de-
pressing hollows and weary lines with *Orange Skin Food*.

*Two versions of
"Everywoman."*

Top: *Elizabeth Arden
advertisement, 1928.*

Right: *Detail, Lady
Esther advertisement,
from* Pictorial Review,
1933.

PARALYZED PORES

**TRUE CAUSE OF
DRY OR OILY SKIN
ENLARGED PORES
AND BLACKHEADS**

HER PORES SAY

I CAN'T BREATHE!

HELP! GIVE ME AIR!

I'M SUFFOCATING!

MAKE THIS TELLING TEST!

RUB YOUR finger tips over your face. Press firmly. Give particular
attention to your chin, forehead, around your mouth, and the little
crevices beside your nose. Now! Is your skin absolutely smooth?
Or do you feel tiny bumps and rough patches? If you do, you have
Paralyzed Pores.

of hands—that brilliantly symbolized the universality of Arden's service. In a similar vein, Tre-Jur developed a series of ads called the
"Unknown Beauty." "Everywoman" pervaded Depression-era cosmetics marketing; ads were filled with ordinary women who looked for
beauty at good prices and shared their worries about "paralyzed
pores," "cosmetic skin," and other complexion problems fabricated in
the world of advertising.[37]

In little more than a decade, an aesthetic of women's freedom and
modernity had narrowed and turned in upon itself. *Vogue* could claim
without irony that bright fingernails offered "a minor adventure" and a
facial "doesn't stop at giving you a new face—it gives you a whole new
point of view on life." What had once been seen as women's vices—
vanity, deceit, desire—were now signs of a "normal mind." Beauty
manuals and women's magazines urged women to encourage narcissism in their daughters to make them care about their looks. Asserting
women's "right to ROMANCE!" advertisements offered cosmetics as
talismans and weapons in the proper pursuit of men and marriage.
"Most men are like babies," stated one beauty guide, and women
should use cosmetics to manipulate them—discreetly. As "the one
topic that every woman has in common with her sister," claimed McDonough in 1937, cosmetics even "spread democracy." In that democracy, goods knitted together a female polity, yet limited choice, rights,
and participation to acts of beautifying and consumption.[38]

As the cosmetics trade sought to reach new consumers, there remained
one boundary some contemplated crossing. "Will he-men ever be a
good market?" wondered industry researchers in 1936. It seemed un-
likely. Of two hundred white-collar New Yorkers queried, one in two
used an aftershave talc or lotion, but most eschewed scents and tints.
More than half disliked fragrances as too "sissified," offensive, or caus-
ing unfavorable comment. The problem, researchers concluded, was
the belief that cosmetics were effeminate. "The man who shuns aftershave talcum in the daytime," they noted, "would use it if he thought it

would add to, not endanger, his reputation as a 'regular' guy."[39]

That reputation had been long
in the making. Just as women who
used cosmetics had to contend with
the image of the painted hussy, so
men interested in beautifying had
to defend themselves against insin-
uations of frivolity, weakness, and
homosexuality.

The late-nineteenth-century "cult
of manliness" offered an emphatic
ideal of male toughness and vitality,
visible in the mania for football and
boxing, the adulation of the cowboy,
and the militarism of Teddy Roosevelt's Rough Riders. Men who
cared too much for their appearance
were perceived to be weak and wom-
anish. The rise of the New Woman
was greeted with reactionary poems
and cartoons of severe, powerful

*Oscar Wilde advertises women's
beauty preparations. Neilson's
Secret for the Complexion trade
card.*

women served by dainty, painted men. Upper-class fops and "exquisites"
wearing rouge and eyebrow pencil, slick-haired salesmen, scented black
dandies, and homosexual "fairies" flourishing powder puffs were all stock
figures in popular culture. Male cosmetics use registered disorder in the
regime of masculinity.[40]

These images had some basis in reality, as different male subcul-
tures adopted a more fastidious and enhanced appearance. At the turn
of the century, the use of hair and shaving products was widespread,
and men of wealth, especially bachelors, conveyed a sense of sophistication and urbanity with the addition of aftershave powder or cologne.
Some black and white working-class men had long put on a stylish parody of the man about town. Most important, male homosexual commu-

nities became increasingly visible in large cities, and as historian George Chauncey explains, the emergent gay cultural style used appearance to signal sexual identity. Significantly, the rouged lips and eye shadow of so-called "painted queens" and "fairies" reflected the makeup styles more of prostitutes and lower-class women than of middle-class ladies. Most gay men did not choose such overt display—typically those who did were young, working-class men with little reputation to protect—but discreet middle-class homosexuals might on occasion use cologne or subtle makeup.[41]

Scattered evidence of men's wary flirtation with cosmetics appears throughout the historical record. Beauty culturists often remarked on how men in the public eye—politicians, actors, salesmen—sought facials and skin treatments. Men visited Madame Velaro's studio in the 1880s to have wrinkles removed and mustaches tinted; decades later, Helena Rubinstein and Elizabeth Arden reported similar forays and sporadically marketed male beauty products and services. At large urban barbershops, *Fortune* noted in 1937, the male visitor received "much the same treatment he might get in the beauty parlor shops, and without seeming faery (except perhaps to the barber)."[42]

Some men covertly used cosmetics, doing "things to their faces in the privacy of their bathrooms which they might not admit to at a teamsters' picnic." They applied their wives' Pompeian night cream in the morning when shaving; they ordered Vauv, a vanishing cream advertised only to women, to remove shine; they raided their wives' cosmetic cases for Covermark to hide blemishes. A business writer described a "successful salesman (and he's a 'HE-MAN') who carries a very small makeup kit with him" and used eyeliner "to enhance impression." A middle-class woman told how her teenage son used Pond's for blackheads: "Keeps it down in his drawer where nobody will see and tease him about it." When men "come to the cosmetics counter and demand 'just powder,' " observed a druggist, they want "face powder, and the wise clerk will assume as much and ask no questions."[43] Some commentators in the 1920s prophesied that women's cosmetic practices would eventually extend to men. "Effeminacy does not mean what it used to mean," said the *Spokane Review* in 1925. "What is going on is the gradual drawing together of the sexes on the common ground of mutual custom." Noting the high salaries paid to handsome male movie stars, it speculated that men might wear eyebrow pencil and lipstick in the future, as appearance became increasingly important to success. But given men's embarrassment and discomfort, transforming idiosyncratic private behavior into publicly acknowledged and accepted practices remained a daunting task.[44]

A genuine opening for men's toiletries came when men first embraced self-shaving. Playing on fears of germs spread in public barbershops, manufacturers promoted the hygiene, privacy, and thrift of the safety razor. They appealed as well to dominant notions of middle-class masculinity: The self-shaver was a self-starter. Gillette, the leader of the industry, glamorized baseball players, soldiers, and young businessmen. "The Gillette is typical of the American spirit," claimed a 1910 ad in the ringing tones of Andrew Carnegie and Horatio Alger. "Its use starts habits of energy—of initiative. And men who *do* for

Gillette advertisement, 1910.

The men who uphold the standards of American sport today are clean men—clean of action and clean of face. Your baseball star takes thought of his personal appearance—it's a part of his team ethics. He starts the day with a clean shave—and, like all self-reliant men, he shaves himself.

Wagner, Jennings, Kling, Donovan, Chance—each of the headliners owns a Gillette Safety Razor *and uses it*. The Gillette is typical of the American spirit. It is used by capitalists, professional men, business men—by men of action all over this country —*three million of them.*

Its use starts habits of energy—of initiative. And men who *do* for themselves are men who *think* for themselves. Be master of your own time. Buy a Gillette and use it. You can shave with it the first time you try. The only perfectly *safe* razor and the only safety razor that shaves on the correct hollow ground shaving principle. No stropping, no honing.

Send your name on a post card for our new Baseball Book—Schedule of all League games, batting records—24 pages of interesting facts and figures. Every fan should have it. It is free.

King C Gillette

GILLETTE SALES COMPANY, 80 W. Second Street, Boston

J. B. Williams advertisement, from American Magazine, *1928.*

themselves are men who *think* for themselves." Manufacturers of shaving supplies invoked good grooming as an entrée into the new corporate economy, the means by which men created their own references. The erosion of local, family-centered businesses and the growth of national commercial networks, corporate industry, and a new professional and managerial class had made questions of probity and loyalty a growing concern. How could businessmen read character in the faces of unfamiliar job applicants or potential partners? Toilet-goods companies answered, "A good face is the best letter of introduction."[45]

Razor manufacturers also used exotic types, albeit in different ways than cosmetic firms selling to women. Seeking to dispel the association of toiletries with effeminacy, an advertisement for Curley's Easy-Shaving Safety Razor claimed that "the first Roman to shave every day was no fop, but Scipio, conquerer of Africa." J. B. Williams compared the "caste marks" of Indian men to the clean-shaven American face. Ironically, these references to the foreign "other" made it more difficult to convince American men to use cosmetics; as one trade analyst put it, toiletries "prepared exclusively for men simply couldn't get by their Anglo-Saxon prejudices."[46]

While razors and shaving soap became a big business, other toiletries remained difficult to sell. Ads for complexion clay or massage cream occasionally addressed both sexes using different appeals: Pompeian cream "beautifies and youthifies" women but enabled men to "win success" and "make [their] own promotion easier" in the business world. More commonly firms classified the products themselves either as women's cosmetics or men's toilet goods. In the late nineteenth century, distributors had sold *mascaro* as an all-purpose dye, useful in touching up gray hair at the temples and darkening eyebrows and lashes; by World War I the product had become *mascara*, an eyelash beautifier for women only. Even when presented with evidence of male demand, firms selling women's beauty wares failed to take advantage. Ads for Cutex manicure preparations in 1918 included keyed coupons for free samples to test the popularity of different appeals; 10 percent of the inquiries came from men but were deliberately discarded.[47]

Having successfully promoted cosmetics use as a natural facet of womanhood, in the 1920s and 1930s the industry labored to cast an aura of masculinity around men's preparations, adopting trademarks, packaging, advertising, and merchandising methods that expunged the feminine. The trade journal *Toilet Requisites* urged retailers to push goods "for men only" by writing ads in men's language, teaching clerks about male buying habits, and creating single-sex boutiques to ease male anxiety. Any evidence of manly grooming was cheered: "Toiletries Effeminate?—Ask the Navy!" Unable to overcome its prejudices, however, the journal continually undermined its own efforts: "It is bootless to argue or advertise the fact that men should have recourse to toiletries in the manner of women. Some do, but, thank Heaven, they form but a meagre company."[48]

Several firms set out to sell face powder to men under the guise of tinted talcum or aftershave powders. The Mennen Company, for example, marketed a Talcum for Men, to be used after shaving: This had a light tint, and despite differences in name and packaging, bore a close resemblance to loose face powder for women. Although the product did well, William Mennen, Jr., remembered that when it was introduced, "the company used to get a lot of bitter mail saying that we were trying to turn men into women." One manufacturer marketed powder puffs in rubber sacks, which could be concealed in the breast pocket of men's jackets. Another made a mitt-shaped Talc-Pad for men's shaving kits and proclaimed hopefully, "Now it's man's turn to be emancipated."[49]

Carl Weeks made the most ambitious attempt to render cosmetics masculine. Apparently male powder users often bought Armand because it was heavy and adherent enough to cover beard stubble. Weeks began thinking about a men's powder as early as 1925, "not a talc to sell to men, but a real face powder made to go on men's faces easily to make them look better." In 1929 Weeks finally launched Florian, a line of men's toiletries that included skin lotion, face powder, and moisturizer. He believed that "men were beginning to realize that, if their faces are smooth and clean, their hair neat, their clothes pressed, and their shoes shined, they gain a sense of well being that is worth money." In the face of much skepticism, Weeks forged ahead. When journalist Charles Muller, swallowing hard, wrote to inquire, "Will appeal be that of health or—I hesitate—beauty?" Weeks nonchalantly (and ambiguously) noted in the letter's margin "sure."[50]

To detach Florian from any taint of the feminine, Weeks spurned French trade names, floral designs, and pastel colors. Florian's red and black containers with zigzag lettering presented snappy and cartoonish trade names, such as Brisk, Dash, Vim, Keen, Zest, and Smooth. Weeks advised druggists to place the line at cigar counters and mount displays featuring boxing gloves, pipes, dice, and footballs. "You will put over the idea that the mascu-*line* is all *stag*," he enthused. "It's for he-men with no women welcome nohow." To create brand recognition and demand, he distributed free samples where men congregated, at

Let's NOT join the ladies!

Detail, Houbigant advertisement for Fougere Royale after-shave, from Esquire, *1934.*

colleges, rotary clubs, fire and police stations, banks, and factories. Still, Weeks's "he-man proposition" could not disguise the fact that men were being asked to adopt female beauty practices. Florian sales-men showed dealers "that slick way of mixing Zest and Smooth so that it powders and stays on and doesn't show," but the products and in-structions differed little from Armand's vanishing cream and complex-ion powder for women.[51]

Although the onset of the Depression made the launch of Florian a classic case of bad timing, few manufacturers were successful in pro-moting even the most limited line of men's skin-care cosmetics, let alone makeup. *Fortune* and *Esquire* ran relatively few toiletry ads in the 1930s, although sales of aftershaves and scented products did rise after 1935. J. B. William's Aqua Velva dominated the mass market for aftershave using a direct and practical appeal—"feels great on your face," "peps up your appearance." In contrast, an elite brand like Houbigant's Fougere Royale offered a "stimulating cocktail for the face" and featured tuxedoed men lingering over postprandial brandies, declaring "Let's NOT join the ladies." The image was sexually ambiguous, potentially viewed as a scene of gay bonhomie, but it drew a clear line between male and female consumption.[52] When it came to cosmetics, most men did not join the ladies. Cosmetics were not readily reconciled with a heterosexual masculine identity.

In the 1920s and 1930s, cosmetics producers, advertisers, and beauty experts shifted the burden of female identity from an interior self to a personality made manifest by marking and coloring the face: Makeup was a true expression of feminine identity, not its false mask, and the makeover was a means of individual self-development. Marketers underwrote consumers' belief in their own modernity, an endorsement that potentially opened a space for women's individuality, social participation, and public presence. Yet that female space, in the imagination of advertisers and advice writers, quickly became an animated world of romantic interludes, leisure activities, social encounters, and narcissistic pleasure, all occurring through commercial exchange. Cosmetics marketing intensified gender distinctions—especially in failed attempts to sell cosmetics to men—even as it acknowledged, in oblique ways, the social changes affecting women's lives. Through powerful beauty images, makeup's aesthetic wedded women's modernity and individuality to a normative female identity. In his "Cosmetic Laws," Carl Weeks wrote that cosmetics must render each woman "entirely herself," yet must express the "glorification of divine femininity."[53] Such incongruity and paradox were not incidental by-products but governing axioms in the mass market for beauty.

Everyday

Cosmetic

Practices

"**F**acial decoration increasing," the trade paper *Toilet Requisites* happily announced in 1920, and indeed the use of beauty preparations, especially makeup, rose sharply in the years that followed.[1] To all appearances, the beauty industry had succeeded in delivering its message to women, that the fulfillment of individuality and femininity required the purchase of cosmetics. Still, these successes do not explain how women felt as they entered into the new consumer culture, how they read advertisements, what motivated them to buy cosmetics, or how they actually used makeup. Not everybody powdered and painted, and participation in the new beauty rituals varied greatly from woman to woman.

Unfortunately most women left few records of behavior so ordinary and taken for granted. But early market research, public debates about makeup use, and women's own letters permit a sketch of female purchasing habits and cosmetics use in the 1920s and 1930s. These sources are problematic and fragmentary, limited to white middle- and working-class women in several localities across the country. Nevertheless, they open to view a picture of women's everyday beauty practices otherwise obscured by the potent and influential images circulated by the cosmetics industry. They suggest how women negotiated the earlier disreputable meanings of paint and shaped our modern perceptions of makeup.[2]

Although the beauty industry claimed that American women everywhere were making up, the consumer surveys they commissioned show a wide spectrum of opinion about cosmetics and distinct patterns of use. Age, marital status, economic class, ethnic origins, and residence influenced women's relationship to the new mass market.

Before World War I makeup had been largely a phenomenon of the metropolis. New York City led the country in the cosmetic arts, as it did in so many other forms of cultural expression. Helena Rubinstein recalled that when she came to New York in 1915 she "was shocked even then by the numbers of young girls who were excessively made up." Cosmetics firms perceived New York to be a distinct market at the heart of the fashion trade, where the latest styles circulated rapidly not only in high society but among working-class retail clerks and dressmakers. At a time when American women tentatively dusted on rouge, New Yorkers painted their lips, flourished compacts, and even bought mascara and eye shadow, considered the most questionable type of makeup. Women in other large cities followed suit. In Chicago, one industry observer reported in the mid-1920s, wealthy women applied makeup "very carefully and sparingly," while working women "use it in astonishing quantities."[3]

In contrast, makeup came only gradually to Main Street. "Such a small percentage use cosmetics to any considerable extent," exclaimed a surprised executive at the J. Walter Thompson ad agency in 1927. In Topeka, Kansas, and Columbus, Ohio, middle-class housewives had begun to use such basic skin-care products as cold cream and vanishing cream, following the regimen promoted by beauty culturists and advertised by Pond's and other mass marketers. A substantial minority had even started to rouge, although, as they reported it, only with a

Small-town teenagers at the cosmetics counter. From Beauty, *1922.*

light touch. In contrast, poor and working-class wives interviewed in Providence, Rhode Island, and Chester, Pennsylvania, showed little use of any beautifier, let alone visible makeup. As late as 1933, low-income housewives, many of whom worked in factories and stores to support their families, did not so much resist beauty preparations as express indifference: Cosmetics were irrelevant to their lives.[4]

Cosmetics were even less prevalent in small towns and farming communities, where one-half of all Americans still dwelled in 1920.

Distribution was uneven. "Towns under 1,000 are hopeless," complained a Thompson investigator, since the general stores carried few beauty preparations, but in larger towns "up-to-date" druggists eagerly began to stock cosmetics. O. N. Falk's drugstore in Stoughton, Wisconsin, for example, sold mainly skin-care products and face powders before the mid-twenties, but then offered an enormous selection of brand-name rouges, lipsticks, and even complexion clay. Beauty shops began to surface in towns and villages, and mail-order sales served many rural women. Market research surveys even reported the occasional small-town woman who purchased Elizabeth Arden's high-priced preparations.[5]

Despite the availability of cosmetics, farm women indulged in skin-care regimens sporadically and adopted visible makeup only reluctantly. Most cleaned their faces with soap and warm water, but a small number had begun to develop the "cold cream habit." Many used powder, which was believed to protect the skin from the elements. City women's rouge and lipstick were uncommon, and one correspondent reported in 1927, "mascaro is just beginning to become a staple item in the smaller towns in the corn belt." It was not until the end of the 1930s that farm women's use of cosmetics approximated that of urban dwellers. A study by the *Farm Journal* of over two thousand rural families in 1941 reported that almost all women used face powder, two-thirds applied cold cream and rouge, and more than half wore lipstick. Even so, the study excluded the class of "illiterates, negroes, or sub-marginal farm families"—one-fifth of all farm women—considered strangers to consumer culture by national advertisers.[6]

These surveys show, in a general way, that makeup use dropped as household incomes declined, especially among married housewives. However, age and activity, broadly defined, appear to be more important indicators of makeup use. Women over forty might use powder but few wore rouge and lipstick; in the Providence survey, not one woman over sixty used any of these cosmetics. Among women under age twenty-five, on the other hand, virtually all used powder daily, three-quarters used rouge, and almost half wore lipstick. Visible makeup was especially pronounced among wage-earners and college students. At Ohio State University and Pembroke College in 1927, makeup applications constituted a daily regimen. A 1931 study of college women similarly reported that over 85 percent wore rouge, lipstick, face powder, and nail polish, and spent about twelve to thirteen dollars a year on these items. Young stenographers, typists, and clerks also applied color regularly to cheeks and lips, transforming the painted face into a business uniform. At Macy's, working women were "the largest consumer of units of rouge and lipstick," crowding onto the selling floor during their lunch hour, sniffing powder compacts and "pay[ing] anything for Tangee, Incarnat, Indelible or Rubinstein's lipstick." Even high school girls had begun buying cosmetics.[7]

The beauty industry embraced national advertising, believing it effectively identified previously unrecognized "needs" and showed Americans how to fulfill their desires. Mass marketers applauded the rising subscription rates of traditional "home journals" and the new confession magazines. In them, women could find page after page of cosmetics advertising, detailed instructions on cosmetic applications, and inspirational stories of beautiful women. According to market researcher Nell B. Nichols, women read beauty columns "religiously" and studied magazines "like textbooks."[8]

Yet women's exposure to advertising was partial, their immersion in commercial beauty culture mediated and incomplete. The circulation of women's magazines varied greatly by economic class. In a 1923 study of Cincinnati magazine readers, 23 percent of professional and business families and 38 percent of clerical and skilled workers' households subscribed to *Woman's Home Companion;* in contrast, only 6 percent of those in low-paid working-class occupations—domestic workers, laborers, and factory operatives—did so. In 1930, while almost one-third of the wealthiest families in the United States (earning more than $10,000) purchased the *Ladies' Home Journal*, the number of subscribers declined steeply among the less prosperous. Even taking into account the fact that magazines were purchased on newsstands and frequently handed around among friends and neighbors, many women, especially among the poor, had little exposure to national advertising.[9]

Low-income women often ignored advertised national brands and looked for "specials" on cosmetics, "house" brands, and cut-price sales. At Bloomingdale's, an investigator contrasted the Lexington Avenue circle that bought on charge accounts with the Third Avenue crowd, mainly foreign born, who "have limited money and buy on a price basis." Many women redeemed the manufacturers' coupons that appeared in advertisements to introduce the brand. Consumers, however, often saw free samples as an end in themselves. "The kinds [of cosmetics] I really like are too expensive, so I don't buy them," observed one woman. "I depend on samples." Farm and small-town women also engaged consumer culture selectively. They purchased some of the same nationally advertised brands as urban women—Pond's creams, for instance—but also bought many mail-order and door-to-door brands not found in urban stores. "In several cases the leaders in city stores attracted little demand in the country trade," one study noted.[10]

Even in the 1920s many women continued to make their own beauty preparations, following recipes handed down in families or between neighbors. Vinegar, cream, lemon juice and bay rum, or rosewater and white Vaseline went into popular homemade face lotions; these concoctions were second in popularity only to Hinds' Honey and Almond Lotion among rural readers of the *People's Home Journal* in 1925. Well into the 1930s, women used old-fashioned honey packs and oatmeal scrubs to improve the texture of the skin. The fans of *Modern Screen* and *Modern Romance,* mainly young urban working women who bought large quantities of makeup, still used many common substances from the kitchen or bathroom cabinet: peroxide and buttermilk to bleach the skin, Vaseline or castor oil to lengthen eyelashes, and witch hazel as an astringent.[11] A decade of aggressive advertising did not silence homespun views of skin care: Many women feared that commercial creams spurred hair growth, advocated "ice [as] the best astringent," or used "white of egg to remove wrinkles and youthify."[12]

Early market research offers some insight into the ways women read beauty ads. Middle-class women seem to have been close readers. They were impressed with ads that gave detailed instructions, told an engaging story, or had striking illustrations. (Elizabeth Arden's ad of a beautiful woman's head wrapped in a towel often elicited comment.) When interviewed, women frequently used the language of commercial beauty culture to discuss their skin-care and grooming habits. Sounding like an advertisement, Topeka housewife Nell Read observed that vanishing cream "makes the powder go on smooth and gives a velvet-like appearance." "I had a very hard, tough skin that 'nobody loved to touch' until I used your soap," wrote a Southern debutante on a Woodbury's questionnaire; "now it is smooth and velvety and everybody loves to touch it."[13]

College students in particular quoted advertising slogans verbatim—"a skin you love to touch," a "school girl complexion"—when describing and evaluating their own faces. In a Thompson study of Vassar students, "again and again phrases that had been used in the Woodbury advertising were used by the girls, with apparent unconsciousness." University of Chicago students wrote on their questionnaires that Woodbury's "actually draws the dust and dirt out of the pores" and "one feels deliciously clean and fresh after using it." One even commented on its "psychological effect": "I always imagine myself *radiant*—like the pink-cheeked girl in the advertisement—after I use it."[14]

However, relatively few college students in these surveys directly connected beauty products to the promise of romance and glamour common in advertisements. A Smith student who "longed for Romance and thought perhaps a beautiful complexion would make me more fascinating" made a rare admission among the respondents. Instead, college women mainly evaluated the promises of beauty ads according to practical considerations—whether their skin was dry or blemished, for instance, or if their area had hard water or sooty air.[15]

This market research, intended to convince manufacturers to invest in advertising, ironically reveals a significant degree of consumer indifference. Although complexion care dominated national cosmetics advertising in this period, most women did not purchase home treatments, massage the face, or follow a beauty "system." An extensive survey of Milwaukee consumers in 1923 found that only 7 percent used the four creams—cold, cleansing, vanishing, and night cream—that composed a complete skin-care regimen. Efforts to sell entire product lines repeatedly failed; at Macy's, four-fifths of cosmetics sales were of single items. Moreover, women tended to use skin-care products according to their own lights. Despite the advertisers' best efforts, women confused cold cream and vanishing cream, often applying them interchangeably and erratically. In the Columbus survey, many women reported they used cold cream or vanishing cream (74 percent and 57 percent respectively), but a much smaller percentage applied them daily (45 percent and 21 percent).[16]

Indeed, many women expressed suspicion of cosmetics ads, seeing them as so much bunk. To the dismay of J. Walter Thompson executives, most women interviewed in Columbus offered "no reaction" to the Pond's testimonial advertisements, and less than one-third remembered them well enough to describe them. Even fewer Chester and Providence women recalled the ads, again a figure that dropped as income declined. Those who did often questioned the motives of the wealthy women who endorsed Pond's creams. For every woman who praised the socialites' testimonials—"it brings the story home to you to read about women whose names are known"—there was another consumer who wondered skeptically, "Why do they do it? What do they get?" Women demanded factual discussion of makeup techniques, not extravagant claims and romantic copy. As radio became a popular medium, they often objected to commercials for cosmetics and personal hygiene intrusively entering the home. Lady Esther's warning of the dangers of "gritty face powder" caused many listeners to turn down the volume. "If I hear 'Lady Esther' tell me to put that powder between my teeth and if I find grits," wrote an irate woman to NBC, "I will be likely to tear my hair out."[17]

Women approached advertising messages not as isolated consumers but as social actors, reading their warnings and advice in light of personal experiences and local contexts. Family and friends, class and social background all came into play as women assessed the salience of an advertisement in their lives. One middle-class woman, for instance, judged a Pond's testimonial advertisement "interesting in a way," but stated she "would be more interested if my next-door neighbor told me what good results she had had." Commenting on the ad's high-society endorser, she continued:

> Some of the wealthy women probably don't have as bad skins to care for as people who have come from large families with small incomes where doctors were too expensive to be called in always, and skins sometimes suffered because diseases were inadequately cared for. So what Queen Marie does for her skin which is probably very smooth to begin with, would not help me as much as what my next-door neighbor uses.

Her comment makes tangible the results of unpublished market studies in the 1920s and 1930s: Women never cited advertising as the primary reason they purchased cosmetics. Consumers repeatedly named free samples, retailers' recommendations, and saleswomen before they mentioned ads as their motivation to buy.[18]

Ultimately, the most important influences on women's cosmetic practices were personal. Sometimes friends discouraged each other from appearing "painted." Sometimes women talked themselves out of making up simply by imagining the censure of their neighbors: They feared to look "ridiculous without knowing it." Mrs. Edwin Austin, a Topeka housewife, expressed "no prejudice" against other women wearing rouge but thought "she would be conscious every minute of the addition and knows all her friends would be remarking about Mrs. Austin and her rouge."[19]

Often women egged each other on, encouraging participation in a practice whose questionable reputation persisted. "Most products are bought by woman to woman advice," confirmed *McCall's* beauty editor. Makeup circulated in familiar rounds of sociability: A sister would make a present of a box of rouge; a friend would advise another to put a little color in her cheeks. At first Rachel Neiswender "thought it was a disgrace to be seen with artificial color," but then her friends started using rouge and she gave in. Mrs. George Chambers received rouge as a Christmas present from a friend who "knew I would never use any if it wasn't given to me so I would make the start."[20]

Children, both young and grown, also persuaded women to take the plunge. The Topeka housewives frequently attributed their first use of rouge to the influence of daughters and sons. Mrs. Sidney Smith's seven-year-old daughter came home from school one day and asked her mother to make her cheeks "pink and pretty," and she complied. An elderly woman who had given little thought to such matters explained that "her children kept urging her to make the start" and her "thought-ful son" had even bought her a box of rouge. "She says she now feels as uncomfortable without it as she does without her powder," the inter-viewer stated.[21]

Advertising promoted cosmetics as a means of winning and keeping a husband. As a cultural *practice,* however, making up more often un-derscored women's ties to other women, not to men. Married women, at least, rarely mentioned husbands as the reason they began to use makeup. Although some spouses "approved the results," more often women identified men as the reason they did *not* wear cosmetics or hid their use. Men's letters to the *Seattle Union Record* in 1925 generally opposed the use of paint, and market researchers recorded male com-plaints about wives' beauty rituals. One woman, for instance, explained she did not use cold cream because her "husband objects to my fussing with [my] face when going to bed."[22]

Women seemed to be engaged in a running conversation about cos-metics with other women, whether nearby friends or distant experts. They sought makeup advice from magazine beauty editors, approached salesclerks and beauty salon operatives, and even asked cosmetic de-bunkers and market researchers to recommend products. In one mar-

Christmas shopping in the toiletries department, R. H. Macy's in New York, 1942.

ket study, New York housewives turned the tables on the interviewers, sought their cosmetic preferences, and tried "to become investigators themselves," the Market Research Corporation reported with amazement. Women bought toiletries in a different way than household goods, wrote another investigator, because "personal preference" played a greater role. "There is a certain joy in the actual shopping," she observed of cosmetics consumers, in which "leisure, comparisons, subtle persuasion and discussion play an important part."[23]

The social pleasures of beautifying certainly received attention from drugstores, beauty parlors, and manufacturers, who believed that "beauty days" and demonstrations promoted cosmetics sales. But women themselves sometimes organized activities around the pursuit of beauty, inserting the products of commerce into their own social activities and cultural rituals. Women's clubs invited beauty experts and manufacturers' representatives to speak on cosmetics. Some women collected free samples to be given away as prizes at church fairs and fund-raisers. Others created party games using cosmetics ads cut out of magazines or went to costume parties dressed as advertisements. The recognition that beauty culture was an influential language among women helps explain this apparent incongruity: During the 1920 election campaign in Brooklyn—the first election after passage of the women's suffrage amendment—a Democratic party worker left small vanity-bag mirrors with each woman voter she canvassed.[24]

Although sometimes derided as "lazy women's tricks," makeup applications ultimately proved much more popular than beauty culture regimens. Face powder, rouge, and lipstick were more frequently used than vanishing cream, astringents, and "skin food." Women purchased many different brands, restlessly looking for new and better tools for the cosmetic arts; no one company commanded a large percentage of the market for rouge and lipstick, and top sellers changed frequently in the 1920s and 1930s. Moreover, almost all women who reported *any* use of visible makeup applied it daily. For young women, whether in college or at work, "putting on a face" had become a routine part of dressing in the morning, a part of their personality.[25]

In letters and interviews, women defended making up as creative work. They made this assertion in the face of a barrage of comments from men mystified and affronted by the makeup craze. In 1925 a man calling himself the "Sick-O'-Paint Father" started a debate in Ruth Ridgway's column of the *Seattle Union Record* with a complaint about his wife's embrace of makeup. Once she was "one of the prettiest girls in town," but now "it takes more stuff to get her ready to go out than it does to cook a five-course dinner." Paint and powder had turned his

A male cartoonist's view of makeup in 1934.

companionate, domestic wife into some strange, unclean creature. All he wanted was "a sweet, clean kiss that we can't eat off our lips afterwards." Abraham Mondamin, an "ornery bachelor," agreed: "Who wants to get his face all gummed up with that sort of 'Goo'?" For these men, the actual texture and look of makeup, as well as its sexual symbolism, triggered male revulsion.[26]

What men ridiculed as "goo" and "junk" commanded an elaborate vocabulary among cosmetics users. Women precisely discussed their features and skin, the qualities of different preparations, and their assessments of brand-name products. Despite advertisers' aggressive promotion of vanishing cream as a base for face powder, women rejected a preparation that "constricted their face," "made the powder lumpy," or "made the rouge blotchy." They commented upon the most obvious characteristic of face powder, its different tints, but also debated more subtle properties, powder's "hand," "weight," and adhesiveness. Creams also came in different consistencies, and women made detailed evaluations. "Old users," one investigator observed, "ask[ed] for their creams with confidence," taking pride in the knowledge of their skin and appropriate treatments. "I like a heavy, waxy cream, such as Hudnuts 'Marvellous' was for many years," wrote Blanche Snyder to consumer advocate M. C. Phillips, "but now that name is given to an oily 'liquifying' cream." Readers' letters, observed the beauty editor of *Smart Set* magazine, "are astonishingly analytical [and] go into most astounding details as though women had studied themselves for hours."[27]

Makeup continued to be understood by many men as the mark of women's artificiality and guile. Writing to the *Seattle Union Record,* Marco B. called it a "method of seeking satisfaction . . . by falseness and deception" and "a confession of women's shallowness and incapacity." In response, cosmetics-using women translated the sign of artifice into the language of artistry. Making up required adroit skill, an aesthetic sensibility, and hard work. "It takes time, care and practice to use cosmetics," Senga R. shot back. "You can't sit down and just 'daub' it on."[28]

The test of that skill in the twenties involved the application of rouge, which had strong symbolic associations with prostitution. In this period, rouge came in three forms—powder, cream, and liquid—and the coloring was very bright, usually red, pink, or orange. Too little made no difference to one's appearance; too much stamped the wearer as vulgar and tasteless. Several Topeka housewives claimed they did not rouge because they could not manage to apply it artistically. Mrs. W. Pattison used rouge on occasion but thought it "a waste of time to work with it, trying to make it appear natural." Another woman, the interviewer reported, said "she tried using liquid rouge once and it gave the appearance of two birth marks on each cheek."[29]

Women stressed that they did not blindly follow ads and advice columns but experimented with different products. "I began remaking my complexion by asking my friends what they used," explained Violet Osler, winner of a *Household* magazine contest on cosmetics use. "What suited one did not always suit me, so I had to try again." The beauty editor of *Harper's Bazaar* observed that women were "quick to realize their own reactions, they will experiment but throw away that which doesn't agree." They often used products in ways not intended by their manufacturers. A surprising number of women working at the J. Walter Thompson agency, thoroughly familiar with cosmetics advertising, nonetheless applied paste rouge to their lips and lipstick to their cheeks. Perceiving little distinction between these products, they were as likely to follow their own muse as the manufacturer's instructions when making up.[30]

Cosmetics users often found in their experimentation and artistry a physical and psychological pleasure. The cosmetic substances and tools themselves delighted the senses. "Women pick up a powder compact and automatically smell it," noted an investigator working at a toiletries department. "I never saw this to fail." Enamelled and painted compact cases, with ingenious compartments for rouge and powder, tempted the hand: "If the shape or decoration of the container pleased, the customer took the compact," often disregarding the unbecoming shade of the powder inside. The new, jewel-like lipstick cylinders also had a magnetic appeal, but old-fashioned pots of lip coloring and large lipsticks with "unsightly paper wrappers" did not sell at all. Little wonder that Armand representatives were taught that getting women to touch the package would make the sale.[31]

Also pleasurable were the moments of relaxation and respite from the demands of work. The surprising popularity of beauty clays and masks in the 1920s may have been due to the pause they sanctioned. After applying the Clasmic Beautifier, instructed Boncilla Laboratories, "then—for 30 minutes if possible—sit down or lie down and rest." It emphasized, "No exercise or effort is required of you." The Watkins Company even promoted a five-minute beauty break for wage earners.[32]

Most important, making up was labor performed for the self, labor that men often could not readily comprehend. The Sick-O'-Paint Father, unable to understand why women did such things to their faces, wondered if it was to please men or to make other women jealous. When he asked his wife, she "gave the funniest reason of all": "She says she does it to please herself. Can you beat that? All that work TO PLEASE HERSELF!" Market studies confirmed women's commitment to these intimate, sensuous commodities: They desired to keep their looks more than they wanted to acquire labor-saving devices; they would buy cheaper groceries before they would give up on skin cream; and they were "much better able to recall names of favorite brands of cosmetics than they were of canned goods."[33] Makeup per se was no longer a matter of immorality, but a right, a necessity, and especially a pleasure. "Of course the 'bad women' cold creamed and powdered and painted," wrote an elderly woman, "but is that any reason why 'decent' women, who are married or otherwise, cannot have the right to make themselves as attractive as possible, instead of making themselves look and feel so miserable."[34]

Even before the widespread dissemination of beauty preparations and cosmetics advertising, women understood care for appearance as a sign of personality, a self-regard neither indulgent nor narcissistic. Farm women in upstate New York, for instance, questioned about physical culture in the early 1900s, equated good appearance with a modern sense of self that was distinct from their roles as wives or homemakers. "I have neighbors who work all day, every day, never [have] time to wash, comb and change dress in afternoon," wrote one farm wife, "so married women seem to lose all pride." When asked how much time she invested in taking care of her body, Edith Enders, married to an abusive husband, scrawled, "not as much as I would were I a free citizen or as I did before I was in bondage to a despot." Another advised her farm sisters to groom and dress carefully after the housework was finished. "It pays to feel that you are keeping in touch with the world, and all the little things count," she said.[35]

Aware of the historic changes in women's lives, those who did not use makeup in the 1920s called themselves "old-fashioned," "homebodies," and "soap-and-water" women. Many of these old-fashioned women had long worn face powder and skin cream to protect the face against hard water, harsh weather, dirt, and soot; they purchased highly adhesive, white or "flesh" colored powder, with a medium or heavy weight. Their resistance was to makeup, used to change appearance. Although some of them stated a moral opposition to rouge, more often they expressed a sense of discomfort with "paint," as they still called it, a poor fit between their sense of self and a made-up appearance. Ashamed and ill at ease, they described rouge as an inexorable force: Although they were "trying to avoid wearing" it, they felt they would be "won over to it" or "have to yield to it sooner or later."[36]

In contrast, the self-proclaimed "moderns" leaped into the culture of beauty with determination and viewed making up as a bold act of cosmetic self-fashioning. "I had always used Kiss-proof powder," observed Violet Osler, "and I got up the courage to use the rouge and lipstick." These women saw makeup not as a protective covering but as a medium of expression. They embraced the idea of matching makeup shades to skin tones and character types. "Young girls know the shade of powder best adapted to their complexion," observed an investigator in 1923, but "older women were not familiar with the names Rachel and Naturelle," two of the newer shades. By 1930 most cosmetics-users wanted face powder to "blend with [the] skin."[37]

Their behavior echoed some but not all the messages promoted in mass-market advertising in the 1920s. Advertisers urged women to maintain youthful beauty, to express their personality, to enjoy the social whirl of dances and beach parties, but most of all, to seek love and marriage. When the Sick-O'-Paint Father wondered if women made up to attract men or incite female envy, he restated a view that circulated throughout American culture. "As a 'feminist' I hate to say it," wrote marketing expert Christine Frederick in *Selling Mrs. Consumer*, but "women's chief business in life still appears to be to charm and hold a man." Articles with such titles as "I Cured My Pimples—and Became a Bride" and "How a Wife Won Back Her Youth—A Surrender to Ugliness That Nearly Cost a Husband's Love" ran often in romance and beauty magazines. Popular movies like *Why Change Your Wife* and *Dancing Mothers* similarly advanced a modern, youthful appearance as the cure for marital problems.[38]

In linking appearance and female personality, however, the agencies of consumer culture denied the full measure of women's experiences. Advertisements promised youth but remained silent about the effects of time, hard work, and illness on the body; they celebrated the modern young woman as a dancing, romancing free spirit, but erased most signs of her status as a wage earner. Modernist drawings of flappers and photographs of movie stars offered commercial ideals of beauty for imitation far removed from the lives of most women.

Women, in contrast, incorporated cosmetics into the "true story" of their lives, adopting the confessional technique of advertisers but changing the subject. "Women proceed to dramatize themselves" when writing for beauty advice, commented a magazine editor. Like the consumer who judged Pond's face cream in relation to poverty and poor health, these women told of everyday experiences, delights, and struggles. Making up indeed figured in women's dreams of love, their pleasures in self-display, and anxieties over male approval. But in their accounts, their desire for youthful beauty had as much to do with aging bodies, loss of vibrancy, the requirements of employers, and the physical demands of housework and child rearing.[39]

Older women, for instance, often discussed skin care and rouge as a means of veiling the real and deeply felt effects of time and labor. Childbearing, illness, and household duties in an era when women had few labor-saving devices all took their toll on the body. Writing for advice they would explain, "I'm run down and my skin isn't in good condition."[40] They did not want husbands to see their artifice, yet expressed a belief that women's work led them to need artificial beautifiers. Mrs. Charles Crabb described her "struggle to avoid" the use of rouge, but that weariness from housework had made her pale. "Rouge is for the woman who has had color which has been lost with the years," observed Mrs. Edgar May. These women viewed the made-up face as their social face, put on when going shopping or visiting, or applied at dinnertime. Crabb "admitted that she did not powder her face in the morning or when working around the house," but did so before going out or after supper; Mrs. Howard Beagle "applies rouge whenever going away from home but seldom uses it unless she is going away or is expecting company."[41]

Working women too placed cosmetics use within a life story. "I'll admit that we use cosmetics a little too strongly," observed the class-conscious Senga R., but "not all people can diet properly, have regular hours and 'proper attire.' No, not on the present wage system." She described why working women might need to make up: "It's hard to get up at 6, work till 5 or 6, rush home, eat, and either step out or do some odd jobs around home, and still have rosy cheeks and sparkling eyes." A young woman wrote consumer activist M. C. Phillips that facial hair had "become almost an obsession," making her a "gullible victim for Koremlu [depilatory] advertising." But it was her job, which placed her "in contact with people all the time in my capacity in a local Newspaper Office," that had kindled her "obsession" and deepened her credulity.[42]

The creative "work" of makeup tended in two distinct directions, toward an embrace of artifice, on the one hand, and toward an aesthetic of the "natural," on the other. Some women applied makeup with a heavy touch, relishing bright colors, reshaping lips, restructuring cheekbones. For them, makeup was makeover, the transformation of appearance and self. Others believed makeup should be undetectable and imitate the "bloom of youth"—an illusionistic and transparent medium through which a woman's true identity could be expressed. They made up to appear "natural," modulating, not making over, the appearance of the face.

Young working women often embraced a flamboyant and conspicuous look. They not only wore ruby lipstick outlining "bee-stung" lips, but regularly accented their eyes with eye shadow and mascara, products few women used in the daytime, if at all. "The shop girl has lost all sense of perspective," one industry observer chided. "Each of her cheeks are a blooming peony. Her eyes are two smudges of dusky, shadowy black. Her lips are cruel with scarlet." The theatrical aesthetic of makeup especially appealed to sexually active and defiant young women—considered delinquents and "problem girls"—whose crimson cheeks and beaded lashes called attention to surface, color, and texture, not the imitation of nature. They used makeup to play with the image of the "hussy," even as they rejected the stigmatizing label others placed on them.[43]

Many women delighted in the display of makeup's artifice. While older women tended to buy loose powder, the young flapper adopted the compact as a fashion accessory and prop in a public performance. Making up in restaurants, on commuter trains, and in movie houses drew attention to the fabrication of appearance. In the workplace as well, women powdered their noses through the day, halting the company's work to indulge momentarily their desire for beauty and, doubtless, to take a break. As they put on a feminine face, these women briefly claimed a public space, stopping the action, in a sense, by making a spectacle of themselves. Making up spotlighted the self in a gesture at once forceful and feminine, as a tale told of aviator Ruth Elder suggests. Crossing the Atlantic, Elder was plagued with trouble in flight and required rescue; when she stepped off the plane, her first act was to powder her nose.[44]

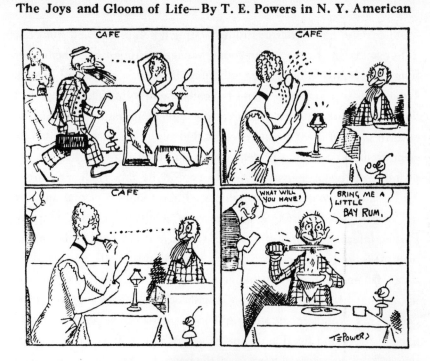

A cartoonist's commentary on "face-fixing" in public. Toilet Requisites, *1917.*

Aviator Phoebe Omlie powders her nose after winning a national transcontinental air derby in 1931.

"Glamour" and "charm" did not so much define different women as different styles. Respectable young women distinguished themselves from "tough girls" through the subtle application of rouge and lipstick. Tangee was especially popular—typically the first lipstick girls were allowed to use—because it appeared to complement natural lip color, not cover it up. But daytime and evening makeup styles also permitted the same women to create different versions of themselves: a ladylike appearance on the job, a more provocative one at the dance hall or cabaret.[45]

For young women, makeup declared adult status—social and sexual maturity—often before parents were ready to grant it. Margaret Parton, later an editor at the *Ladies' Home Journal,* battled her mother over makeup, permanent waves, and heels in the 1930s, and one summer, "driven by an urge to change my school girl image," she "dressed up as what I thought a prostitute might look like, complete with charcoal on my eyelids, a spit curl, and a cigarette."[46] The sudden appearance of rouge and lipstick on a teenage girl's face often accompanied a demand to keep more of her wages, to choose her boyfriends, and to enjoy greater autonomy in leisure activities.

Many daughters of immigrant parents put on makeup to look "American," expressing their new sense of national identity and personal freedom by consuming beauty preparations. In the novel *Bread Givers,* Anzia Yezierska carefully depicts a young Jewish immigrant woman's desires and confusion over appearance. Her protagonist, Sara Smolinsky, works long hours in a laundry, goes to night school, and looks, to her eyes, prematurely old and ugly. Crying "I want to be looked at, longed for, followed," Sara buys lipstick, powder, and rouge to "let loose the love of colour in me." Looking in the mirror at her red lips and cheeks, she proclaims, "Now I was exactly like the others!" But unsettled by her workmates' derision and her own doubts, Sara quickly rejects her painted "American" face as untrue to herself.[47]

Some parents erupted at what they considered an emblem of sexual waywardness, if not outright prostitution. In one 1937 study of high school girls, over half reported family fights over lipstick. Makeup use especially vexed immigrant parents, who considered makeup one more sign of the breakdown of familial control and moral standards. A daughter of Hungarian Catholic parents complained bitterly about her tradition-bound parents, who refused to let her go dancing, date men unchaperoned, or wear makeup. "All this is vanity and God doesn't like it," she quoted them as saying. "God wants every girl to be just like he made her." Some of these conflicts ended up in juvenile court: One Los Angeles judge barred an "incorrigible" eighteen-year-old girl "from any use of make-up, such as rouge and pencil, which she has been using against the mother's desire for some time past." For Mexican-American parents, the popularity of Hollywood film stars and barrio beauty pageants made opposition to makeup a losing battle by the late 1930s.[48]

But beautifying did not always create generational conflict: If the younger generation pioneered in cosmetics use, some mothers tried to keep up. Mother-and-daughter skin-care regimens were common in the Topeka households. Mrs. W. Pattison "never gave much time to caring for [her skin] until her daughter started to take an interest in such matters." The daughter, who attended high school, was a manufacturer's dream consumer, regularly using Pompeian night and day creams and rouge. Her mother was less habitual, putting on the day cream when leaving the house and applying rouge occasionally. This mother believed that maintaining an attractive appearance was a maternal duty, one which gave pleasure to her children and modeled proper behavior. During a period when the gap between the generations appeared to be widening, a number of mothers reached across the chasm by appearing more up-to-date, in the belief that their influence would be strengthened through modern looks. Mrs. Sidney Smith observed that "she is trying to use cosmetics wisely so Harriet and Mary Louise will do the same when they are grown."[49]

A few mothers seem to have gone beyond their daughters in embracing the modern style of "flaming youth," despite traditional proscriptions. Massachusetts caseworkers reported a woman right out of *True Story*, who went to the big city, painted her face, and abandoned her children. Latino immigrants bemoaned the influence of American culture on their wives. "Even my old woman has changed on me," went a popular ballad. "She wears a bobtailed dress of silk, goes about painted like a piñata, and goes at night to the dancing hall."[50]

For many women, makeup was a way of expressing class identity. Posing as clerks behind the counter, J. Walter Thompson investigators in the early 1920s often remarked on class and ethnic variations in cosmetics purchases. Jewish wage earners, Park Avenue socialites, and Brooklyn housewives all had particular looks and brand preferences, often recognized and reinforced by salesclerks. Saleswomen quickly sized up their patrons and judged what they could afford. A clerk selling Arden, Elcaya, and Pond's creams at Lord and Taylor said that "she could tell by the appearance of the customer which cream to offer." But the crafting of consumer identities was not reducible to price. Scent, color palettes, and packaging carried elusive but legible signs of status. The wealthiest patrons looked for, and were shown, high-priced or imported brands with light scent and natural tints. "Jewish flappers," in contrast, typically bought white powder in compacts and deep red or orange lipstick made by Angelus. "All Jewish girls use" it, a Walgreen's clerk in downtown Chicago explained: "She never asks what brand they want but gets the Angelus drawer out when she sees them coming." Bright red lipstick and glossy nail enamel, new products in the early 1920s, won acceptance slowly among "refined" middle-class women. As one Thompson staffer a decade later recalled, "I thought it was extremely vulgar to go around with 'varnish' on the nails."[51]

Viewed as a form of aesthetic expression embedded in life stories, applied in many different ways, makeup asserted no single or uniform meaning. Women used makeup with many different, contradictory ends in mind: to play the lady or the hussy, to look older or younger, to signify common identities as "American" and "respectable," or to invoke class and ethnic distinctions. Supple and negotiable, makeup could always be washed off and applied anew.

Ideals of beauty were shaped not only by the messages of the cosmetics industry and the everyday scrutiny of husbands and children, neighbors and friends. As Helena Rubinstein observed, there were many audiences to please and impress. From state fairs to beauty contests, dance pavilions to street corners, women's appearances drew eyes that looked and judged.[52]

Beauty contests had evolved from modest May Day celebrations to the spectacle of the Miss America pageant in 1921, where physical proportions, facial beauty, and appealing personality delineated the feminine ideal. By 1930 beauty contests were even held in high schools, as one Fresno superintendent explained, to make students more interested in personal care; a physical education teacher rated girls' skin, hair, muscle tone, and general appearance, among other criteria. At the Iowa state fair, judges measured young women against a yardstick of health and rural virtue. The winner in 1926, reported the *Des Moines Register,* "uses no powder or rouge, cares nothing for boys and dates, does not dance, and rarely goes to the movies."[53] Very different standards applied elsewhere.

The movies—with their highly made-up stars, glamorous lighting, and close-ups—particularly influenced the way American women and men looked at women. Female fans took pleasure in actresses who were "always first with the latest" and copied their appearance and gestures. In a massive study on movies and conduct, led by sociologist Herbert Blumer in the late 1920s and early 1930s, three-fourths of the "delinquent girls" said they heightened their sex appeal by imitating movie stars' clothes, hair, and cosmetics. Said one, "I learned how to put on make-up and how to do different ways of make-up and how to make my make-up and clothes go together." Going to the movies, they gained a sense of themselves not as "bad girls" but as romantic, glamorous heroines. Fan magazines, addressing young urban working women, reinforced the appeal of emulating the stars. As reformer Hazel Ormsbee accurately observed, these magazines understood that their readers "possess little or no capital or savings and . . . their assets are personal qualities."[54]

At the same time, "movie autobiographies" written for the Blumer study suggest that women's relationship to the screen was less direct imitation than a negotiation between one's sense of self and the ideal female images. While one fan enjoyed "reveling in pictures where beautiful clothes are displayed," another got "an inkling of what I could do with that sense of adventure of mine" from watching serial heroines. Women tried out Greta Garbo's hair style or Clara Bow's perky looks, but clearly recognized the gap between their appearance and the stars'. One woman admired actress Vilma Banky: "I sure wish I could look like her! I've tried, but it's impossible." Another, after seeing Lillian Gish in *Way Down East* at age twelve, even resolved "to refrain from using any cosmetics so as to appear as frail and ethereal as she."[55]

Men also learned new ways to look at and assess women from the movies. A male college student explained that he chose his "girl friends on the basis of [his] favorite actresses." Italian street-corner youth revealed that movie beauty—the immoral platinum blonde and the chaste brunette—influenced their perceptions of women off the screen. These ways of seeing in turn influenced women's decisions about fashioning their appearance. As one college woman wrote, the movies had intensified her awareness that "men place a high premium on the physical aspect of woman."[56]

If women learned to see their faces in the "looks" of movie stars and in the stares of male companions, they also found that appropriate appearance was an unspoken requirement on the job. "Here in America," said Helena Rubinstein, "women's employers, or their customers, are often the audience they want to please." Such requirements were not new, of course. Restaurant owners had often sought attractive waitresses as a lure for male customers. "In one place the pretty girls were put downstairs, where the men were served," stated reformer Louise de Koven Bowen, "and the homely girls were put upstairs, in the room reserved for women customers." With the mix of immigrant and second-generation women seeking jobs, the requirements often took on an ethnic tinge. Clerical workers and saleswomen with Anglo-Saxon features and genteel manners were favored, while women of Southern European ancestry complained that "their dark skin was against them" in gaining employment.[57]

Such appearance requirements at work became increasingly regimented in the 1920s and 1930s. The expansion of personnel management and vocational guidance codified judgments about the proper fit between face and job. Employment tests appraised bodily appearance; one prototype included spaces for recording an applicant's use of makeup and hair dye, "the peroxide blonde being always looked upon with suspicion." In an article ostensibly about job skills and placement, a New York State Employment Service staffer blamed stenographers' unemployment on their personal appearance: The jobless included a woman with a "broken-out and pimpled complexion" and an applicant wearing "a blood-red hue of nail polish, a frilly dress and high heels." Guidance counselors at Smith College routinely noted graduating students' "attractiveness" in their records.[58]

Cosmetics played an essential part in the new business look. Executives wanted to hire "a girl who looks normal," which included tasteful cosmetics on the job, but not glamour. "No eye shadow, no mascara, no mauve powders or orange rouge for the business girl in office hours!" warned one advice manual.[59] Some companies integrated beauty protocols into training and job performance. Telephone operators, although unseen by the public, faced many requirements for on-the-job appearance and demeanor; A.T.&T.'s newsletter *Long Lines* stressed personal grooming, modern clothes, and attractiveness. Although its founder wrote in 1917 that "a natural smile beats all the artificial decoration in the world," two decades later Statler Hotels directed waitresses to appear at their stations wearing "light makeup." The H. J. Heinz Company even instituted weekly manicures for its pickle packers. Initially a sanitary measure, the program proved so popular it expanded to instruct workers on proper makeup.[60]

For young women about to enter the workforce, commercial colleges and YWCAs began to offer "self-development" courses with instructions on skin care, makeup, manicuring, and hair styling. By the early 1920s, YWCA clubs for young wage earners no longer required that members "refrain from using rouge and face beautifiers" and cautiously endorsed "wholesome" makeup and noon-hour beauty demonstrations. These programs were considered especially important for daughters of immigrant parents, who, it was presumed, had little exposure to proper "American" standards of grooming. At the same time, instructors hoped that lessons in beautifying would improve morale and productivity on the job.[61]

Working women well understood the hidden rules of appearance. Many made up fully when they went to work in the morning, and they touched up often. Florence Miller, an ambitious stenographer "much interested in appearing her best," applied rouge and powder four times a day, "before going to work in the morning, when going to lunch at noon, before leaving the office at night and after dinner in the evening." Some waitresses might wear a made-up, glamorous look to increase their tips, but many big-city clerical and sales employees put on subdued face colors, taking such care in making up and dressing well that they would not be readily identified as working girls. One Russian immigrant stated clearly the economic consequences of ignoring appearance requirements, even as she acknowledged the psychic cost of following them. She had failed repeatedly to find a job, because employers took one look at her leather jacket, a treasured "symbol both of Revolution and elegance," and rejected her as a troublesome Bolshevik. After a year without work, "I dressed myself in the latest fashion, with lipstick in addition, although it was so hard to use at first that I blushed, felt foolish, and thought myself vulgar," she wrote. "But I got a job."[62]

Educational institutions increasingly saw themselves as caretakers of female appearance. Most schools in the 1920s tried to deter teens from wearing makeup or applying it in public, and some banned it outright. Home economics courses, taken by one-third of all girls in public high schools by 1928, preached cleanliness, body care, and good taste. It was not long, however, before beauty and cosmetics became an academic subject.[63]

Women's magazines, manufacturers, and retailers worked with home economics instructors to teach grooming and quietly insinuate their names into budding consumer awareness. The *Ladies' Home Journal* and *Woman's Home Companion* produced how-to booklets, *McCall's* developed a "Charm Group Program," and Helena Rubinstein sent representatives to speak in schools. Several toiletries manufacturers had long distributed instructional materials on hygienic body care, including toothbrushing and manicure. By 1940, an explicit beauty appeal had become acceptable enough in schools that cosmetics firms like Revlon promoted this noncommercial tie-in. Consumer activism also appeared in classrooms. Students read exposés of the beauty industry or worked on scientific investigations. Excessive cosmetics use tended to be discouraged and sometimes disciplined. "We had a nail polish removal in assembly this morning," wrote high school senior Helene Harmon Weis in her 1939 diary. "Miss Braley always enjoys them so."[64]

Soon beauty education was everywhere. Home extension services gave rural wives lessons on making an attractive appearance; 4-H clubs provided girls with "self-checking" charts and ran fashion shows; the Alma Archer House of Smartness and International Charm Insti-

A lesson in grooming at Cornell University.

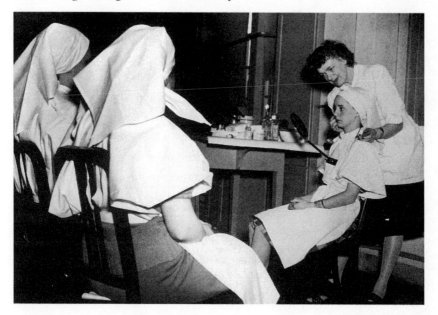

tute taught New York women how to succeed in business through better grooming. In colleges and universities, deans of women gave first-year students grooming instructions. At Cornell, where incoming coeds often appeared on campus wearing too much makeup ("lipstick an inch thick—you couldn't miss it," complained a sorority sister) or too little, home economics courses offered units on facial care. In 1936, one junior college even hired a clothing stylist and cosmetician to start a beauty consultation service for its students.[65]

Vocational experts, home economists, and psychologists all agreed that good looks had developmental and aesthetic as well as commercial value. In the mid-1930s, social scientists reported that personal appearance significantly influenced young women's self-expression and self-esteem, findings publicized in magazines for parents. The Depression itself weighed less heavily on those who took beauty lessons, the experts claimed, because such lessons might offer an edge in the job market and, in any case, would lift the spirits of young women "who are finding themselves in a world which seems to have little or nothing for them."[66] Educators and professionals responsible for socializing girls, and often contemptuous of the beauty industry, had come to accept one of its basic premises.

In 1930, the beauty editor of *Smart Set* observed that the cosmetics consumer is "out after something and is disillusioned on empty promises." Her comment heralded a shift in attitudes toward beauty products. Criticisms of commercial cosmetics as overpriced, injurious, and fraudulent spread widely. These had been heard before, but now they circulated in a very different context, in which making up was rapidly becoming the feminine norm. If not depression-proof, cosmetics sales remained strong. Women who went without new clothes could still afford to indulge in a new lipstick. Most families spent only small amounts on personal care items, about 2 percent of their household income, but this added up to a total outlay of $750 million nationally on cosmetics and beauty shops in 1931.[67]

"American Chamber of Horrors" poster.

Consumer advocacy groups, physicians, and New Dealers began to lobby diligently for government regulation of the beauty industry in the aftermath of several well-publicized incidents of cosmetic poisoning and injury. In 1930, the American Medical Association reported that the depilatory Koremlu contained rat poison; three years later, Lash-Lure, an eyelash beautifier containing aniline dye, blinded and disfigured a young society woman from Dayton, Ohio. The "American Chamber of Horrors," an exhibit sponsored by the Food and Drug Administration and then turned into a book by Ruth Lamb, increased public awareness. The before-and-after makeover, normally a device to sell beauty preparations, here was used to unmask their dangers. Efforts to ban dangerous ingredients, register the content of products, and license beauticians succeeded in some states. Women's groups, organized under the umbrella Joint Women's Congressional Committee and supported by Eleanor Roosevelt, pushed for passage of a federal law, enacted as the Food, Drug, and Cosmetic Act of 1938. The Act was intended to make cosmetics safe for consumption by bringing them under the regulatory arm of the government.[68]

Significantly, activists in the consumer movement, except for the most radical, did not reject beautifying wholesale. Rather they distinguished between "honest cosmetics" and "criminal cosmetics," called for rational consumption, and promoted the state's interest in protecting its female citizens from harm. M. C. Phillips's *Skin Deep*, a 1934 exposé of the beauty industry that did much to whip up the demand for cosmetics regulation, reflected the temper of the times. Phillips denounced the "cosmetics racket" for selling illusions, and she claimed women's right, as voters and taxpayers, to safe, honest cosmetics. Women's clubs, YWCAs, labor unions, high schools, friends, and coworkers debated Phillips's revelations of cosmetic hazards and shams. "The girls in our office have been reading your book, 'Skin Deep,' with great interest," wrote Mabel Moats. After its publication, about 150 readers wrote to Phillips about beauty products and the cosmetics industry. Their letters still offer an occasion to ponder how hopes, anxieties, and prosaic pleasures converged upon jars of cream and boxes of powder.[69]

Some readers frankly questioned Phillips's credentials. Because Phillips had written under her initials instead of her given name, a few thought the author was in fact a man who had neither the understanding nor the authority to criticize cosmetics. Nelle Mordoff questioned the motives of Consumers' Research, the organization that had sponsored Phillips's work, and "wonder[ed] how any woman could have made" the critical conclusions of *Skin Deep*. "She could not have if she had ever had her face improved as I have had," she stated. "Is this Club composed entirely of men?"[70]

Many readers, however, took a different tack in letters of almost formulaic similarity. They thanked Phillips for guiding them down the righteous, and cheaper, path to beauty. They told of women's victimization by the cosmetics industry: They had been "suckers," spending un-

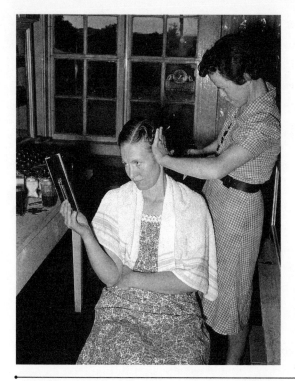

Migrant women in New Mexico fixing each other's hair in the absence of a beauty parlor.

necessarily large sums on worthless products. In the 1930s, women had many options for purchasing cosmetics, including inexpensive door-to-door products and ten-cent brands sold in variety stores. High-priced cosmetics sold in exclusive salons and department stores nevertheless enticed a number of middle- and working-class women. One *Skin Deep* reader observed that "women are actually frightened into buying" expensive preparations, then listed all the Charles of the Ritz products *she* had purchased: "I need not tell you that this adds up to more than a week's salary."[71]

They confessed their own self-delusions and gullibility. Phillips had confirmed "what I already knew down in my heart," Alice Breitenbach sadly wrote, "I've been deluding myself that certain cosmetics I have been using suited me." Some proudly repudiated their past in favor of consumer rationality. "Our family has thrown out jars of cosmetics and are buying the few which you recommend," wrote Mrs. Earl Kerwell.[72]

Then as if hearing a siren's call, women turned back to the beguiling world of beautifying, pouring out their hearts to Phillips, closely questioning her advice, revealing long lists of products they used. Although reading *Skin Deep* had caused them to "lose all confidence in cosmetics," women repeatedly asked Phillips for the name of a safe rouge, the formula for an expensive cream, an assessment of their beauty routines. Whatever the hyberbole of the cosmetics industry, admitted one woman, "there is no doubt that a wave and a little makeup helps a lot."[73]

Agnes Hoffman, a college graduate and teacher, was typical. Writing in the confessional style so common to women's discussions of cosmetics, she called herself "a nervous, high strung person, as are many school teachers." "I don't always keep regular hours and sometimes can't," she wrote. "I feel in general a mess." She used the expensive Arden line and had "spent money out of all proportion to my salary." "I don't really so much believe what saleswomen tell me as I hope that what they tell me will come true," she said ruefully, but *Skin Deep* had "quite shattered my illusions" about cosmetics. Still, in a lengthy postscript, she wrote question after question about complexion care.[74]

By the 1930s, makeup had become an aesthetic expression woven deeply into women's daily life, a life increasingly entwined with commodities, advertising, and mass media that promoted, in Charles Revson's famous phrase, "hope in a jar." Uttered with different inflections in the 1930s, those words could cynically capture the deepest disappointments of a consumer culture, or give voice to the utopian promise that cosmetic alchemy might transform deficiency into triumph.[75] But advertising was not the only—or the decisive—influence on women's cosmetics use. Its message was reinforced and refined in the workplace and in school, at home and at leisure, as women experienced growing pressure to adjust their looks to new norms of feminine appearance.

If women increasingly internalized a "regime" of scrutiny, assessment, and instruction, they did not simply copy the images they saw

In these banquet photographs, sorority sisters put on a glamorous, made-up look, while the Daughters of the American Revolution wear plain faces and suffer the camera. (Detail, Beta Chi Sorority, 17th Annual Banquet, 1935, and DAR Convention, April 1931, photographer Schutz. Courtesy George Eastman House.)

but adapted them to the requirements of their own lives. Some had begun to recognize that the discipline of appearances heightened their anxieties and undermined their self-confidence. Others discerned in beautifying new possibilities for play, self-portrayal, and participation in modernity. They took sensory delight in makeup, enjoyed the sociability it engendered, and lucidly perceived what appearances the labor market and social life demanded of them. Even when they proclaimed themselves dupes and victims of consumer culture, women did not renounce makeup, for it had become a common language of self-expression and self-understanding.

Shades of

Difference

The term "mass market" implies both a standardized product and a standardized consumer, but in fact it conceals important differences along racial lines, not only in Americans' buying habits, but in their responses to the culture of consumption. For African Americans, commercialized beauty was not only an aesthetic, psychological, and social matter, but, from the outset, explicitly a problem of politics. Cosmetics were never far removed from the fact of white supremacy, the goal of racial progress, the question of emulation. Unlike mass-circulation magazines aimed at white audiences, African-American periodicals often debated the political meaning of cosmetics. Black critics excoriated an exploitative cosmetics industry, gullible consumers, and a white-dominated society that imposed its beauty standards on all. "Good Looks Supremacy," Chandler Owen, editor of the *Messenger*, called it: If people of color ruled the world, white people would curl their hair and darken their skin.[1]

Advertisers, manufacturers, and advice writers—all part of a nascent black consumer culture—defended the beauty trade with their own claims. Casual readers of the 1928 *Oklahoma Eagle*, for instance,

beheld a two-page advertisement in the rotogravure section, its headline announcing: "Amazing Progress of Colored Race—Improved Appearance Responsible." Amid images of businesses and banks,
prosperous farms and churches, the Madam C. J. Walker Company offered an assessment of African-American history since Emancipation.
"In 64 short years our people have cast aside the shackles of slavery—
have risen to the heights of social and commercial supremacy," the ad
noted. To what did black Americans owe "such epochal progress"?
"PRIDE OF RACE, APPLIED INDUSTRY and BETTERED APPEARANCE."
"Add Beauty to Brains for Success" was the simple recipe for living in
a modern world where first impressions counted as much as wealth.
"Radiate an air of prosperity and who is to know if your purse is lined
with gold or not?" the ad maintained. "Look your best . . . you owe it to
your race."[2] With a few potent images, the Madam C. J. Walker Company advanced a sweeping historical, psychological, and political interpretation of the role of beauty in everyday affairs. Caught up in its
story of uplift and hope, a reader might be forgiven if she overlooked
that this was, after all, a sales pitch for hair grower, bleach cream, and
face powder.

A public dialogue about the meaning of cosmetic preparations and
beautifying practices accompanied the entry of black women into consumer culture. While many fashioned their appearances by following
in some measure the aesthetic of European beauty, they frequently understood their beauty rituals in ways that modified, undercut, and even
challenged the charges of white emulation. Powder boxes and porce-
lain jars became the battleground in a contest of cultural visions, political concerns, and individual desires.

Even before the emergence of a mass beauty trade, black reformers, educators, intellectuals, and journalists had begun to speak out about the political meaning of appearances. In the late nineteenth century, as Jim
Crow tightened its grip on black Southerners, the color line was drawn
more starkly: Caricatures of unruly hair, oily skin, and apelike features

circulated throughout American culture. New cosmetic preparations promised relief from such stereotypes. By claiming to turn African Americans white or many shades lighter, a number of manufacturers—white and black—in fact reinforced racial bigotry. Others, however, especially the pathbreaking women beauty culturists, stressed racial pride and dignity in their appeals; Madam C. J. Walker and Annie Turnbo Malone refused to sell skin bleach and emphasized hair care, not straightening, in their beauty systems. Among African Americans, the body itself—physi-

The New Negro Woman, in Voice of the Negro, *1904.*

cal features, cleanliness, and demeanor—had become a subject in the debate over collective identity and action. As lecturer and author Azalia Hackley put it, "The time has come to fight, not only for rights, but for looks as well."[3]

Black writers rejected the physiognomic equation between looks and character as long as white Americans were setting the aesthetic standards. Morality had no color, they argued, and racial definitions based on the "one drop" rule of African "blood" consigned African Americans to a life of degradation. At the same time, the black elite pictured a "New Negro" to counter the plantation and minstrel stereotypes, envisioning a figure of modernity who embodied changed historical circumstances and future prospects. In a 1904 issue of the magazine *Voice of the Negro,* John H. Adams, Jr., sketched the New Negro Woman, her physical beauty and purity claiming the moral ground long held by the white lady. She possessed "the sober consciousness of true womanhood the same as her white or red or olive sisters." Nevertheless, Adams could not imagine her appearance apart from the pose, expression, and features of white Victorian womanhood, the governing image of refinement and culture.[4]

The contradictory rejection and embrace of Euro-American aesthetic standards surfaced repeatedly as black writers, reformers, and educators responded to the new beauty culture that spread throughout black communities in the early twentieth century. Azalia Hackley declared that "kinky hair is an honorable legacy from Africa," yet hoped African features would evolve into more desirable European ones through good grooming: "Constant care of the hair will cause an improved condition of the texture which will in time be inherited." Similarly a *Voice of the Negro* editorial suggested that civilizing culture and education had "smoothed down" the "rough, savage features that our African ancestors had."[5]

Like the beauty culturists, African-American etiquette books and beauty manuals situated beautifying within the political mission of black uplift. Improved appearance expressed self-respect, registered collective progress, and would expedite social acceptance. "On the streets and as the street cars pass our homes," observed Hackley, "colored people should give the best pictures possible of themselves." Refined looks particularly defended black women against the slander of promiscuity that had long explained away predatory sexual behavior by both white and black men. Hackley harangued girls at Tuskegee to dress neatly, appear subdued, and not let their faces be a "public bulletin" inviting male attention. This advice, which recognized that black women represented both their race and their gender, became more urgent as their presence in public life increased.[6]

At issue were not only the prejudices of white Americans but a perception by educated black Americans that stereotypes had some basis in lower-class reality. The poor rural woman who came to town each Saturday and learned "her lessons in manners, dress, and morals from what she sees in the streets" needed training in hygiene, grooming, and proper dress. Also under attack was the urban "street" style of young working-class black women, who dressed in yellow and red gowns, and promenaded New York's "African Broadway" with male "dudes" and "run-arounds" in silk hats and figured waistcoats. Advice writer E. M. Wood decried the "hired girl" who painted her cheeks "much after the fashion of the wild Indian." Oiled hair, "primping the face," and "cologning it down" instead of bathing were all marks of the street to be eradicated.[7]

Although black leaders advocated grooming and cleanliness in their crusade for social acceptance, they denounced the "wholesale bleaching of faces and straightening of hair." Emphasizing race pride, educators considered these practices a degrading bid to deny African heritage and to look like white people. Ministers railed against those who practiced and profited from these unnatural and ungodly habits. Like their white counterparts, middle-class reformers distinguished between cosmetic artifice and the cultivation of real beauty. Nannie Burroughs called upon women to spurn cosmetics, arguing that self-improvement lay in education and culture:

> Many women who bleach and straighten out make as their only excuse that it improves the appearance. A true woman wouldn't give a cent for a changed appearance of this sort—a superficial nothing. What every woman who bleaches and straightens out needs, is not her appearance changed, but her mind. She has a false notion as to the value of color and hair in solving the problem of her life. Why does she wish to improve her appearance? Why not improve her real self?

She reminded her readers that women's identification with purity derived not from appearance but "the straightness of life and the whiteness of soul."[8]

These critics spoke directly to a burdensome but repressed issue raised by cosmetics, the existence of color hierarchies among African Americans. "Many Negroes have colorphobia as badly as the white folk have Negrophobia," Burroughs pointedly observed. During slavery, light-skinned African Americans received preferential treatment in work assignments, becoming household servants and sometimes receiving training in skilled trades. Because many were the offspring of plantation owners, they were more likely to be manumitted. After Emancipation, these advantages gave them greater job security, independence, and influence. "Good" hair and light skin affected everything from employment to club and church memberships. By the 1890s, the "mulatto elite" were suspected of trying to become a separate caste or pass into white society.[9]

The status hierarchy based on color figured in the most intimate relationships between men and women. In a particularly acute analysis, women reformers argued that the white aesthetic ideal, by representing only white women's purity and supposed need for protection, implicitly supported the defamation and sexual abuse of black women by white men. This aesthetic also corrupted black men, who judged women on the basis of outward appearance, not inner character, and scorned those with dark complexions. All black men required in women, Anna Julia Cooper charged, were "the three R's, a little music and a good deal of dancing, a first rate dress-maker and a bottle of magnolia balm [i.e. skin whitener]." Nannie Burroughs sarcastically remarked, "The white man who crosses the line and leaves an heir is doing a favor to some black man who would marry the most debased woman, whose only stock in trade is her color, in preference to the most royal queen in ebony."[10]

With the rise of new movements for racial solidarity in the 1910s and 1920s, skin color and hair texture—and the use of cosmetics to alter them—became ever more charged political issues. A newly assertive political leadership pointed to the use of straighteners and bleaches as ipso facto evidence of self-loathing and the desire to appear and be white. Marcus Garvey's United Negro Improvement Association (UNIA) proclaimed not only a new political destiny for the masses of African Americans, but a new aesthetic for dark-skinned people. The militant journal *Crusader* featured dark-skinned girls and beautiful African women, wearing traditional hair arrangements and dress, on its covers and noted the enthusiastic response of readers. The Negro Universal Protective Association even denounced Madam Walker upon her death in 1919 for having promoted white emulation; although Walker had always stressed growing and grooming the hair, her critics charged that her system amounted to straightening.[11]

Condemnations of bleaching and straightening rang out in African-American political journals. George Schuyler, columnist for the *Messenger*, spent much of the 1920s blasting skin bleach, "one of the chief Aframerican industries and customs"; chiding women who swallowed arsenic tablets or calcimined their faces; and denouncing "race conscious Negroes who spend huge sums in skin whiteners." Schuyler's hostility to those who exploited racial awareness—white and black—led him to write a satiric novel *Black No More*, whose title was the trade name of an actual skin bleach. In it, inventors produce a device that turns African Americans white, thus creating a crisis for both "race leaders" and the Ku Klux Klan. Often cosmetics appeared to be weapons in an escalating war of words, as black leaders charged each other with skin-color hypocrisy. Schuyler rebuked the Garveyite *Negro World* for advertising skin lighteners: "Evidently Brother Marcus has hit upon a new plan for solving the race problem." Chandler Owen attacked Garvey's followers as two-faced: "To take this very crowd away from the world would bankrupt Madame Walker, the Poro, Overton, Dr. Palmer's, [and] the Apex . . . in a few weeks."[12]

There was more than enough hypocrisy to go around. Black leaders and journalists were deeply ambivalent about the African-American beauty industry, caught in the irony that an exemplary model of black economic development profited, in their view, by exploiting the desire to be white. Although the *Crusader* and *Negro World* criticized bleaching and straightening, they advertised whitening creams, pressing oils, and similar preparations made by African Americans. Critics of Madam Walker's business were largely silenced in the face of her political activism and financial success. Thus even Schuyler lavished praise on Madam Walker as a "Race Wonder Woman" who had emancipated her sisters from economic and psychological slavery. And when the Walker Company ran a contest to reward a "race leader" with a trip to the Holy Land in 1925, UNIA official Percival Burrows, with Garvey's blessing, sold Tan-Off and other Walker preparations containing ballots, and exhorted consumers to "give me your votes."[13]

Similar contradictions marked such black newspapers as the Chicago *Defender*, the New York *Age*, and the Pittsburgh *Courier*. These weeklies played a critical role in shaping and mobilizing black public opinion. They not only served their own cities but circulated throughout the South, Midwest, and Southwest as "national" newspapers. The Chicago *Defender*, for example, had a circulation estimated to be at least 130,000 in 1919. These publications vaunted the achievements of African Americans, protested discrimination and lynching, and encouraged black Southerners to migrate north. Their "race news," features, and assertive editorials epitomized freedom and modernity for thousands of African Americans.[14] At the same time, advertisements for beauty products and services dominated their pages. The Plough and Walker companies often bought full-page advertisements and the ads of smaller firms dotted newspaper columns. In the 1920s, cosmetics and toiletries, including bleaches and straighteners, accounted for 30 to 40 percent of black newspaper advertising, and in a few cases as much as 50 percent.[15]

The incongruity was not lost upon critics and observers: How could newspapers that propounded black advancement run "anti-kink" and "bleach your skin" advertisements? Two "conflicting forces" warred within black America, one social scientist remarked in 1924, "an attempt to efface racial characteristics" and "an unmistakably powerful force, race pride, which is everywhere evident in Negro life." Noting that the ads particularly "reflected on our women," the *Half-Century*, a black women's magazine, condemned the "Bleaching Imposition" and scolded the press to "take out the kinks."[16]

If the political debate over bleaches and straighteners offered fervid charges and countercharges, black commercial culture complicated the picture. African-American manufacturers, newspapers, tastemakers, and consumers defined hair and skin preparations in ways that limited and resisted the charge of white emulation. They denied the contradiction between racial solidarity and cosmetics in three ways: by positioning cosmetics within a race-conscious economic nationalism, by proclaiming black women's beauty as a sign of racial pride, and by asserting that African Americans had the same "natural" right as all women to be beautiful.

Many commentators and consumers determined the value of beauty preparations by distinguishing between racist white companies and race-conscious black ones. Whatever questions African Americans may have had about goods produced by their own, public controversy erupted specifically over the activities of white-owned companies. The *Crusader*, among others, called for boycotts. Viewed as unscrupulous exploiters of black consumers, white-owned companies stood accused of selling fake or hazardous preparations that ruined the skin and even led to death. The *Half-Century* charged that white manufacturers would never produce good products for African Americans because they wanted to preserve the racial order. "Too many of our people have the same features," the magazine noted. "Whiten the skin a little, and the white people would not know white from Colored—the result of such a condition is plain." Concerning a chemical hair treatment, one female pharmacist asked, "now if they don't use it themselves, why put it on other people's heads with rubber gloves?" Some black manufacturers encouraged views that displaced general anxieties about cosmetics onto white manufacturers. Anthony Overton pointedly observed, "We do not ask you to let us experiment on you."[17]

Letters to the *Half-Century* from 1919 to 1921 denounced white-owned cosmetics firms. Liane de Witt of Augusta, Georgia, told of a friend who used a skin bleach and whose "skin became sore and peeled off in great patches and where it is dark, it is darker than ever." She concluded, "I don't believe a Colored concern would be so dirty as to deliberately place on the market a preparation to ruin the beauty of their women." Mary Vaughan described a visit to a white-owned factory in Paris, Tennessee, and criticized the company's disfiguring bleaching powder. An Oklahoma reader wrote about the illness and death of a woman with a "clear, red-brown" complexion who had used a cosmetic made by a white manufacturer.[18]

It is difficult to assess the accuracy of these charges. They appeared, after all, in a magazine subsidized by Anthony Overton, who had a direct interest in discrediting his competition. But although undoubtedly selected for their critical content, these letters do seem authentic expressions of concern, and some of their allegations may well have been true. Skin bleaches received particularly close scrutiny from the American Medical Association in the 1920s and the Food and Drug Administration in the 1930s. Nadinola bleach cream, it turned out, contained 10 percent ammoniated mercury, a concentration high enough to cause serious skin irritation and damage. The National Toilet Company had received complaints about it from consumers through the 1920s and 1930s but did not deviate from the original formula, taken from a textbook, until 1937. Under pressure, the company decreased the ammoniated mercury to 6 percent and finally reduced it to 1.5 percent in 1941. According to the company's vice president, the lower concentration made no difference in the product's efficacy, but diminished consumers' complaints. In contrast, extant formulas and product labels indicate that at least some black-owned firms produced relatively mild forms of skin bleach: the Kashmir Chemical Company's formula included small amounts of borax, while one of Overton-Hygienic's bleaches used hydrogen peroxide.[19]

Some critics related the cavalier treatment of black consumers to discrimination in the workplace. In a letter to the *Half-Century* about Plough, reader Amos Turner complained that "we are so thoughtless, careless and ignorant that we are piling up $60,000 a year for a white company that will not give you a dime's worth of employment." Liane de Witt charged that white-owned businesses did not employ black workers because "they don't want them to see what awful things they mix up in these toilet preparations that they put out for the exclusive use of Colored people." Whether or not this was the case, black workers were rarely hired except in menial positions, as Claude Barnett, journalist and owner of Kashmir, confirmed after a visit to Plough's headquarters. "In their offices alone they have, I should say, ten times as many employees as Poro has," he wrote Annie Turnbo Malone. "Not a black face was to be seen."[20]

The promotion of beauty preparations also came under sharp attack. Black public opinion condemned cosmetics advertisements that used before-and-after pictures and degrading language, and white-owned companies were deemed the worst offenders. Plough, for instance, shamelessly invoked racist imagery and the memory of slavery in its early advertising: "Bleach Your Dark Skin; Race Men and Women Protect Your Future. Be attractive! Throw off the chains that have held you back from the prosperity and happiness that belong to you." Too many ads "smack of ante-bellumism, disrespect, and a low grade of intelligence," the *Half-Century* complained. And the *Chicago Whip* warned its readers not to trust advertisements for dangerous preparations made by white men, concluding: "Be beautiful if you can, but don't burn your brains out in the attempt."[21]

As if in direct response to the devaluation of African-American appearance, the assertion that black women *were* beautiful became an important declaration of cultural legitimacy. The African-American press had long reported on women's work in clubs, churches, and other organizations, documenting their wide influence in community affairs. In the 1910s and 1920s, women represented the race in an added way, through a well-groomed and attractive appearance. Racial pride often took the guise of a beautiful woman on display.

Photographs of beautiful female performers, celebrities, and fashion models—generally with light skin and European features—ran in black newspapers and magazines as icons of race pride. The Pittsburgh *Courier* in the 1920s typically placed a photograph of an African-American beauty in the upper-left corner of the front page, a prominent location bespeaking the image's importance. "Must the Flapper Go?" one caption read, "We hope not." The radical *Messenger,* which defined the New Negro as a man demanding political and economic equality, now recognized the "arrival" of the New Negro Woman with appealing portraits of "beautiful, intelligent, successful" women.[22]

African-American beauty contestants from Howard and Lincoln Universities.

This New Negro Woman did not spurn manufactured beauty, as Nannie Burroughs had hoped. Fashion news and beauty tips had begun to appear in African-American periodicals as early as 1890. The *Colored American Magazine,* devoted "to the higher culture," brought the fashion column of a Madame Rumford to middle-class readers. Cleveland journalist Julia Ringwood Costen began publishing the pioneering but short-lived *Afro-American Journal of Fashion* in 1891; several other magazines succeeded it, modeled on the home journals read by white women. By 1920 most black newspapers featured women's pages with beauty columns, fashion plates, and free publicity for cosmetics firms. Even publications with a radical political agenda, such as the *Crusader* and Marcus Garvey's *Negro World,* followed the trend.[23]

Beauty contests sponsored by newspapers, magazines, and cosmetic companies proved especially popular. "The most beautiful women in the world are those of the Negro race!" exclaimed the New

York *Age,* and its 1914 beauty contest, held in conjunction with an amusement and advertising exposition, occupied the front page for weeks. African-American women's beauty was even celebrated by the white-owned Golden Brown Company. In the same year that Walker ran a contest for the greatest "race leader," Golden Brown invited customers to vote for the most beautiful woman with coupons inserted into cosmetics packages. Madam Hightower, the company's fictive spokeswoman, credited beauty contests with "the awakening of our racial pride, through the publicity given the beauties of our race in America." Answering the whites-only Miss America pageant, a national Miss Bronze America beauty contest was held for the first time in 1927. Typically finalists had a light complexion and smoothly styled hair, but sometimes the contests sparked debate over the winning image. When the New York *Age* headlined its desire to establish a "Basic Standard for Racial Beauty," one correspondent suggested rather that it should include the full range of skin colors and features.[24]

Cosmetics firms did much to promote the centrality of beauty in black women's racial identity. As manufacturers turned increasingly toward media-based marketing, how to represent African-American beauty in advertising became a key question. In the early days of the industry, Anthony Overton's goods pictured respectable, well-groomed girls and refined, light-skinned women. Criticizing white manufacturers who considered cheap designs "good enough for Negroes," Overton remarked: "From the beginning we have been pioneers in putting out high-grade packages with creditable Colored faces which would be a pride to the race."[25]

The early advertisements of Madam Walker and Annie Turnbo Malone took a different tack, emphasizing the efficacy of their preparations, the creation of job opportunities, and the vast size and scope of their enterprises. Madam Walker's ads in 1912 contained a plain promise to cure hair loss and eczema. Although by 1918 the ads had a more stylish design, they continued to focus on the products themselves, with copy explaining the benefits of the Walker system and warning of adulterated preparations. Some advertisements indicated

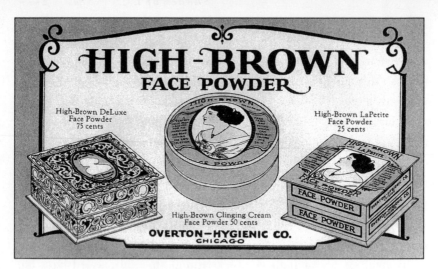

Overton-Hygienic powder sample envelope.

Walker advertisement, from the Crisis, *1919.*

Walker's popularity with maps of the hemisphere or images of arms stretched up to the rising sun. "We Belt the World," announced one headline tinged with nationalist pride. Photographs of Malone and Walker appeared on their package labels and ads for hair grower and pressing oil. These images personified the entrepreneurs' claims and reinforced their accountability to customers.[26]

Claude Barnett's promotion of Kashmir played a signal role in changing African-American beauty advertising. Acknowledging the beauty culturists' considerable business success, Barnett nevertheless criticized their ads as throwbacks to the old-fashioned patent remedy style. "These ads had always repulsed me," he later maintained. The larger transformation of national advertising in the 1910s and 1920s— the rise of advertising agencies, modernist graphic design, and psychological appeals—reverberated within black commercial media. The expansion of a black consumer culture in Northern cities led Barnett to mimic mass marketers' appeals to modernity, beauty, and heterosexual romance.[27]

Barnett devised a savvy advertising campaign that replaced the patent remedy style with the visual innovations and sophisticated copy of the nation's large advertising firms. He recruited attractive black actresses and singers as models, used "perfumed language," and commissioned "original paintings of beautifully turned-out Negro women and elegant males in exquisitely proper surroundings." Addressing a more urbane, well-heeled consumer than did Walker and Malone, Barnett's Nile Queen advertisements opened up a dream world of fur-clad women, automobiles, and other icons of luxury. The resulting ads were so striking, Barnett claimed, that Malone and Walker "expressed great interest in this new concept of advertising beauty products for the Negro market and soon the entire field had switched to the positive approach pioneered by Kashmir."[28]

Indeed, after Walker's death, her company's advertising strategy changed dramatically. Early Walker ads had done little to elaborate consumer fantasies; in one, "social enemies" and "proven friends" were respectively hair diseases and Walker treatments. But by the

*Walker advertisement, from
the* Messenger, *1924.*

Opposite: *Cover of the
Kashmir Chemical
Company's* Nile Queen
pamphlet, 1919.

mid-twenties, the company actively promoted idealized beauty with
images of charming and alluring women. "Beauty's Synonym," an ad
that appeared in the *Messenger,* featured the hallmark of a modern
appeal: The products disappeared entirely, replaced by an illustration
of a stylish young woman gazing into her mirror as consumers gazed at
her. Such images were interchangeable with those of white women's
beauty promoted in mass-circulation magazines, except that black
women often wore long hair—known as the Indian mane—rather than
the white flapper's bob. Advertising copy sometimes praised the
diversity of African-American looks. "Only by the most careful makeup can the Caucasian equal the creamy yellow, the matchless browns,
and the satiny, glossy dark skin of the Colored Woman," stated a Nile
Queen brochure. However, illustrations invariably portrayed women
with straight or wavy hair, light brown skin, and features more
European than African. Despite the growing consciousness of Africa

fostered by Garveyites in these years, advertisers found it difficult to create visual forms that acknowledged the African heritage of black Americans.[29]

Claude Barnett's provocative advertising for Nile Queen is telling. Using Egyptian images and hieroglyphic symbols, Barnett yoked the larger cultural meaning of Cleopatra—an ancient emblem of women's beauty and fascination—to the ongoing debate within black intellectual circles over the African origins of Western civilization. If Cleopatra was African, then African-American women inherited her legacy of beauty. As a *New York Age* editorial in 1934 put it, "Cecil B. DeMille may depict 'Cleopatra' how he pleases but we know and history tells us that she was a Negro woman, and the prettiest of them all." Yet the Nile Queen was not African: Indeed, she seems more the houri of a Persian harem—as DeMille would have depicted her. The name "Kashmir" added to the odd, rich mixture by evoking the luxuries of India. Barnett used "Africa" as white manufacturers celebrated Mediterranean and even Asian beauty cultures—as exotic and universalizing counterpoints. This orientalism effaced any specific African representation, yet affirmed Africa's inclusion—and that of "women of color" generally—in the geography of female beauty.[30]

Kashmir's beauty pamphlet juxtaposed a hand-drawn fantasy of sensuous female pleasure with a photograph of a well-groomed, brown-skinned American girl. The photograph's "reality" returned black consumers to the paramount need for a respectable, clean appearance in daily life. Through the Nile Queen, black women's sensual desire was projected—and thus confined—within a mythic time and place. Like the white-oriented mass market, the African-American beauty industry generally sought to curb the association of cosmetics with sexual expressiveness: Columnists compared overly made-up women to prostitutes; advertisements linked beauty to courtship and marriage. Although some black women had found an erotic voice in the blues, advertisers dealt gingerly with the sexual sell and insisted that cosmetics used properly channeled male attraction into wedding vows. "From boudoir to beach," a Walker ad stated, beautifying led to a paradise of

Walker advertisement, from the Messenger, *1925.*

heterosexual romance and self-fulfillment—"what every woman justly desires, masculine admiration and matrimony."[31]

Achieving racial pride, the industry claimed, was a step in achieving racial progress. "Glorifying our Womanhood," Walker advertisements implied, was integral to African-American advancement. Barnett, for his part, tied Kashmir cosmetics to the mobilization of black soldiers during World War I, which had given a new edge to demands for equality. When the *Defender* celebrated the return of the "Fighting Eighth Regiment," Barnett ran ads which featured heroic black soldiers who, reunited with their lovely sweethearts, exclaim, "Those French Mam'selles haven't a thing on my Kashmir Girl."[32]

If beauty mattered as a symbol and instrument of racial pride and advancement, then black producers and consumers of cosmetics were innocent of the charge of white emulation. But perhaps the most striking strategy that consumer culture offered black women was an insis-

KASHMIR
PREPARATIONS
FOR HAIR AND SKIN
" They Can't be Beat "

Our new colored officers are as gallant and dashing and game a set as ever wore a puttee. They've a keen eye for beauty, too. Of course KASHMIR GIRLS are the ones who attract them.

"Colored officers" with "a keen eye for beauty." Kashmir advertisement, from the Crisis, *1918.*

tence on the pursuit of beauty as a universal ideal. Advice columns carefully distinguished between emulating and beautifying. "If [a woman] uses a cosmetic with the express purpose of 'getting white' I feel that she shows a serious lack of self respect and race pride," observed "Aunt Pat" to the young readers of the *Dallas Express* in 1921. "I believe very few women guilty of this offense." Beauty experts instructed women to apply bleach only for spots and discolorations, not to peel off the top layer of skin. Face powder, they urged, should harmonize with skin color and produce a " 'finished' look," not whiten the face. "A light skin is no prettier than a dark one," the *Half-Century* insisted; "the beauty of any skin lies in the clarity and evenness of color." Aunt Pat agreed: "I heartily endorse the use of any cosmetic which will give the face a smooth, clear surface."[33] Although the women's pages in the African-American press occasionally offered tips addressed specifically to black women, much of the advice was identical to that in such mass-circulation magazines as the *Ladies' Home Journal.*[34]

Black manufacturers in this period developed full product lines for the African-American market and adopted a sales pitch similar to that of national advertisers. The Walker Company's bleach Tan-Off vowed an end to "sunburn, freckles and skin discolorations," a commonplace promise of skin-care advertisements. Ads for Poro simply duplicated J. Walter Thompson's "two creams" campaign for Pond's. Walker's ads were not much different from Armand's in praising a powder that "imparts an olive tint to fair complexions and harmonizes bewitchingly with darker skins." Manufacturers also assimilated dark skin to mass-market taxonomies of beauty. African-American women became Spanish, Creole, Mediterranean, and "brunette types" in ads for Carmencita face powder, LaCreole hair preparations, and others.[35]

Many white-owned firms in the 1920s, perhaps feeling the heat of black public opinion, rewrote their advertising in less explicitly racist language. Plough's ads in black publications simply promised the "tint of youthfulness . . . and an unblemished complexion." Golden Brown explained that its ointment "won't whiten your skin—as that can't be done," but it would produce a "soft, light, bright, smooth complexion." This use of the word *bright* had a double meaning: By smoothing rough or uneven skin, creams did brighten, in a sense, by improving the reflectivity of light, but among African Americans the term had a distinct connotation, that of light brown skin.[36]

To its promoters, African-American women's beautifying expressed a natural and universal female desire and proper attention to fashion. Ironically, fashion slavery was evidence of the New Negro Woman's freedom and equality. Black women used bleaches and light powders just as white women did, the *Half-Century* editorialized, "in the same spirit that they wear some of the most ridiculous [Paris] Fashions." Altogether skin color seemed to be drifting from its biological moorings, with white sunbathers cultivating deep tans, European women taking "henna baths," and brown-skin choruses singing on the Great White Way. "In the cycle of Vogue . . . this is the Bronze Age," wrote Eulalia Proctor in the *Messenger*, but after the fad for dark exoticism had ended, "will it be assimilation of a more intensive nature, or is after us—the deluge?"[37]

Between irony and unease, Proctor recognized that fashion was not a system unto itself, outside the harsh realities of racial discrimination and skin-color prejudice. Claims about beauty's universality were political assertions of female equality, but advice writers and consumers knew well that good looks supremacy affected white and black women in different ways. They noted that white women with kinky hair or swarthy skin could go to black hairdressers, use their hair-care systems, apply skin bleaches, and then return to white society with no loss of prestige. Attention focused especially on Jewish women, who were perceived to be a distinct race by both white and black Christians. The extent of Jewish crossover into the African-American consumer market is impossible to measure, but it was visible enough that the Walker Company placed several ads in the *Jewish Daily Forward* in 1925. Black commentators zeroed in on Jewish women's use of African-American grooming techniques to achieve the standard look of white beauty. "There's an awful lot of Colored women straightening Jewish women's hair and teaching them how to straighten their own," one woman wrote the *Half-Century*. "Then with the suspicious, too-tight curl removed from the hair, these women can move into exclusive districts and scorn the Colored people with whom they come in contact." The democracy of mass-produced beauty still stopped short at the color line.[38]

Focusing on race pride and the universality of female desire, the commerce in beauty products softened the political debate, downplaying the impact of white supremacy on black women's everyday cosmetics practices. How most black consumers interpreted the ads and advice directed at them remains, however, an open question. No survey research tells us which women bought the controversial cosmetics, what their intentions were, or whether they were more influenced by political rhetoric or commercial appeals. It would be important to know, for instance, whether skin bleaches were used more frequently by middle-class or working-class women, in the North or the South, in cities or small towns. Cosmetics use in private may not have accorded with public expressions of ideology. Even "extreme race loyalists," one writer observed, "artfully avoid the unkempt, unimproved hair and the poorly 'attended-to' skin." For every tirade against bleaching and emulation, many tubes of Black and White ointment were sold. Indeed, the controversy over bleaches and straighteners as signs of white domination obscures the fact that black women, like their white counterparts, were buying and using a wide range of other cosmetics. Pond's vanishing cream was popular, for example, because it reduced the oiliness and shine of the skin. White emulation was hardly the issue in this and many other beauty rituals.[39]

While race leaders and beauty experts interpreted cosmetics in symbolic and political terms, consumers assessed beautifying more in light of their own physical condition and social circumstances. Personal letters to Madam Walker, attached to order forms in 1918, discuss in great detail the substances, tools, techniques, and specific effects of beautifying. Written by women all over the country, they mainly concern the trouble many black women had with scalp diseases and hair growth, and rarely refer to straightening and styling. They describe frequent hair loss and breakage, problems that may have been exacerbated by poor nutrition and ill health, traditional hair straightening techniques, and the use of patent remedies. One woman had "the fever" and could never grow back her hair. Another said her hair "combs out by hands full an[d] a i[tc]hing scalp and very much dandruff." Others were driven to wearing wigs and switches. Many expressed a simple, heart-wrenching plea to have their hair restored to normal. For them, their very ability to be sociable, to be looked upon as respectable, depended on the magic of Wonderful Hair Grower.[40]

Hair grower, not the glossine used in pressing the hair, was the most popular preparation the Walker Company sold until the late 1920s, according to customer order forms and company account ledgers. Although a few women expressed disappointment in the product, many women wrote the company to report the precise number of inches their hair had grown: The treatment "mad[e] my hair improve so much about 2 inches," wrote a "surprise[d]" Annie Dervin. Bessie Brown was on her fourth box of hair grower when she wrote, "I am wonderfully pleased with your goods and my hair has improved no little." Women certainly "pressed" their hair using hot combs and oil, but perceived this practice as the final step of an overall beauty system.[41]

Unfortunately, comparable letters about skin bleaching and skin-care products have not been found. Sales of Walker's Tan-Off rose steeply in the late 1920s, and judging from the large investment of white-owned companies in advertising, a sizable market for these preparations existed. Some consumers indeed may have wished to bleach their skin white, as the most extreme advertisements promised and critics charged. But as we have seen, skin bleaches appeared on the market in different formulas and strengths, and were used for different purposes. Moreover, women applied bleach in various ways: Some dotted it on spots or blemishes to even the skin tone; others sought to fade or dissolve unwanted hair; still others spread bleach across the entire face to peel off the darker epidermis and reveal the lighter layer below. Consumers might have rendered different verdicts on these practices, approving of fade creams, for instance, but looking critically upon those who peeled their skin.[42]

Many of the women purchasing hair and skin preparations were newcomers to commercial culture and frequently mingled the modern language of consumption with older traditions. Despite Walker's efforts to "uplift" her products in the minds of consumers, the rural women who wrote often referred to them as "hair grease" and "remedies." Some combined the use of Walker products with traditional hair-styling techniques: Marie Cane ordered hair grower but asked Walker if plaiting or twisting the hair made it grow more quickly. A number of Walker's customers expressed an ideal of beauty rooted in traditional religious precepts, an ideal they now could realize in the marketplace. Although critics charged that the hair craze reflected a desire to look white, these women echoed the teaching of the Bible. "[I] must Give thanks to the Dear Co," said Lillie Byrd, "for i Do know Hair is the Glory of a Woman." When the "evangels" of Poro and Walker promoted their wares in rural churches, customers responded to the call. "Praise your wonderful hair grower," exclaimed one woman. Women who believed in the agency of dreams and prayers repeatedly used the word "wonderful" in their letters to Walker, gathering brand name, company, and the product's efficacy within the aura of the miraculous.[43]

A complex blend of modern advertising, word of mouth, and faith led these women into the market for beauty products. "I have taken one of your pamphlet with me home from a cousin of maine and have red it closely," wrote Virgie Brown of News Ferry, Virginia, to Walker about the hair preparation; "my cous[i]n Amalie Madley says she likes it fine so I want to try it." Walker's promotional literature tempted Mamie Bass, a woman from Greenville, Mississippi, but the Holy Spirit moved her to buy:

> I saw adv[ertisement] in the Chicago Definder also a friend
> Lady of myn gave me one of your books to read and after read-
> ing your great testimonial has a great confidence in it[.] believe
> it will do me lots of good I really beleive it will. . . . you saw this
> in a dream su[re]ly the good Lord has sent such a woman and [I]
> am a christ[ia]n my self and has dream of your great hair oil so it
> rested with me so untill I cant help but take a trile.[44]

Others had already tried different hair preparations without success. Helen Bell wrote from Sheridan, Wyoming, about "a colored woman here in this town that used some kind of glossy stuff that makes the ha[i]r slick and nice looking but turns it red." The product might have been O-zo-no, whose ads tried to reassure customers that it "will not turn hair red," "the smarting sensation has been reduced to the smallest minimum," and "every objectionable feature has been removed." Bell wrote, "please Madam do not feel offended at me," when she asked if Walker's glossine had the same effect. Bell judged Walker's sincerity and the product's merits on the caliber of her advertising. "I saw your hair remedies advertised in the Crisis book as I am a continual reader," she wrote, "and as I have used so many different things they have in drug stores for the hair decided I would like to give your remedies a trial." In May 1918, just before Bell wrote her letter, Walker had placed a full-page ad in the *Crisis*, the popular journal of the National Association for the Advancement of Colored People. The ad explained the function of each product, depicted the Lelia College of Hair Culture (named after Walker's daughter), and affirmed Madam Walker's "genius." It clearly convinced Bell: "I will be more than glad to recommend your remedies here to any of my color as I feel so assured in them that they will do all you claim."[45]

Woman arranging hair in Earle, Arkansas, 1936.

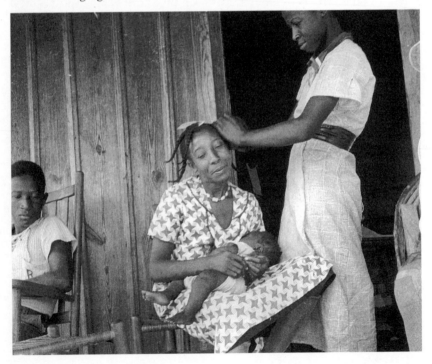

Wife of a Mississippi sharecropper dressing her hair, 1938.

African-American consumers seem to have approached the black press differently than social scientists and political commentators, who saw an irreconcilable conflict between the editorial emphasis on racial solidarity and the advertisements for skin bleaches and hair straighteners. Most readers took pride in their newspapers, believing them to be factual and trustworthy representations, relying upon them to open up a world of accomplishment and hope. "I got a heap to tell you but I feal so sad in hart," a Macon, Georgia, woman wrote to a Chicago friend, "my definder diden come yester[day] . . . it['s] company to me to read it." Readers like Mamie Bass and Helen Bell viewed advertisements in a similar way, paying careful attention to their messages, responding eagerly to their claims, and showing a willingness to "take a trial."[46]

Across the rural backwaters and hamlets of the South, Southwest, and Midwest, black women embraced the new beauty rituals. Share-croppers and domestic workers mailed the Walker Company substantial sums for hair growers and glossine, eked out from washing clothes, selling eggs, or cooking meals. Women from all walks of life—those who earned meager wages, lived on isolated farmsteads, or had only rudimentary schooling—participated in this new consumer culture.[47]

The Great Migration further heightened black women's self-consciousness about appearance. Deepening poverty, segregation, and violence, combined with perceived opportunities in the North for jobs and just treatment, sparked an African-American exodus from the South after 1915. Migrants took with them a sense of destiny and their capacity to shape it. They represented themselves as highly motivated workers, "honest people & up to date," as an Alabama man put it: "The trash pile dont want to go no where."[48]

The élan of the migrants often took an aesthetic form—an aware-ness of self-presentation, closely linked to a new sense of physical freedom and economic possibility. When they described their physical qualifications for employment, men mentioned weight and strength, but women highlighted a well-groomed, respectable, and fit appearance. A Natchez woman catalogued her features for potential northern employ-ers: "I am a body servant or nice house maid. My hair is black and my eyes are black and smooth skin and clear and brown[,] good teeth and strong and good health and my weight is 136 lb." Descriptions of ap-pearance came up repeatedly in applications for work. A domestic from Jacksonville similarly asked the Defender to help her find "a job with some rich white people who would send me a ticket," adding "I am brown skin just meaden size."[49]

It is little wonder, then, that a number of black women believed cosmetics were a prerequisite to the journey north, the makeover at once claiming a new status and helping to make it possible. One Walker agent in St. Petersburg, Florida, mailed an order to the company's headquarters with an urgent request to "send these things at once." Her customer "is expecting to go north as soon as she get[s] them," she wrote. "She is only waiting on you to send them that she might have them before starting." Even a journalist for the *Saturday Evening Post* commented upon this phenomenon: "The first thing every negro girl does when she comes from the South is to have her hair straightened." Elizabeth Cardozo Barker, who ran a Washington, D.C., beauty salon with her sisters, recalled the girls from the South who came in with unkempt hair. She gave them "croquignole" waves, the fashionable hairstyle of the time. "What it did for their ego," she exclaimed. Beauty culture operations as well as mass-market retailers expanded to meet the demand. By the early 1920s, over one hundred beauty parlors and nine toiletries companies served black

A Walker client reads Modern Beauty *magazine as she has her hair done.*

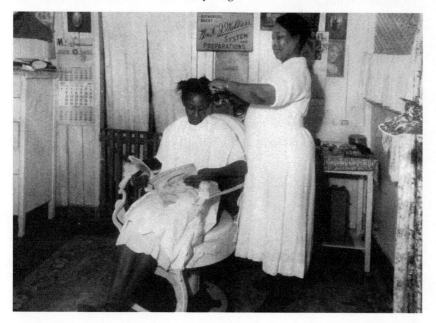

Chicagoans; beauty parlors in Harlem were reportedly three times more numerous than elsewhere in New York.[50]

Migrants learned quickly to adopt a style of self-presentation suited to urban life. Echoing earlier reformers, long-time city dwellers warned the new migrants that their country ways might inflame white antagonism. Black newspapers and social service agencies issued instructions on proper appearance and deportment, proscribing the rural customs of head rags, boudoir caps, aprons, and house slippers in public. The *Chicago Advocate* urged parents in the city's "Black Belt" to send their daughters to school clean and well groomed: "Do not wrap her hair with strings, but comb it out, or else your child will be made a laughing stock for the whole school." The flashy style of the street still beckoned. Harlem residents believed "you must look sharp as a tack, a city slicker," recalled one woman; "many Negroes were 'immigrants' and didn't want to look like it."[51]

Waitressing, clerking, theatrical work, and other urban occupations honed an awareness of the body and appearance. "One must have looks to-day," observed Louis George in the *Messenger.* "The colored girl to-day would greatly limit her opportunities did she not make use of hair dressing, manicuring and facial massaging." But even those who worked as maids and cooks—the chief form of employment for black women at the time—approached their work with a new sense of style. "Gone are the neat housekeepers in guinea blue calicoes, starched until they rattled," one disgruntled white commentator griped, replaced with women who wore fashionable clothes. Refusing a servile identity, black women carried their uniforms in "freedom bags" and changed in their employers' homes. As Evelyn Northington observed, "The woman who cooks all day in the restaurant, the women who scrub in the department store, even the farmer's wife is making every effort she can to be beautiful."[52]

The heated political rhetoric about emulation did not appear in the comments of these black women, but most adapted their beauty practices to immediate social realities, an adaptation that straighteners and bleaches might facilitate. Complexion certainly pigeonholed white

*A well-groomed
appearance on the job.
Lewis W. Hine's portrait
of a print-shop worker,
circa 1920. (Courtesy
George Eastman
House)*

women—witness the immigrant women whose dark skin marred their job prospects—but these handicaps might be overcome. For African Americans, however, physical attributes continued to have explicit social, economic, sexual, and psychological effects. Both men and women were still classified by an elaborate lexicon of skin tones (yellow, smooth-brown, creamy, black, bright, blue-veined) and hair textures (good, bad, halfway good, halfway bad, nappy, kinky). As the writer Pauli Murray put it, "The sliding scale of color bedeviled everyone, irrespective of where one stood on the color chart."[53]

Interviewing rural black Southerners in the 1930s, anthropologist Hortense Powdermaker discovered that "without being asked about color, women are very likely to include it in describing the virtues or defects of their husbands." Photographs were "invariably lighter than the original, and sometimes the features and hair [were] made to appear less Negroid," with some women even holding in their lips to make them look smaller. Urban African Americans too were "color struck" or "partial to color." Sociologists Horace Cayton and St. Clair Drake discovered many Chicagoans in the same period whose marriages, employment, and social activities were affected by color distinctions. As one dark-skinned man, describing the kind of woman he wanted to marry, said, "I don't want her too dark—just dark enough so she can't call me black." A very dark complexion especially hampered women seeking work as secretaries, waitresses, doctor's assistants, actresses, or other positions involving face-to-face contact with the public. "I have a policy of hiring only real light girls with good hair," said the owner of an exclusive restaurant. "A dark girl has no drawing power." Those with lighter skin tones were viewed as more refined, while their darker sisters were considered better manual laborers.[54]

It was possible to find alternative views. A poem in the *Messenger* praised the black girl who used no artificial beautifiers as the most authentic representative of the race:

> No vulgar grease or heated iron ever touched
> Your tangled hair;
> No rouge your full red lips, no powder
> Ever streaked the midnight blackness of your skin.[55]

In the blues, "high yellow" and "coal black" competed for the roving eye of the singer. "Teasin' browns," however, were most popular.

Indeed, "a veritable cult of the brown-skinned woman" had emerged, the Chicago sociologists found, reflected in the appearance of dolls, movie stars, and beauty queens and in the attitudes of high school students. This ideal was the Brazilian *moreno* with brown skin, soft features, and "good hair," similar to the respectable girl in the Kashmir ads. She was no simple avatar of white emulation, but rather the product of a shift in African-American self-perceptions—if not a black girl, then certainly not a white one either.[56]

The ideal of brown-skinned beauty was vigorously promoted by the African-American beauty trade. One window display at a Harlem beauty shop invited women to "come in and become a brown-skinned tulip." Manufacturers produced powder in shades ranging from white and rose-flesh to golden brown, but not colors to match very dark complexions. In a rare study of black consumers' response to advertising, economist Paul Edwards found that African Americans detested antiquated images like Aunt Jemima, who "looks too much like old-time mammy," but approved of the well-groomed, brown-skinned woman depicted in cosmetics advertisements for Madam Walker's face powder: "Here the Negro was dignified and made to look as he [*sic*] is striving to look and not as he looked in antebellum days . . . here was the New Negro." As they left behind the world of servility and inferiority, consumers adopted beautifying as an essential aspect of becoming modern African-American women. Still, the ideal they favored remained a painfully restrictive one.[57]

African-American beauty had become a commodity to trade not only in the marketplace of goods but in the exchange of political ideas. For black women themselves, however, beautifying was much more. Although opposed by some as a sign of emulation and falsity, cosmetics offered others a way of negotiating new experiences and expressing a new sense of self. For those who embraced it, the culture of beauty asserted desires for dignity, respect, and social participation in a world in which these basic human imperatives were all too often denied.

Through the 1930s, black women continued to purchase beauty products and services, while black cosmetics firms struggled to stay afloat. Remarkably, in the midst of the Depression, one investigator tallied 382 hairdressing shops in Harlem storefronts. Countless women did hair work in their own kitchens or parlors, and itinerant operators carried their straightening combs and supplies door to door. As they had thirty years earlier, women looked to the beauty trade for employment, and beauty systems like Sara Spencer Washington's Apex urged women

Valmor Products Catalog cover, 1936.

to "plan your future by learning a depression-proof business." This hopeful proposition belied women's actual prospects—low earnings and long hours driven by competition and the oversupply of beauticians. Most clients were household workers, themselves hard hit by the Depression. Still, going to the hairdresser had become a ritual, and women would pay with food if they did not have cash. The salons offered beauty, relaxation, and sociability in a troubled time. At the establishment where she first learned hair work, Elizabeth Barker recalled, customers would "sit in there for hours, sometimes. They'd play cards; sometimes they'd gossip . . . they just came expecting to sit."[58]

Beautifying continued to be a central economic and cultural activity, but the message of female dignity and racial advancement allied with it became more subdued as the decade wore on. Walker and Malone's pioneering conception of beauty culture, merging commerce, philanthropy, and politics, suffered as newer companies, such as Snow White and Valmor, came out with cheaper products. Salon operatives remained important figures in civic affairs, but the commercial images projected by the beauty business were increasingly depoliticized. When Sara Spencer Washington began publishing the *Apex News* in 1929, beauty columns ran alongside stories on politics and notable African Americans; by the mid-thirties, these had disappeared, replaced by articles on romance, marriage, and the psychological effects of beautifying. Valmor, a mail-order firm selling Sweet Georgia Brown preparations, went even further, explicitly sexualizing the sale of beauty products. Illustrations of steamy embraces, passionate kisses, and women in negligees, along with old-fashioned before-and-after pictures and lighten-your-skin copy, appeared throughout its catalogs. Here black women's identity was centered on achieving beauty to attract a man. Sweet Georgia Brown became a leading brand in the African-American market in the 1930s and 1940s, and according to New York retailers, aggressive promotion explained its success. How consumers themselves understood Sweet Georgia Brown advertising remains an unanswered question, but there is no doubt that Valmor's rise signaled the end of an era.[59]

Identity and

the Market

By 1940, manufactured beauty formed a major sector of the economy and informed the everyday practices of women. In the decades that followed, mass media tied cosmetics ever more closely to notions of feminine identity and self-fulfillment, proliferating images of flawless female beauty—mostly youthful, white, and increasingly sexualized. The made-up face would now be regulated by fashion seasons and firmly bound to the internal workings of the female psyche. Nevertheless the postwar look of perfect femininity disintegrated in the last third of the century. Ironically this development owed something to the efforts of the mass beauty industry itself, which linked distinct social identities to cosmetics consumption through market segmentation. However, it was also the mounting discontent among African Americans, feminists, and gay activists that challenged the widespread acceptance and commercial exploitation of the governing beauty ideals. From the 1960s onward, ideas that had long shaped Americans' understanding of cosmetics were challenged anew in a vigorous political debate.

• • •

When the United States entered World War II, some questioned whether women should continue to seek "glamour as usual" in a world bent on destruction. In the *New York Times* novelist Fannie Hurst criticized frivolous, self-absorbed women who tarried in beauty salons and complained over shortages of silk stockings and makeup. Observing that women were on the threshold of a new era, she said, "The history of their role in this desperate struggle will not be written in lipstick." Replying to Hurst, a "red-blooded, red-lipped" housewife countered that American women's brave response to the national crisis was not diminished but enhanced by reasonable attention to appearance. Beautifying showed "women's own sense of pride" and respect for the men "we try most to please." She asked, "Would we help them more if, when they are about to perish for freedom's sake, we showed ourselves to them worn with sorrow and dejection?" Lipstick worn as a badge of courage signified "iron in our hearts," the "red blood of the true American woman."[1]

In the wake of the Depression and rise of fascism, the attractive, made-up woman of the 1940s bespoke the "American way of life" and a free society worth defending. Indeed, she had become a global commodity and symbol, exported in Hollywood movies and promoted by cosmetics firms. American women were "beautifying themselves according to the 'American plan,'" Max Factor, Jr., proclaimed. "The women in most of the other countries in the world have been, too." Even before Pearl Harbor, journalists had worried that a "national glamour shortage would seriously lower national morale." Once the United States entered the war, pinups and snapshots of the glamorous girl next door served to remind soldiers of the home front and women's service to national ideals.[2]

Cosmetics advertising during the war continued to use the old sales pitch of love and romance, now set in USO camps and seaports. But increasingly a conscious message emphasized women's part in winning the war. These new appeals were not directed at "those who have noth-

*Doing your Bit...
and a Little Bit More?*

ing to do but sit around and look pretty for the returning warrior," a trade journal noted, but at the "new cosmetic market—women war workers."[3]

Among the memorable wartime ad campaigns was Tangee's, which appeared in major women's magazines in 1943 and 1944. Tangee exalted the function of such "mysterious little essentials" as lipstick in a world at war, praising women's success in "keeping your femininity—even though you are doing man's work." Tangee conceded that "neither our cosmetics, or anyone else's, will make you a better WAC, or a better war-worker, or a better wife." But it claimed a large symbolic and psychological boost from lipstick, which enabled women to "do" as a man and "appear" as a woman. Lipstick helped women to put on a brave face, "conceal heartbreak or sorrow," and gain "self-confidence when it's badly needed." Picturing the Venus de Milo with the Statue of Liberty, Tangee equated the protection of freedom and democracy with the protection of beauty. Lipstick symbolized "the precious right of women to be feminine and lovely—under any circumstances," and this, Tangee concluded, was "one of the reasons why we are fighting."[4]

It is tempting to dismiss these views simply as the work of ingenious advertisers, but they carried far beyond the pages of magazines. The national emergency unsettled conventional ideas about women's capabilities. As they tackled jobs traditionally held by men, women faced strong pressures to maintain their femininity through grooming and makeup. Even the All-American Girls Professional Baseball League, organized during the war, ordered women ballplayers to take makeup lessons from Helena Rubinstein and to appear ladylike on the

War, Women and Lipstick—

by CONSTANCE LUFT HUHN
Head of the House of Tangee

*A recent portrait of Constance Luft Huhn
by Maria de Kammerer*

For the first time in history woman-power is a factor in war. Millions of you are fighting and working side by side with your men.

In fact, you are doing double duty—for you are still carrying on your traditional "woman's" work of cooking, and cleaning, and home-making. Yet, somehow, American women are still the loveliest and most spirited in the world. The best dressed, the best informed, the best looking.

It's a reflection of the free democratic way of life that you have succeeded in keeping your femininity—even though you are doing man's work!

If a symbol were needed of this fine, independent spirit—of this courage and strength—I would choose a lipstick. It is one of those mysterious little essentials that have an importance far beyond their size or cost.

A woman's lipstick is an instrument of personal morale that helps her to conceal heartbreak or sorrow; gives her self-confidence when it's badly needed; heightens her loveliness when she wants to look her loveliest.

No lipstick—ours or anyone else's—will win the war. But it symbolizes one of the reasons why we are fighting...the precious right of women to be feminine and lovely—under any circumstances.

The Tangee Satin-Finish Lipstick of your choice will keep your lips smoother...longer! It will bring an exclusive grooming and a deep glowing "life" to your lips that defy both time and weather.

BEAUTY—*glory of woman*...
LIBERTY—*glory of nations*...
Protect them both...

**BUY WAR BONDS
AND STAMPS**

TANGEE *Lipsticks*
WITH THE NEW SATIN-FINISH

Above and opposite: *Tangee advertisements*, Ladies' Home Journal, *1944, 1943.*

RASHES FROM GLUE KEEP GLAMOUR FROM YOU

USE GLUE SOAP
AND CAUTION

SAFETY SERIES

Pratt and Read poster.

field. With the sudden increase of women war workers, psychiatrists and efficiency experts alike testified to the importance of cosmetics in countering fatigue, improving morale, and increasing productivity. Lockheed and Sperry installed beauty salons and cosmetics stations; Boeing offered charm classes in its factories; the Seattle Navy Yard's management and unions provided advice on good looks.[5]

While feminine beauty was promoted as a powerful tool to spur output and lift morale, it was circumscribed by carefully defined boundaries. At Pratt and Read's aeronautical division, one placard, urging women to be cautious with adhesives, used the slogan "rashes from glue keep glamour from you," but another warned that glamorous looks—long curls, frilly blouses, and high heels—had no place on the production line where "it's smart to dress the part." As if to underscore women's temporary place in defense plants and heavy manufacturing, workingmen often complained about women "prettying up" on the job, suggesting that they were more devoted to the mirror than the welding torch.[6]

Earning high wages but faced with shortages of clothing and other

Women war workers making up, 1941 and 1942.

style goods, working women did spend heavily on cosmetics. Leg makeup, produced since the 1920s as a substitute for stockings, became commonplace. "Victory Girls," seeking fun, companionship, and sometimes sexual encounters with servicemen, openly declared themselves with flirtatious gestures and heavily painted faces. At some war plants, their looks exacerbated tensions within the community over single women's sexuality and autonomy. A company official at Moore Dry Dock in Seattle, apparently pressured by his wife, "went about among the girls in his jurisdiction with a bottle of acetone and a handkerchief and forced them to remove their nail polish and lipstick."[7]

The centrality of cosmetics in women's lives became a pressing issue for the federal War Production Board, charged with restricting the manufacture of consumer goods to conserve metals, chemicals, and other materials needed for the war effort. Some government officials voiced skepticism about cosmetics, believing that demand was produced artificially by the advertising industry. Trying to decide whether to ration beauty products, the board questioned magazine editors and consumers about cosmetics use, especially the "influence of age, race, [and the] changing of women's sphere of activity to [the] war effort." Many women stated their willingness "to give up wrinkle eradicators, nail polish, and what not if it will help sock the Axis." In a 1942 survey of Baltimore consumers, women over forty declared that most beauty preparations were inessential; they had come of age just before cosmetics had become a mass industry. Younger women, however, viewed powder, rouge, and cold cream as necessities. And there was one item deemed indispensable by nearly all—lipstick.[8]

In July 1942, the War Production Board's Order L-171 restricted some cosmetics manufacturing and packaging and banned new products from the market; production of the most popular cosmetics was to be reduced by about 20 percent. Relative to other limitation orders, L-171 was quite mild. Nevertheless, within four months the board rescinded its order and called for women to curtail cosmetic purchases voluntarily. Certainly the cosmetics industry had exerted steady pressure on the government, and some board officials argued that needed materials, like metals used in powder compacts, could be adequately conserved through existing regulations. But at the same time, the War Production Board, sensing public opposition even to the limited order, had undoubtedly come to appreciate cosmetics in a new light—as vital to securing women's commitment to the war effort.[9] Beautifying had evolved from an everyday grooming habit into an assertion of American national identity.

Following World War II, the beauty industry entered a rococo period and, like other consumer industries, began to produce a limitless array of goods, colors, and styles. By 1948, 80 to 90 percent of adult American women used lipstick, about two-thirds used rouge, and one in four wore eye makeup. "Women are now constantly buying additional shades of Lipstick, even *before* they completely use most of them up," Max Factor reported. Although department stores and drugstores remained the leading outlets for cosmetics, growing numbers of women shopped for glamour at new self-service supermarkets, discounters, and shopping malls. Door-to-door firms expanded from their traditional rural territory into middle-class suburbia: as 70,000 Avon Ladies rang doorbells, the company's sales skyrocketed from $10 million in 1940 to almost $87 million in 1956. Many firms still followed the prewar style of operation, depending on "cookbook magic"—the "intuition and hunch of a few cosmetic chemists"—but increasingly the largest corporations invested in scientific research and systematic product development.[10]

The promotional strategies cosmetics firms had developed in the 1920s effloresced in the postwar years—extended product lines, coordination of cosmetics with fashion seasons, tie-ins, and fads exploited as a matter of course. High-powered advertising remained fundamental to the industry. Revlon exemplified these trends: Charles Revson, the American-born son of Jewish immigrants, joined with his brother Joseph and chemist Charles Lachman to form a nail enamel company in 1932. By the 1940s Revlon introduced new colors of lipstick and nail polish each fall and spring fashion season, developing elaborate campaigns around original and enticing color names. These proved so popular that women named their bowling teams the "Fatal Apples" and the "Pink Lightnings." In record time, the company pushed one new product after another into the market. Locked in fierce competition with Hazel Bishop, a chemist who had burst into the cosmetics market in 1950 with an indelible lipstick, Revlon waged "lipstick war" on television; when the firm sponsored the television quiz show "$64,000 Question" from 1955 to 1958, sales tripled. By the end of the 1960s Revlon had become the cosmetics industry's equivalent of General Motors, with six separate product lines intended to appeal to different classes of consumers.[11]

From its earliest days, the cosmetics industry had practiced market segmentation by dividing its customers into class, mass, and African-American markets. In the 1940s a more nuanced effort to define consumers according to demographics and lifestyle took shape. Women's magazines like *Seventeen* and *Charm* targeted high school girls and working women respectively. Consumer panels and cosmetic juries— early focus groups representing distinct demographic sectors—enabled businesses to tailor their advertising to housewives, students, and other categories of women. Teenagers and even children emerged as distinct segments of the market. "We should recognize teenagers on their own," urged one marketing expert, "develop products, develop packages, prices that fit the teenagers." Ten-cent sizes, originally promoted as samples, soon sold expressly to teens. In the early 1950s, Tinkerbell pioneered the sale of grooming aids for children, at first mainly bath products but later powder and lip gloss. The African-American market also gained new attention from mass-market firms; black newspapers, magazines, and consumer surveys promoted the view that African-Americans' wartime experience had not only escalated the demand for civil rights and better jobs, but had intensified their desire for consumer goods. Cosmetics manufacturers even renewed their interest in marketing to men.[12]

Still, adult women remained the most important consumers of

beauty preparations. Cosmetics use continued to vary across the country, with expenditures highest in urbanized areas and lowest in the rural Northeast and South. Many Southern white women followed the prewar practice of applying vanishing cream as a powder base, but Northern and urban women purchased modern tinted foundations. Surveys of African-American consumers found striking regional differences in the late 1940s: In Knoxville black women reported few cosmetics purchases, but in Philadelphia over two-thirds used hair products and over half used skin preparations.[13]

Following strategies of persuasion codified before World War II, advertisers delivered a therapeutic sales pitch, illustrated ads with images of flawless beauty, and made consumption integral to achieving the feminine ideal. Directing attention to both facial surfaces and psychological depths, the beauty industry sharpened its paradoxical pitch. Pond's, for instance, promised that cosmetics would produce a "real, warm Inner You."[14] One *became* a woman in an act of making up that was, incongruously, *inherent* to feminine nature.

Makeup products and styles in the 1950s served this notion of a performance that disguised its performance. As Coty put it, women could "wake up beautiful." Indelibility became a cosmetic ideal. Hazel Bishop captured one-quarter of the lipstick market with a product that "stays on you, not on him." Here was a lipstick that did not come off on napkins and men's collars, that need not be reapplied, that a woman could even wear to sleep. Unlike the flapper of the 1920s, who reveled in the public cosmetic gesture, the woman who chose indelible lipstick effaced makeup's artifice.[15]

Liquid and cake foundations that provided "coverage" also permitted an illusion of permanence. Widely used since Max Factor introduced Pan-Cake makeup in 1938, water-soluble foundation in cake form gave the face a certain look: It concealed uneven skin tones—which were, indeed, natural for most women—under a matte, uniform, and finished surface. Women often perceived foundation to be too heavy or even dirty, however, and by the late 1950s cosmetics firms were touting foundations that were sheer yet covered the skin. Cover

Girl perfectly captured the contradictory goals, advertising itself in the 1960s as "clean makeup," "so natural you can't believe it's makeup."[16]

The simple act of putting on lipstick or foundation became even more aligned with therapeutic claims than it had been in the 1930s. Psychologists and social scientists weighed in, warning women that too much paint reflected the unresolved psychodynamics of childhood, a misplaced effort to attract father and attack mother. One psychiatrist called makeup a female pathology, a form of "extreme narcissism" through which women "reduced themselves to a symbol of the genitalia." However, most supported the cosmetics industry's view that lipstick and mascara were natural signs of maturing femininity. In one article on "mentally healthy beauty care," stories of average women using cosmetics were illustrated with photographs of patients in mental institutions, both groups gaining a psychological lift through makeup. Advocating a "middle road," psychiatrists advised each woman to use all the cosmetic aids possible to create the appearance of her real self.[17]

The war's end was the catalyst for this psychological interpretation of cosmetics. Movies, advertising, and advice literature reflected the view that women were bound to experience "harsh inner conflicts" as they faced the traumatic return of husbands and boyfriends, the death of loved ones, and their own job losses. Now, a Pond's executive explained, they were searching "not for romance alone, not for marriage and children alone, not for beauty alone, but for something far deeper." Martin Revson, Charles's brother and a Revlon executive, similarly spoke of a reservoir of emotion and desire that could not be tapped by the old advertising appeals. Invoking Henry David Thoreau and oddly anticipating Betty Friedan's description of the "problem that has no name," he observed that "most women lead lives of dullness, of quiet desperation." The answer lay not in seeking educational and employment opportunities, as Friedan would later argue, but in a "wonderful escape" into the fantasy world of feminine beauty.[18]

In the postwar years, sexual allure and desire were celebrated as key attributes of the normal female psyche. "By femininity I mean all the aspects of sexuality which permeate the female personality," wrote G. M. White in the *Ladies' Home Journal,* "including her 'way of thinking,' dressing, walking, talking . . . her tone of voice, her gestures, the faint perfume of soap and cosmetics and lack of whiskers."[19] This conception greatly influenced how the cosmetics industry addressed women consumers in the late 1940s and 1950s. For years advertisers had acknowledged women's sexuality but contained it safely in the story of heterosexual romance and marriage. They dealt gingerly with women expressing their sexual desires, relying on double entendre and flirtation. Even movie and romance magazines, whose beauty ads explicitly connected makeup and sex appeal, maintained a logic that downplayed women's sexual assertion: A woman acted upon her desire for a man by making herself beautiful, in order to catch his attention and awaken *his* desire.

Fire and Ice, a Revlon lipstick color introduced in 1952—"for you who love to flirt with fire, who dare to skate upon thin ice"—definitively changed the sexual resonance of cosmetics advertising. The "innermost essence of Woman" included her fantasies and sex life, Charles Revson maintained, for "the genuinely sexy woman is the 'good' woman." With Fire and Ice, Revlon portrayed a fantasy of the "high class tramp" who "somehow you know [is] really a nice girl." The ad featured a beautiful model in a low-cut, sequined gown, sporting a come-hither, knowing expression. Revlon women had "lips parted and moist," and wore "molten fabrics as extra skin," breathlessly wrote a journalist in *Printers' Ink.* Accompanying the photograph was a questionnaire for consumers to see if they were "ready for Fire and Ice." It asked conventional questions about heterosexual romance but also quizzed women on their desire for sensuous pleasure, their adventurousness, and their iconoclasm: Do you dance with your shoes off? Do you secretly hope that the next man you meet will be a psychiatrist? If tourist flights were running would you take a trip to Mars? "Every woman in the civilized world" answered the questionnaire, observed Beatrice Castle, Revlon's fashion director. "It was like having a cheap analysis."[20]

for you who love to flirt with fire...
who dare to skate on thin ice...

Revlon's "Fire and Ice"

for lips and matching fingertips. A lush-and-passionate scarlet
...like flaming diamonds dancing on the moon!

"Indelible-Creme" Lipstick...Regular Lipstick
Frosted Nail Enamel...
Improved-Formula Nail Enamel

Revlon's "Fire and Ice" advertisement, 1952.

Strikingly, Fire and Ice portrayed a moment of pure glamour, featuring, as one advertising executive put it, a model "totally floating in space . . . in a complete world of her own." There was no heterosexual encounter here, no romantic scene, just a self absorbed—or self-sufficient—woman. How ordinary consumers perceived Fire and Ice is not documented, but the ad itself offered a mix of visual and verbal cues. In one sense, Revlon had transported the image of the eager sexpot, common in men's magazines such as *Esquire,* into the marital and domestic milieu of women's magazines. But the advertising women who developed the campaign claimed that the new postwar Italian movie stars—"tough" but "all woman"—had inspired them. The ad was intentionally tongue-in-cheek, they insisted, and presented a playfulness in which women were in on the joke, not a "burlesque" that demeaned and objectified them. Warning other advertisers to maintain that distinction, Revlon advertising executive Kay Daly observed that "the difference is devastatingly different to women." Daly's perceptive comment nevertheless failed to acknowledge how hard it was to draw that line in a culture increasingly saturated with perfect images of sexually alluring women.[21]

The sensual Revlon woman who "only went out at night" was one of several beauty types in the postwar decades. The old taxonomic convention of the cosmetics trade responded to the increasingly calculated effort to carve out markets, position products vis-à-vis competitors, and create specific brand personalities and looks. When Noxzema developed Cover Girl as a medicated makeup for teens as well as adults, it knew that a frankly sexual appeal would anger girls' parents. So advertisers consciously established the product's image against the Revlon woman with a consistent look of daytime, wholesome beauty. Interviewed about the campaign years later, they repeated the mantra that Maybelline was "for not too intelligent girls," "Revlon was for tarts," and "Cover Girl was for the nice girls."[22]

For all their differences, the Cover Girl and the Revlon Woman were both standards of perfection against which most women would come up short. Many contemporary writers have vividly recalled the pressures to conform to those beauty images as they came of age, their feelings of helplessness and inadequacy in the face of them. As early as the 1940s, social scientists reported that the quality teenage girls most wanted to change in themselves was their physical appearance. This anxiety was surely aggravated in the next two decades—a period of relatively confining roles for women—as advertising, magazines, and television produced a succession of feminine images that were often contradictory and sometimes even undermined the ruling models of beauty that young women strove so hard to match. Changing the face each fashion season, producing an array of beauty requisites, delineating narrower markets based on lifestyle, and making a therapeutic appeal the cosmetics industry compelled consumers to continually interrogate, experiment with, and renew their looks.[23]

These contradictions are especially apparent in the socialization of girls into cosmetics use. Where to draw the line—between proper grooming and unseemly glamorizing, between children's make-believe and adult makeup—vexed parents, schools, and manufacturers. Girls were taught the lesson of better appearance through cosmetics, yet cautioned against looking too sexual and mature. Most firms refused to sell eye shadow, rouge, and tinted lipstick to young girls, although Tussy did market a Budding Beauty Glamour Set. In the name of good grooming and personality development, schools, girls' clubs, and stores offered classes in beautifying, a trend that had begun in the 1930s but steadily accelerated in the postwar years. Pond's, Noxzema, and other mass marketers distributed booklets and filmstrips on "teen beauty," prepared grooming units for home economics classes, and hired beauty consultants to talk to teens.[24]

The girls themselves made experimenting with makeup a central part of teen culture in the 1950s. A sizable minority of preteens began to wear makeup to school and social events, around the time that they experienced the onset of menstruation and other physical changes of puberty. More so than in earlier decades, the passage into "womanhood" was anticipated and certified through the visible use of makeup. By the mid-sixties, teenage girls, who comprised 11 percent of the population, bought nearly one-quarter of all cosmetics and beauty preparations.[25]

As was true in the 1920s and 1930s, makeup styles marked the generations, but teens in the sixties created strikingly distinct looks. Eye makeup, used relatively infrequently into the 1950s, became extraordinarily popular, and the "big eye look" altered the balance and appearance of facial features. Thick bands of black eyeliner, glittering eye shadow, and white lipstick sharply distinguished girls from their mothers, whose taste ran to red lipstick, light mascara, and a matte complexion. Generational differences in makeup styles mirrored more radical conflicts over sexuality, social life, and politics.[26]

At the same time, makeup fashions identified cliques and cultural groups within the teenage world. Sociologist Jessie Bernard contrasted the clean-cut, middle-class cheerleader, "a breathing replica of a *Seventeen* model," to the working-class "majorette" wearing "gaudy" makeup; the former were often college bound, while "twirlers" clustered in the secretarial courses. Makeup traced bonds of friendship among girls who shared the exuberant triumphs and dismal failures they encountered in their efforts to achieve the right look. Indeed, the embrace of cosmetic excess—not only the vast quantities of makeup applied but the time spent in doing so—led some schools in the early 1960s to forbid makeup, extreme hairdos, and tarrying in the rest rooms.[27]

The beauty trade was deeply implicated in these trends, as it sought to navigate parents' concerns and girls' desires. Cover Girl, Maybelline, and Revlon all created beauty images that meshed closely with the ways high school students themselves classified girls into cliques and codified their evolving sense of personal identity. Yet experimentation and play were possible, and in many ways encouraged, by the profusion of ads and advice, the variety of makeup ideals, and the endless supply of new products.[28]

Encouraged by manufacturers, even male consumers revised conventional views of masculine identity by incorporating toiletries into their postwar appearance. Military service during World War II had transformed men's formerly haphazard grooming habits. Neat hair, a close shave, clean body, and polished shoes were all subject to inspection and policing. Indeed, for servicemen such matters could upset traditional hierarchies: Farm boys and working-class youth could attain status and rank in part by attending to good grooming. Army PXs stocked a wide variety of aftershave lotions, skin creams, deodorants, talcum powders, sunburn remedies, and lip pomades. Seaforth distributed a Commando Kit filled with miniature grooming aids for men at the front who went without showers and a change of clothes. Even cologne was "used by the G.I.s as a substitute for water when there are no bathing facilities handy." Soldiers wearing loud or exotic scents and sailors with pirate-style hoop earrings—called "Asiatics" by their shipmates—may have found a sub-rosa means of expressiveness in regimented lives that mixed danger with drudgery. Like women's cosmetics during the war, men's toiletries were promoted as "morale boosters." Observed the president of Shulton, maker of Old Spice: "It is our feeling that toiletries are necessary for men and women to maintain their self-confidence and their courage."[29]

Promising "better living through better grooming," postwar firms produced a new array of men's toiletries with "no froufrou." Reinforcing masculine stereotypes, package designers rejected pastels for plaids, red, gold, and black, and made colonial apothecary jars, Scotch whiskey jugs, and practical Lucite containers to "fit a man's hand." A variety of scents were marketed as manly: Pine suggested the great outdoors; cognac and leather evoked the men's club; citrus was invigorating. The fastidious man of quality may have promoted expensive aftershave in the 1930s, but two other masculine images now appeared in toiletries advertising: the military hero and the romantic male, whose use of aftershave enhanced his lovemaking abilities. By the late 1950s, major women's cosmetics companies began to develop male product lines, such as Arden for Men, which included face cream, cleansing mask, lip pomade, and hair spray.[30]

Journalists noted the breakdown of men's inhibitions with a bemused tone that masked a certain uneasiness with the new "vanity of the American male." "After priding himself for generations on his stale old hunting shirt and his stubbly beard, he has suddenly grown self-conscious," *Business Week* reported in 1953. Its survey found that men shaved on average five times a week, much more regularly than before the war; half used aftershave, and over one-third used deodorant—a figure the magazine called "startling." Most strikingly, the connection between fragrance and effeminacy weakened: The "Scented Sixties" were celebrated as the "decade of the male breakthrough."[31]

The commercialization of men's appearance was often explained, paradoxically, by men's need for a sharp look in corporate America *and* by a new hedonism that rejected the conformity demanded by the business world. Important elements in this market were teenagers and college students, who, beginning in the 1950s with the fad for Canoe, had by the 1960s become major purchasers of men's grooming aids. The advertising manager for Swank's Jade East, a popular aftershave, explained: "I was told on one southern campus that girls wouldn't date boys who didn't use them."[32]

Although men's toiletries had earlier played with sex appeal—Mennen's slogan was "the he-man aroma that wows the ladies"—the theme became pervasive in 1960s ads that "imply a dash of fragrance leads to a rash of heterosexual activity." Believing in its power as an aphrodisiac, men made musk surprisingly popular. But in much of this marketing to men, the need to counter effeminacy turned romance into sexual aggression and violence. Swagger, Si Señor, Macho, and Score were typical trade names. "What helps a man handle a woman?" one ad asked. "Dante knows. This time treat yourself to Dante. Next time she won't forget." In television commercials using clips from the James Bond movie *Thunderball,* an announcer intoned: "When you use 007, be kind," "careful, it's loaded," and "licensed to kill . . . women." The initial advertising campaign for Jade East, running as the government began to build up military forces in Vietnam, depicted a sensual Asian woman in a jungle fantasy of Oriental exoticism, female desire, and submission. The commercial's closing line: "If she doesn't give it to you, get it yourself." Stripping the beauty image of notions of mental health, self-improvement, and romance that dominated women's cosmetics marketing, these ads put women firmly in their place.[33]

Criticism of cosmetics was muted in the 1950s and early 1960s. Although sometimes seen as symptomatic of the baleful influence of consumerism, cosmetics rarely earned activists' or social critics' sustained attention. Indeed, when the obscure socialist journal *Militant* attacked the cosmetics industry in 1954 for selling women useless products, the editor was astonished to receive a stream of protest letters from women readers, "the kind of response that only an important issue deserves." Readers' defense of cosmetics echoed that of working women decades before. "I'm no sucker for beauty-aid ads," reader Helen Baker wrote, "but economic pressure—I have to earn my living—forces me to buy and use the darned stuff." Older or unattractive women needed cosmetics to compete in a job market where office work required glamour and factory bosses expected women to present an "illusion of the necessary vigor and youth." Many criticized the *Militant*'s paean to the moral beauty of ordinary working women: "There is nothing beautiful in the dishpan hands, the premature wrinkles, the scraggly hair, the dumpy figures in dumpy housedresses." Hard work, monotony, poor health, and the struggle to survive robbed working-class women of the beauty and self-fulfillment to which they were entitled. "I wish to improve and enjoy my physical appearance and at the same time improve and develop all the other sides of my personality," wrote one reader. "And I think all women have a *right* to both these things."[34]

The most penetrating criticism of the American beauty ideal continued to come from African Americans. Poet Gwendolyn Brooks exposed the racism and violence behind the mask of white femininity in a 1959 poem on the death of Emmett Till. Brooks imagined the inner monologue of the white wife whose beauty served as a symbol of white supremacy and pretext for lynching African-American men. She carefully puts on her makeup before serving breakfast to her husband, a participant in Till's murder:

Whatever she might feel or half-feel, the lipstick necessity
    was something apart. He must never conclude
That she had not been
worth It.[35]

African-American appearance dramatically reemerged as a public
issue after the war. Expenditures for personal care products among
African Americans rose steadily. A new generation of black entrepreneurs capitalized upon the growing market. The place Walker and
Overton had once had in the industry was now held by George Johnson,
S. B. Fuller, and Rose Morgan. *Ebony,* a glossy general-interest magazine for African Americans appearing in 1945, made beauty a central
preoccupation. The civil rights movement sparked a renewed attack on
discriminatory practices in commercial beauty culture. Black women
filed lawsuits against white-owned salons that refused them service,
and industry workers fought to eliminate race-specific requirements for
hairdressers and cosmetologists. By the mid-1960s, beauty salons in
urban business districts were increasingly integrated, with about one-
quarter of black beauticians working in white-owned shops or on white
customers. This was a "double-edged sword," *Ebony* noted, since integration drained business from neighborhood shops run by black
women. Those shops still served as community institutions, and during
the civil rights era they spread news of protests and organized voter
registration drives.[36]

African Americans also protested their exclusion from the mass
media's promotion of American beauty. Black manufacturers purchased spot commercials on local radio but could not sponsor television shows. In 1954, when Rose Morgan wanted to broadcast a "series
of 'sing-offs' among church choirs" that would include ads for her
beauty preparations, she "ran into a stone wall" at the Dumont television network. Segregated beauty pageants, modeling agencies, and
women's magazines also came under attack. An African-American
agency, Brandford Models, opened in 1946, with models posing in
bathing suits and sportswear Brandford called "freedom clothes."

However, large agencies and mainstream fashion magazines did not hire even the occasional black model until the late 1960s. *Mademoiselle* featured the first makeovers for "distinct racial beauty types" in 1967. It was not until 1974, however, that the first black model, Beverly Johnson, appeared on the cover of *Vogue*.[37]

In the late 1950s and early 1960s, observers began to notice a decline in African Americans' use of hair straighteners and bleaches. The growing political and cultural interest in Pan-Africanism and black nationalism found expression in appearance. Opera tenor George Shirley wore "his hair quite long and natural, in a manner which has already become identified with a number of leading diplomats from Africa," wrote a columnist for the *Amsterdam News* in 1962, and "even more startling is a similar trend among the ladies" started by South African singer Miriam Makeba. In perhaps the most famous hair-care scene in American letters, Malcolm X described the physical and psychic pain of hair conking, a straightening process using lye and other chemicals that created the stylish hair of zoot-suiters. In Malcolm's view, conking signified the depths of black alienation from body and spirit. Only on joining the Nation of Islam did Malcolm X claim his true black identity, with a new appearance that included short, unprocessed hair.[38]

By the mid-1960s, young civil rights workers were adopting natural, unprocessed hair as an expression of black solidarity and authenticity. "We, as black women, must realize that there is beauty in what we are, without having to make ourselves into something we aren't," explained Suzi Hill, an organizer in Chicago. She hoped to end the frustration and self-loathing of black women who "go through a lifetime of hiding themselves." Black nationalists repudiated a white aesthetic felt to be oppressive with the phrase "black is beautiful," the raised fist, and the iconic Afro. With little awareness of a complex history, black critics condemned the African-American cosmetics industry for colluding with white supremacy, destroying African pride, and exploiting the "pitiable escapist dreams of the black masses" by selling hair straighteners and skin bleaches.[39]

At first the mainstream African-American press featured few images of the new natural style. Straighteners and bleaches continued to be widely advertised. Catching *Ebony*'s editors by surprise, readers in 1966 complained about the magazine's long-time depiction of black women, which featured models and beauty queens with European features, light complexions, and straightened hair. Shirley Works wrote, "I am sick of seeing Negro women 'lift' makeups intended for the 'natural' look on white skin, transformed to the 'unnatural' look on us." She worried that her daughter would see only bleached blonde models in the mass media. "I've looked at white fashion and glamour magazines," she wrote, "and go through mental gymnastics trying to figure what and how much can be appropriated." When *Ebony* ran a cover story called "Are Negro Girls Getting Prettier?" angry letters assailed its choice of models. "Why don't you put some Negro girls on your front page so we can see," fumed one reader, while another sarcastically commented, "It should be titled 'Are Negro Girls Getting Whiter?' " Soon thereafter, *Ebony* featured the revolution in African-American beauty in a story on "The Natural Look," with a twenty-year-old civil rights activist, not a professional model, on the cover.[40]

The natural look was "more than mere style," even to those who were not activists. "I just feel more black and realistic this way," said an art student who no longer straightened her hair, while a model noted that "it was the natural thing to do." Members of an older generation, however, sometimes perceived earlier stereotypes in the new style. "The ladies who are practicing this look are just plain, lazy, nappy-haired females," complained one man. In a Chicago church, a minister spontaneously preached a sermon on a woman with natural hair: "I have spotted something in our midst that is *evil!*" (Ironically, sixty years earlier Madam Walker had struggled to convince the clergy of the morality of her hair-care system.) One *Ebony* reader criticized the natural as a return to primitivism: "Let's not lead our women back to grass huts." Another questioned the reduction of aesthetics to politics. "Why should Negro women be obliged to prove their racial pride by wearing their hair natural?" she wrote. "Why should Negro women have a mission to extol their ancestry by sporting a certain haircut?"[41] The natural look had brought about a reappraisal of black appearance; first as a radical symbol, then as fashionable style, it retained its political associations with black pride, authenticity, and freedom.

The 1960s marked a decisive break in the way American women made and understood their appearances. After that decade, the regime of fashion fractured: Women no longer changed their hemlines, silhouettes, and colors in lockstep response to Paris designers and fashion oracles. Beautifying became highly politicized in a climate where social movements recast personal matters as public issues. The counterculture promoted an ideal of the "natural body," evident in men growing long hair and beards and women rejecting makeup. The natural body was considered authentic, real, erotic, and beautiful, a challenge to the artifice and repression of postwar society. Although not always espousing the philosophical underpinnings of this aesthetic, many high school and college students adopted its look as a form of expression, or simply as fashion.

Animated by the counterculture and the example of black women activists, young white feminists mounted an attack on beauty ideals and the beauty industry. Tellingly, the first public action of the women's liberation movement was a demonstration in 1968 against the Miss America beauty pageant. Protesting women's enslavement to commercial beauty standards, one hundred feminists filled a trash can with makeup, curlers, hair spray, bras, and other beauty aids, and crowned a live sheep America's beauty queen. In her classic, *The Feminine Mystique*, Betty Friedan had already blamed mass consumer culture, including women's magazines and advertising, for deflecting women's aspirations and limiting their roles in society. Only in the late 1960s, however, did feminists indict the beauty industry as a cornerstone of women's oppression.[42]

The Miss America protesters equated the "commercialization of beauty" with the more generalized categories of sexism and racism.

Women succumbed to the "temptation to be a beautiful object," observed activist Dana Densmore; "many of us are scarred by attempts as teenagers to win the promised glamor from cosmetics." Criticizing the dominant view that beautifying fostered women's self-esteem, she wrote: "Somehow it always just looked painted, harsh, worse than ever, and yet real life fell so far short of the ideals already burned into our consciousness that the defeat was bitter too, and neither the plain nor the painted solution was satisfactory." The more women try to achieve beauty and admiration, "the less reality our personality and intellect will have," she argued. "How can anyone take a manikin seriously?"[43] Combining an assault on consumer culture with a new emphasis on patriarchy, these critics charged that the male-dominated capitalist economy manipulated female desires and anxieties in ways that served men's personal and political control of women. Unattainable standards of beauty had an effect at once intense and narcotic: Women were driven into an absorption with appearances, into making themselves the objects of men's visual pleasure. Thus beauty practices simultaneously diverted and excluded women from intellectual work, meaningful social participation, and politics.

Feminists' condemnations of commercialized beauty reached deeply into American culture in the 1970s and after. Many young women began to use makeup more sparingly, with some giving it up entirely. Books on how to make natural cosmetics at home proliferated, their recipes reminiscent of the cosmetic tradition of earlier centuries. By 1980 toy manufacturers came under attack for selling makeup kits designed for young girls. A vast literature indicted the merchandising of women's faces and bodies in the mass media, the growth of plastic surgery, and the pressure to purchase an endless array of preparations.[44]

The "no makeup look" startled cosmetics producers and, according to a Cover Girl publicist, they initially pretended the sweeping attack on beauty products "wasn't happening." But the industry soon regrouped. Responding selectively to elements of the feminist and countercultural critique, manufacturers ingeniously repackaged products and redefined advertising to address the increasingly politicized understanding of appearance. They embraced the natural look with organic cosmetics and invoked the "liberated" woman as a beauty type. Revlon's breezy advertisements for Charlie perfume received praise within the trade press for showing that "women quite obviously had become emancipated." The view manufacturers had long promoted—that identity was an aesthetic choice any woman could put on and wash off—proved surprisingly malleable.[45]

A new focus on scientific skin care as a necessary grooming practice deflected criticism that cosmetics objectified and demeaned women. Introduced by Estee Lauder in 1967, Clinique projected its hygienic, asexual message in a number of ways, from its trade name and antiseptic green packaging, to its neutral color palette and advertising. Its "Twice a Day" ad, likening skin care to the regular use of a toothbrush, focused exclusively on the product, not on glamorous models or sexual situations. "Our consumer doesn't want to live her life through someone else," the company's president explained. "She looks at makeup as information." Clinique became the cosmetic line of choice for many professional women and feminists.[46]

Even Mary Kay Ash, an entrepreneur who gloried in "selling femininity," promoted pink Cadillacs and cosmetics home parties not as a reaction against social change but in recognition of it. Although she criticized feminists for effacing sex differences in the pursuit of equality and opportunity, Ash deliberately reached out to displaced homemakers and other women rocked by the social and economic turmoil of the 1960s and 1970s. Lauding female ability, opening job opportunities in her own organization, addressing women's needs as mothers—all the while avowing women's desire to appear feminine—Mary Kay fused feminist economic aims with traditionalist ideals of womanhood.[47]

Mass-market cosmetics firms responded more slowly and often reluctantly to criticisms from women of color about racist beauty images and exclusionary marketing. They remained financially and psychologically invested in distinctive images that represented both product and corporation. Cover Girl's advertising agency, said one staffer, went to "an extraordinary effort to get a specific look—that look is middle American, it's young, it's fresh, it's clean, it's vibrant." By the late 1960s, that look had narrowed to blonde hair and light skin, typified by celebrity models Cybill Shepherd and Cheryl Tiegs. For many years Cover Girl offered only seven shades of foundation, which suited the complexions of most white women but few women of color. Interviewed in 1991, normally eloquent advertising executives mainly voiced discomfort about discussing the racial implications of the look they had created, a look they knew had alienated a number of black consumers.[48]

Under increased pressure from women of color—and in hope of securing their business—the cosmetics industry translated the political demand for inclusion and diversity into a strategy for market expansion and segmentation. Major white-owned mass-market firms entered the "ethnic" cosmetics field after 1970. As they had in the 1920s, they often masked their identity behind an African-American facade: Alberto-Culver introduced TCB (Taking Care of Business) hair preparations, while Revlon adopted packaging similar to black-owned Soft Sheen, leading Operation PUSH to initiate a boycott of the company. Revlon also introduced Polished Ambers makeup in 1975 specifically for black women, but it did not sell well.[49]

Avon pioneered what proved to be the most successful strategy, extending existing product lines to include a wider range of foundation shades and makeup colors. Market research indicated that most women of color "didn't want to be singled out" with goods identified by race or ethnicity, but preferred to be approached "as an American." Avon also hired African-American sales agents and produced Spanish-language catalogues to improve distribution. By the 1980s, magazines and advertisers had begun to perceive multiculturalism as a fashion aesthetic. "Everybody's all-American," *Vogue* suddenly discovered. "The face of American beauty has changed to reflect the nation's ethnic diversity," the magazine exclaimed. "It's a new ideal . . . and it's big, big business." After the 1990 census revealed that one in four American women described themselves as nonwhite, Prescriptives' All Skins and Maybelline's Shades of You, each with an expanded range of foundation tints, appeared on the market.[50]

Critics with a politicized understanding of beauty often condemn the market, but they do not live outside it. Ironically, the cosmetics industry's parade of products and looks in a time of identity politics has fostered a newly anarchic attitude toward self-display. "In the bombardment of new female images," writer Marcelle Clements comments, "it has become impossible to hold on to a unified esthetic."[51] In recent years, the political aesthetic of the natural has yielded to an intense and multifaceted reconsideration of appearance, not only among women but also among men.

Even as market researchers continued to uncover "closet moisturizer users" who secretly applied Nivea and Oil of Olay, skin treatments specifically for men began to sell well in the 1980s and represented about one-sixth of male toiletries sales overall.[52] Stepping up their efforts to align cosmetics with masculinity, Clinique started to market Skin Supplies for Men in the mid-1980s, with skin-care products similar to their women's offerings but packaged in steel gray and renamed in "simple, direct, clear language." Thus an exfoliating liquid became Scruffing Lotion, the men's moisturizer, M Lotion. Designers at Macy's renovated the men's toiletries department "to create a separate identity . . . a strongly masculine feeling." Manufacturers sought alternative sites for distribution—health clubs, gyms, and sporting goods stores—in a misplaced attempt to avoid a "gay image." Some companies even tried to masculinize rouge or blushers by calling them "bronzers." Guerlain's Terracotta for Men replaced the women's compact with a container shaped like an Apollo spaceship; an ad promised "natural color, so matte and transparent, you'll be the only one to know." Marketing No-Color Mascara to women, Max Factor found that the shiny colorless gel was being purchased by men "who want eye-definition without detection."[53]

Although men's cosmetic practices, particularly involving face makeup, still remain largely hidden from view, there are signs that some cosmetics use may be becoming a more accepted part of male identity. A *Gentlemen's Quarterly* survey in 1989 reported men's awareness of the advantages of a "more polished appearance," and ascribed it to the influx of women into business and the professions; indeed, young professionals constitute the largest market for men's high-priced toiletries and fragrances. The increased visibility of the gay community has also influenced masculine appearance. Vivid feminine makeup styles continue to appear in the ongoing gay tradition of camp and drag. More generally, however, many gay men purchase and use cosmetics as part of a regimen of maintaining physical health and attractiveness. The short hair, muscular body, and attention to skin care adopted by many gay men have been widely promoted by high-style men's magazines, models, and fashion designers. "A man still has to be a man," a fragrance manufacturer insists, but being one—and looking like one—now definitely involves preparations and practices once shunned as unmanly.[54]

For many women, there has been a striking reassessment of the links between identity and appearance. When the Noxell Corporation, maker of Noxzema and Cover Girl, studied the impact of feminism on consumers' views in the late 1980s, they found that "cosmetics still play the same roles in their lives that they've always played." As an advertising executive explained, "It's what allows them to get out the door in the morning, it's what allows them to feel good about themselves, it makes them feel dressed." But if women still sought the pleasures of makeup, they were increasingly suspicious of the therapeutic view of cosmetics. They stressed a new need for personal and financial control in their lives, a striving for security and independence. They criticized beauty advertising—the Cover Girl happily posing for the camera—for failing to reflect the aspirations and looks of "real people" like themselves. When women were asked to invent an obituary for the Cover Girl, they expressed both cynicism and hostility toward her flawless image. As one stated, she "died from too much oil control makeup." To these women, perfection "was something someone else looked for in them, as opposed to what they looked for [in] themselves." Their stated desire to look attractive, now expressed in the language of feminism, had been subtly redefined.[55]

This reassessment has occurred especially among women outside white middle-class culture. It is not that women of color have rejected beauty wares: Indeed, African Americans spend three to five times more on personal-care products than do white Americans. The explanations they offer form a continuity with views expressed decades earlier. "If you're black," said one woman, "you are trying your very best to make sure there is no reason you might be disregarded or thought less of." But in addition, they have begun to question both the mass media's normative beauty ideals and the dominant feminist critique. Latina, Asian, and other women of color have joined black women in exploring the meaning of self, community, and appearance. Long stereotyped as exotic, or excluded altogether from beauty representations, they have announced their refusal to portray white women's "other" and called instead for commercial images in which they could recognize themselves.[56]

The multicultural look, and the self-congratulatory tone of its promotion, has been censured by such critics as bell hooks as a new form of exploitation masquerading as inclusion. Commercial media, in her view, cynically depict racial diversity to profit from a liberal image. African Americans still do not control the terms of their representation, she emphasizes: Models with light complexions and hair weaves still signify African-American beauty in magazines and on television, while those with dark skin or African features are often stereotyped as hypersexual or primitive. Although equally critical of advertising and media, other writers have begun to explore the creativity and pleasures of beautifying among women of color. They have come full circle, recalling the straightened hairstyles and hairdressing rituals of their youth with great poignancy: the smells of hair pressing, the movement of hands expertly applying oils and combs, the talk and laughter of black women in the kitchen or the beauty parlor. "Was it an enactment of a degradation inspired by a bitter inferiority," asks critic Gerald Early, or "a womanly laying on of hands where black women were, in their way, helping themselves to live through and transcend their degradation?"[57]

Women from all walks of life now express an awareness of complexity and ambiguity in the culture of beauty. In Los Angeles in the early 1990s, women of color interviewed by sociologist Natalie Beausoleil attacked both the beauty industry and moralistic white feminists and professional women who insist on "natural" makeup. Students and secretaries alike described the rejection, anger, and self-loathing they have experienced over features that did not match the white, blonde ideal. Yet they also proudly fashioned their looks by drawing upon traditional aesthetic practices and by inventing new styles. Working-class Latinas cherished visible makeup and the art of applying it as part of their cultural heritage. A new sense of choice seems to have surfaced. Some black women wore cornrows, while others who straightened their hair denied that their beauty practices implied white emulation. When asked by the *New York Times* why she dyed her hair blonde, an African-American college student explained, "I just wanted to see how it looked, not because I was trying to be white." This "freeing up of style," as Alvin Poussaint has called it, has incorporated looks formerly despised as inauthentic and suspect into an aesthetic that expresses both individuality and cultural identity.[58]

Nowhere has this "freeing up" been more pointedly rendered than in the lesbian community. In the 1970s, many lesbian feminists adopted the natural aesthetic, simultaneously rejecting the look of heterosexual femininity and the tradition of butch-fem role-playing. By the mid-1980s, however, a new appreciation for camp and drag, and a fervent debate over sexuality, caused a reassessment of androgynous looks. As gay theorists in their academic writings condemned notions of the natural, "lipstick lesbians" appeared all made up on the street. Did they destabilize dominant ideals of beauty and sexuality, or were they sellouts who passed as heterosexual?[59]

Women, gay and straight, claimed self-fashioning as a political right in the 1980s and 1990s. African-American women wearing cornrows and beads, fired from their jobs for not conforming to the corporate image, sued employers for racial discrimination. A few college campuses and municipalities imposed regulations against "lookism" or "looksism." After a boisterous debate, the city council of Santa Cruz, California, passed an ordinance in 1992 barring discrimination based on appearance in employment, housing, and public accommodations. "Because I have a tattoo on my head, I'm treated like a cretin," testified one young woman, protesting employers' refusal to hire her. High school students, sent home from school for appearing in "costume style makeup or hair colorings," also claimed their constitutional rights had been violated. "This is a freedom of speech issue and an issue of identity," said one mother defending her pink-haired daughter.[60]

Even Mary Kay's corporate identity could be turned on its head, albeit briefly, by a zealous Cincinnati distributor calling herself FeyKay, whose Go Grrrrl! Cosmetics for Queers, "the first lesbian on-line cosmetics service," surfaced on the Internet in 1994. FeyKay claimed she was "the only out gay girl in the organization" to serve transsexuals, transvestites, and lipstick lesbians. Stating "we are here, queer and fabulous," FeyKay attacked "the heterosexual hegemony of the makeup industry" that had identified the made-up woman solely with the pursuit of men and marriage, rendering gay men and lesbians invisible. She redefined the Mary Kay home party as "a place for glam slams, insights, and good beauty advice with the possibility of a political cutting edge"; a percentage of the profits would support AIDS research and activism. Significantly, FeyKay did not reject cosmetics but played upon a notion of makeover promoted decades earlier: "Cosmetics are fun, they are about creating identities, representing our ideas about ourselves to others." This view admitted no state of nature: In a society in which looks, display, and goods are pervasive and inescapable, beauty standards could only be disrupted from within.[61]

The public debate over cosmetics today veers noisily between the poles of victimization and self-invention, between the prison of beauty and the play of makeup. The feminist argument continues to be widely heard. Naomi Wolf's recent best-seller *The Beauty Myth* recapitulated the 1960s critique for contemporary women. Beauty standards, Wolf argued, are a "political weapon against women's advancement," a "violent backlash against feminism." Through them, a capitalist and patriarchal "power elite" controls modern women who have begun to make political and economic gains. Women who are beautiful or who achieve beauty according to the imposed standards are rewarded; those who cannot or choose not to be beautiful are punished, economically and socially.[62]

Certainly this critique has increased women's skepticism toward the beauty industry, but it has hardly stopped them from buying cosmetics, reading fashion magazines, trying out new looks, and sharing makeup tips with friends. The connections between appearance, identity, and consumption, forged initially by women beauty culturists at the beginning of the century, have inexorably tightened at its end. Moreover, the cosmetics industry has hastened to absorb and profit from the challenges mounted against it, even as it produces the normative ideals of beauty for which it is criticized. If image and style have long offered women a way to express cultural identities, now those identities offer business a new set of images to sell.

Still, the power of those commercial beauty images and the vigorous critique directed against them obscure the many forces that shape the cultural practice of beautifying. Employers make appearance a job requirement; families and peer cultures socialize girls into the necessity of maintaining a public face; differences in social class, region, and ethnicity mark themselves on eyes and lips. But the culture of beauty has never been only a regimen of self-appraisal and surveillance. Women have used makeup to declare themselves—to announce their adult status, sexual allure, youthful spirit, political beliefs—and even to proclaim their *right* to self-definition. As in the past, cosmetics offer aesthetic, sensory, and psychological pleasures to those pressed by the obligations of home and work. And women still perceive beautifying as a domain of sociability, creativity, and play.

When women put on a face, they continue to express ideas of naturalness and artifice, authenticity and deception, propriety and danger, modernity and tradition. Making up remains a gesture bound to perceptions of self and body, the intimate and the social—a gesture rooted in women's everyday lives.

Notes

ABBREVIATIONS FOR NOTES

BCL   Bella C. Landauer Collection, New-York Historical Society
CAB   Claude A. Barnett Papers, CHS
CHS   Chicago Historical Society
CW   Carl Weeks Papers, University of Iowa Library
DD   Dorothy Dignam Papers, SHSW
GLB   *Godey's Lady's Book*
JWT   J. Walter Thompson Company Archives, Hartman Center for Advertising History, Duke University Library
LHJ   *Ladies' Home Journal*
MCJW   Madam C. J. Walker Papers, Indiana Historical Society
MPA   Manufacturing Perfumers Association
MFMB   Max Factor Museum of Beauty, Hollywood, California
MFPG   Max Factor Collection, The Procter & Gamble Company, Cincinnati
NMAH   National Museum of American History, Smithsonian Institution
NNBL   National Negro Business League
NWA   N. W. Ayer Advertising Collection, Archives Center, NMAH
PI   *Printers' Ink*
SHSW   State Historical Society of Wisconsin, Madison
TR   *Toilet Requisites*
WCBA   Warshaw Collection of Business Americana, Archives Center, NMAH

INTRODUCTION

1. *Mademoiselle* 7 (June 1938): 13. John J. Pollock, "Smart Merchandising and Fashion Tie-Ups Multiply Volupté Sales," *Sales Management*, 20 April 1939, 17.
2. See, for instance, Naomi Wolf, *The Beauty Myth* (New York: Morrow, 1991); Sandra Lee Bartky, *Femininity and Domination* (New York: Routledge, 1990); Dean MacCannell and Juliet Flower MacCannell, "The Beauty System," in Nancy Armstrong and Leonard Tennenhouse, eds., *The Ideology of Conduct* (New York: Methuen, 1987), 206–38. For a more complex view, see Susan Bordo, *Unbearable Weight: Feminism, Western Culture and the Body* (Berkeley: Univ. of California Press, 1993).
3. For insights into women, modernity, and consumption, see Anne Friedberg, *Window Shopping: Cinema and the Postmodern* (Berkeley: Univ. of California Press, 1993); Gilles Lipovetsky, *The Empire of Fashion: Dressing Modern Democracy* (Princeton: Princeton Univ. Press, 1994); Victoria de Grazia with Ellen Furlough, ed., *The Sex of Things: Gender and Consumption in Historical Perspective* (Berkeley: Univ. of California Press, 1996); Hilary Radner, *Shopping Around: Feminine Culture and the Pursuit of Pleasure* (New York: Routledge, 1995); Janet Wolff, *Feminine Sentences: Essays on Women and Culture* (Berkeley: Univ. of California Press, 1990). See also Judith L. Goldstein, "The Female Aesthetic Community," in George E. Marcus and Fred R. Myers, eds., *The Traffic in Culture* (Berkeley: Univ. of California Press, 1995), 310–29.

CHAPTER ONE

1. Helen Crawford, "Beauty Culture for the Belle of '64," *TR* 14 (April 1929): 26.
2. P. V. Schenck, "Chronic Lead Poisoning Following the Use of Cosmetics—With Cases," *St. Louis Courier of Medicine and Collateral Sciences* 1 (1879): 514–16; Laird's advertisement, *Harper's Bazar* 14 (9 July 1881): 447.
3. *The Book of Health and Beauty, or the Toilette of Rank and Fashion* (London: Joseph Thomas, 1837), xvii; *Etiquette for Ladies* (Philadelphia: Lea & Blanchard, 1839), 126.
4. Constance, Countess de la Warr, ed., *The English Hous-wife* (1653: reprint, London, Grosvenor Library, n.d.), 1, 59–68; Gervase Markham, *The English Housewife* (1615; reprint, Kingston, Ont.: McGill-Queens Univ. Press, 1986), 125, 131. This history is explored in Virginia Smith, "The Popularisation of Medical Knowledge: The Case of Cosmetics," *Society for the Social History of Medicine Bulletin* no. 39 (1986): 12–15; Londa Schiebinger, *The Mind Has No Sex? Women in the Origins of Modern Science* (Cambridge: Harvard Univ. Press, 1989), 112–16.
5. Henry Howard, *England's Newest Way in All Sorts of Cookery*, 5th ed. (London: J. Knapton, 1726), 180; Nicholas Culpeper, *Pharmacopoeia Londinensis; or, The London Dispensatory* (1650; Boston: John Allen, 1720), 297.
6. John Gunn, *Gunn's Domestic Medicine* (1830; reprint, Knoxville: Univ. of Tennessee Press, 1986), 225. See also Peter Smith, *The Indian Doctor's Dispensatory*

(1813; reprint, Cincinnati: Bulletin of the Lloyd Library, 1901). On African-American grooming practices, Mamie Garvin Fields, *Lemon Swamp and Other Places* (New York: Free Press, 1983), 187, 218; Shane White and Graham White, *Stylin': African-American Expressive Culture from Its Beginnings to the Zoot Suit* (Ithaca: Cornell Univ. Press, 1998); Barbara M. Starke et al., eds., *African American Dress and Adornment* (Dubuque, Iowa: Kendall/Hunt, 1990). On beauty in West Africa, see Sylvia Ardyn Boone, *Radiance from the Waters: Ideals of Feminine Beauty in Mende Art* (New Haven: Yale Univ. Press, 1986).

7. Beatrice Roeder, *Chicano Folk Medicine from Los Angeles, California* (Berkeley: Univ. of California Press, 1988), 298–99; Gunn, *Gunn's Domestic Medicine*, 225. See also Clarence Meyer, *American Folk Medicine* (New York: Thomas Y. Crowell, 1973), 224–28.

8. Receipt Books of Mrs. Lowell and Mrs. Charles Smith, Garrison Family Papers, Sophia Smith Collection, Smith College; Eleanor Custis Lewis to Elizabeth Bordley Gibson, 21 October 1825, Mt. Vernon Collection (TS courtesy Patricia Brady); Patricia Brady Schmit, ed., *Nelly Custis Lewis's Housekeeping Book* (New Orleans, 1982), 80–81.

9. Smith, "Popularisation of Medical Knowledge"; Guenter B. Risse et al., eds., *Medicine Without Doctors: Home Health Care in American History* (New York: Science History Publ., 1977).

10. Dozens of encyclopedias and ladies' guides were published in the mid-nineteenth century. Typical were Sarah Josepha Hale, *Mrs. Hale's Receipts for the Million* (Philadelphia: T. B. Peterson, 1857); Thomas Webster and Mrs. Parkes, *The American Family Encyclopedia of Useful Knowledge* (New York: Derby & Jackson, 1859); Eliza W. R. Farrar, *The Young Lady's Friend* (1836; reprint, New York: Arno, 1974); *The Toilette of Health, Beauty, and Fashion* (Boston: Allen & Ticknor, 1834). See also Eleanor Lowenstein, *Bibliography of American Cookery Books, 1742–1860* (Worcester: American Antiquarian Society, 1972).

11. Owsei Temkin, *Galenism: Rise and Decline of a Medical Philosophy* (Ithaca: Cornell Univ. Press, 1973), 17, 164–79; Roy Porter and Dorothy Porter, *In Sickness and in Health: The British Experience, 1650–1850* (London: Fourth Estate, 1988); Margaret Pelling, "Appearance and Reality: Barber-Surgeons, the Body and Disease," in A. L. Beier and Roger Finley, eds., *London 1500–1700: The Making of the Metropolis* (London: Longman, 1986), 82–112. On humoralism's continued salience, see Davydd J. Greenwood, *The Taming of Evolution* (Ithaca: Cornell Univ. Press, 1984), 99–101; Joanne Finkelstein, *The Fashioned Self* (Philadelphia: Temple Univ. Press, 1991).

12. Sir Hugh Plat, *Delights for Ladies* (London: William Dugard, 1651), n. pag.

13. *Ibid.* [Pierre Buc'holz,] *The Toilet of Flora* (London: J. Murray, 1775), 13, 59; Markham, *English Housewife*, 125.

14. On the humors, Mrs. A. Walker, *Female Beauty* (New York: Scofield & Voorhies, 1840), 181. For recipes, see L. E. Craig, *True Politeness* (Philadelphia, 1848), 45; Sir James Clark, *The Ladies Guide to Beauty* (New York: Dick & Fitzgerald, 1858), 92. On the continuing belief in these practices, see "On Cosmetics," *Penny Magazine* 7 (8 December 1838): 477; Wayland D. Hand et al., *Popular Be-*

liefs and Superstitions: A Compendium of American Folklore, vol. 1 (Boston: G. K. Hall, 1981), 162, 171, 230. On medieval recipes, see Fenja Gunn, *The Artificial Face: A History of Cosmetics* (London: David & Charles, 1973), 66, 100–101.

15. Culpeper, *Pharmacopoeia*, 298; Gunn, *Domestic Medicine*, 110–11; Craig, *True Politeness*, 43; Walker, *Female Beauty*, 61. On hygienic regimen, see Ginnie Smith, "Prescribing the Rules of Health: Self-help and Advice in the Late Eighteenth Century," in Roy Porter, ed., *Patients and Practitioners: Lay Perceptions of Medicine in Pre-Industrial Society* (London: Cambridge Univ. Press, 1985), 249–82; Susan Cayleff, *Wash and Be Healed: The Water-cure Movement and Women's Health* (Philadelphia: Temple Univ. Press, 1987).

16. *Attractions for Ladies* (n.p., n.d.); Potter Drug and Chemical Co., *Diseases of the Skin and Blood and How to Cure Them* (Boston, 1885), Cosmetics, WCBA.

17. *The American Family Keepsake or People's Practical Cyclopedia* (Boston, 1849), 73; *Arts Revealed, and Universal Guide* (New York: H. Dayton, 1860), 11; Marcus Lafayette Byrn, *Detection of Fraud and Protection of Health* (Philadelphia: Lippincott, Grambo, 1852), 139–40.

18. Edward S. Townsend formula book (1860–1897), 39, 81, Hagley Museum and Library. See also Wm. King's Receipt Book (1842–[1901]), Hagley Museum and Library; George H. White, Pharmacist's Book of Recipes ([1857–1872]), Special Collections, Rutgers University Library; Philadelphia College of Pharmacy, comp., *The Druggist's Manual; Being a Price Current of Drugs* (Philadelphia: Solomon W. Conrad, 1826).

19. George E. Putney, Druggist's Invoice Book (1857–1882); Bryan Hough Daybook (1856–1861), Special Collections, Rutgers University Library. See also Edwin Jennings Stores Accounts, books 1 and 2, Rare and Manuscript Collections, Cornell University Library.

20. *TR* 16 (April 1931): 51. Compare cosmetic stock in John Day & Co., *Catalogue of Drugs, Chymical and Galenical Preparations* (Philadelphia: Dunlop, 1771); Apollos W. Harrison, *Harrison's Columbian Perfumery, Cash Prices* (Philadelphia, 1855), Scrapbook 18, BCL; W. H. Schieffelin & Co., *General Prices Current of Foreign and Domestic Drugs* (New York, March 1881). See also Nydia M. King, *A Selection of Primary Sources for the History of Pharmacy in the U.S.* (Madison: American Institute for the History of Pharmacy, 1987).

21. T. W. Dyott, *Approved Patent and Family Medicines* (Philadelphia, 1814), 22.

22. F. A. Souillard, *The Pharmaceutic Practical Recipe Book* (New York, 1849), i–ii, 66–71, 82–83; H. Dussauce, *A Practical Guide for the Perfumer* (Philadelphia: Henry Carey Baird, 1864), 41; Lois Banner, *American Beauty* (Chicago: Univ. of Chicago Press, 1983), 43.

23. *New York Daily Tribune*, 4 June 1845. On the history of patent medicines, see James Harvey Young, *The Toadstool Millionaires* (Princeton: Princeton Univ. Press, 1961).

24. Carroll & Hutchinson, *Things of Beauty, Set with Gems of Verse* (New York: C. W. Benedict, 1853), 48, 54.

25. *New York Daily Tribune*, 3 June 1845. On millworkers' appearance, see Thomas Dublin, *Women at Work: The Transformation of Work and Community in Lowell, Massachusetts, 1826–1860* (New York: Columbia Univ. Press, 1979), 8.

26. *Humbug: A Look at Some Popular Impositions* (New York: S. F. French, 1859), 39; H. Burchstead Skinner, *The American Prize-Book* (Boston: J. B. Hall, 1853), 160.

27. Lola Montez, *The Arts of Beauty; or Secrets of a Lady's Toilet,* (New York, 1858), xii–xiii. For warnings on hazardous cosmetics, see Webster and Parkes, *American Family Encyclopedia,* 1013; A. I. Mathews & Co., *Hints on Various Subjects Connected with Our Business* (Buffalo, 1856), 72–73.

28. Lydia Maria Child, *Letters from New York,* Second Series (New York: C. S. Francis, 1845), 248–50. On the early meaning of commercial cosmetics, see Pelling, "Appearance and Reality."

29. On eighteenth-century cosmetics, see Gilbert Vail, *A History of Cosmetics in America* (New York: Toilet Goods Association, 1947), 34–38, 49–53, 74–78; Fenya Gunn, *The Artificial Face,* 104, 111. On the general cultural practices of the period, see Richard L. Bushman, *The Refinement of America* (New York: Knopf, 1992).

30. On male display, see David Kuchta, "The Making of the Self-Made Man: Class, Clothing, and English Masculinity, 1688–1832," in Victoria de Grazia, ed., *The Sex of Things: Gender and Consumption in Historical Perspective* (Berkeley: Univ. of California Press, 1996), 54–78. On Franklin, see John Kasson, *Rudeness and Civility: Manners in Nineteenth-Century Urban America* (New York: Hill & Wang, 1990), 29. On Van Buren, see John Niven, *Martin Van Buren: The Romantic Age of American Politics* (New York: Oxford Univ. Press, 1983), 462. For Ogle's speech, *The Regal Splendor of the President's Palace* (Boston, 1840).

31. Quoted in William R. Leach, *True Love and Perfect Union: The Feminist Reform of Sex and Society* (New York: Basic, 1980), 217; J. Scoffern, "Cosmetics," *Belgravia* 4 (December 1867): 208. For men's toiletries, see J. C. Schenk, *The Barbers' Recipe Book* (Buffalo: Mathews, Northrup, 1884); Strutz and Clottu Company, *Our Drummer* (n.p., n.d.), 20–27, Barbering, WCBA; see also shaving and toiletries artifacts in Medical Sciences Division, NMAH.

32. "Woman's Beauty: How to Get and Keep It," *Harper's* 37 (1868): 116. On feminine ideals, see Banner, *American Beauty;* Karen Halttunen, *Confidence Men and Painted Women: A Study of Middle-class Culture in America, 1830–1870* (New Haven: Yale Univ. Press, 1982), 56–91, 158–63.

33. Alexander Walker, *Beauty; Illustrated Chiefly by an Analysis and Classification of Beauty in Woman* (New York: Henry G. Langley, 1844), xix, 31. See also Wilson Flagg, *Analysis of Female Beauty* (Boston: March, Capen, & Lyon, 1833). On physiognomy, Patrizia Magli, "The Face and the Soul," in Michel Feher, ed., *Fragments for a History of the Human Body, Part Two* (New York: Zone, 1989), 86–127.

34. Hannah Lindley Murray and Mary Murray, *The American Toilet* (1827; reprint, Washington, D.C.: W. Ballantyne, 1867), n. pag. "Something About Fairs," *Harper's Bazar* (17 February 1872): 131.

35. Emma C. Embury, "Lucy Franklin," *GLB* 29 (July 1844): 32, 35. Also "Beauty, and How to Gain It" [series], *GLB* 62 (April 1861): 367–68; (May 1861), 462–63; (June 1861): 557–58. See the excellent analysis in Halttunen, *Confidence Men and Painted Women,* 88–89.

36. Mary F. Armstrong, *On Habits and Manners* (Hampton, Va.: Normal School Press, 1888), 31.

37. Countess de Calabrella, *The Ladies' Science of Etiquette and Handbook of the Toilet* (Philadelphia: T. B. Peterson, [1860]), 45; Mrs. Walker, *Female Beauty,* color plates.

38. Thomas Tuke, *A Discourse Against Painting and Tincturing of Women* (London: Edward Marchant, 1616), 2; Frances E. Dolan, "Taking the Pencil out of God's Hand: Art, Nature, and the Face-Painting Debate in Early Modern England," *PMLA* 108 (March 1993): 224–39 (Donne quoted on 233). The Parliamentary Act is quoted in Gunn, *Artificial Face,* 124. On female deception, see Edward Ward, *Female Policy Detected; or the Arts of a Designing Woman Laid Open* (New York, 1792). On cosmetics and witchcraft, see Thomas Hill, *Natural and Artificial Conclusions* (London: A. M., 1670), n. pag.

39. Mrs. Walker, *Female Beauty,* 13. On Jezebel, John Peter Lange, *A Commentary on the Holy Scriptures; Vol. VI of the Old Testament* (New York: Charles Scribner's Sons, 1887), 99–108; II Kings 9:30–37; Ezekiel 23:40–49.

40. George G. Foster, *New York by Gas-Light and Other Urban Sketches,* ed. by Stuart M. Blumin (1850; reprint, Berkeley: Univ. of California Press, 1990), 154; Mary Ryan, *Women in Public* (Baltimore: Johns Hopkins Univ. Press), 29. The Hangtown Gals ballad is in Marion S. Goldman, *Gold Diggers and Silver Miners: Prostitution and Social Life on the Comstock Lode* (Ann Arbor: Univ. of Michigan Press, 1981), 100.

41. James D. McCabe, *Lights and Shadows of New York Life* (Philadelphia: National Publishing Co., 1872), 154. George Ellington, *The Women of New York* (1869; reprint, New York: Arno, 1972), 42–51, 82–90. Caroline Lee Hentz, "The Beauty Transformed," *GLB* 21 (November 1840): 194–202; Hentz, "The Fatal Cosmetic," *GLB* 18 (June 1839): 265–79; S.S.B., "Not a Puff for Quack Remedies," *GLB* 65 (July 1862): 40–42.

42. H. J. Rodgers, *Twenty-Three Years Under a Sky-Light, or Life and Experiences of a Photographer* (Hartford: H. J. Rodgers, 1872), 192–94; Arnold J. Cooley, *The Toilet and Cosmetics Arts in Ancient and Modern Times* (1866; reprint, New York: Burt Franklin, 1970), 295.

43. Ellington, *Women of New York,* 230. On these cultural anxieties, see Carroll Smith-Rosenberg, *Disorderly Conduct* (New York: Oxford Univ. Press, 1985).

44. Robert F. Lucid, ed., *The Journal of Richard Henry Dana, Jr.* (Cambridge: Harvard Univ. Press, 1968), 79–80.

45. Walter M. Merrill, ed., *The Letters of William Lloyd Garrison,* vol. 1 (Cambridge: Harvard Univ. Press, 1971), 78–79.

46. *Ibid.,* 329, 351.

47. Harry T. Finck, *Romantic Love and Personal Beauty* (New York: Macmillan, 1887), 458; "Notions of Personal Beauty in Different Countries," *Penny Magazine* 14 (6 December 1845): 475–77; Captain Mayne Reid, *Odd People* (Boston: Ticknor and Fields, 1864).

48. Robert W. Shufeldt, *Indian Types of Beauty,* pamphlet reprinted from *The American Field,* 1891, in Rare and Manuscript Collections, Cornell University Library.

See also Melissa Banta and Curtis M. Hinsley, *From Site to Sight: Anthropology, Photography and the Power of Imagery* (Cambridge: Peabody Museum Press, 1986).

49. Finck, *Romantic Love and Personal Beauty,* 43–48, 60–62, 452–59.

50. Edward M. Estabrook, *The Ferrotype, and How to Make It* (Cincinnati: Gatchel & Hyatt, 1872), 41, 174–75, 181; L. C. Champney (1843) quoted in Beaumont Newhall, *The Daguerreotype in America* (New York: New York Graphic Society, 1961), 69; Rodgers, *Twenty-Three Years Under a Sky-Light,* 177, 217.

51. George P. Rawick, ed., *The American Slave, A Composite Autobiography,* vol. 6 (Westport, Conn.: Greenwood, 1972), 44–45, 47, 130.

52. Harriet Jacobs, *Incidents in the Life of a Slave Girl* (Cambridge: Harvard Univ. Press, 1987), 11. See also White and White, *Stylin';* Gwendolyn Robinson, "Class, Race, and Gender: A Transcultural Theoretical and Sociohistorical Analysis of Cosmetic Institutions and Practices to 1920" (Ph.D. diss., Univ. of Illinois Chicago, 1984), ch. 2.

53. See, e.g., Eric Lott, *Love and Theft: Blackface Minstrelsy and the American Working Class* (New York: Oxford Univ. Press, 1995); Robert Jay, *The Trade Card in Nineteenth-Century America* (Columbia: Univ. of Missouri Press, 1987); Stephen Jay Gould, *The Mismeasure of Man* (New York: Norton, 1981); and on the origins of racial stereotypes, Winthrop Jordan, *White over Black: American Attitudes Towards the Negro, 1550–1812* (New York: Norton, 1977). Gussie Davis, "When They Straighten All the Colored People's Hair," in *Remember That Song,* vol. 3, no. 8 (October 1983).

54. Robert Tomer, *The Bazar Book of Decorum* (New York: Harper, 1876), 51; *Beauty: Its Attainment and Preservation* (New York: Butterick, 1890), 232–33. See also Clark, *Ladies' Guide to Beauty,* iv–v; E. G. Storke, *Family and Householder's Guide* (Auburn, NY: Auburn Publ. Co., 1859), 179. Cf. Hagan's Magnolia Balm advertisement, Cosmetics, WCBA.

55. Samuel Otter, "A Case of Measure for Measure," paper presented at the American Studies Association Annual Meeting, November 1991. See also Hazel Carby, *Reconstructing Womanhood: The Emergence of the Afro-American Woman Novelist* (New York: Oxford Univ. Press, 1987), 121–59.

56. Dr. Gouraud's Oriental Cream advertisement, in J. W. Hartz, comp., *Phillips' Elite Directory, 1881–1882* (New York: W. Phillips, 1881), 495.

CHAPTER TWO

1. Harold Earl Hammond, ed., *Diary of a Union Lady, 1861–1865* (New York: Funk & Wagnalls, 1962), 134, 321–22, 331–32.

2. *Ibid.,* 322; Allan Nevins and Milton Halsey Thomas, eds., *The Diary of George Templeton Strong,* vol. 1 (New York: Macmillan, 1952), 313, 317; Louis Auschincloss, *The Hone and Strong Diaries of Old Manhattan* (New York: Abbeville, 1989), 126.

3. Nevins and Thomas, *Diary of George Templeton Strong,* 334–35, 327.

4. C. H. Crandall, "What Men Think of Women's Dress," *North American Review* 161 (August 1895): 253; Hilary Evans, *Harlots, Whores and Hookers: A History of Prostitution* (New York: Taplinger, 1979), 157; Alexander Walker, *Beauty; Illustrated Chiefly by an Analysis and Classification of Beauty in Woman* (New York: Henry G. Langley, 1844), 329–39; John Kasson, *Rudeness and Civility: Manners in Nineteenth-Century Urban America* (New York: Hill & Wang, 1990), 96–100.

5. N. P. Willis, *The Convalescent* (1859), quoted in Beaumont Newhall, *The Daguerreotype in America* (New York: New York Graphic Society, 1961), 78.

6. John F. Marszalek, ed., *The Diary of Miss Emma Holmes, 1861–1866* (Baton Rouge: Louisiana State Univ. Press, 1979), 192–93, 213–14, 280–81, 290, 331.

7. On beauty ideals, see Lois Banner, *American Beauty* (Chicago: Univ. of Chicago Press, 1983); Karen Halttunen, *Confidence Men and Painted Women* (New Haven: Yale Univ. Press, 1982); Robert C. Allen, *Horrible Prettiness: Burlesque and American Culture* (Chapel Hill: Univ. of North Carolina Press, 1991). On fashion extremes, see *GLB* 78 (March 1869): 296; *New York Times*, 18 October 1868, 22 November 1868, 28 March 1869.

8. Frances Trollope, *Domestic Manners of the Americans* (New York: Knopf, 1949), 299–300; *TR* 9 (January 1925): 41; Marie Mott Gage, *How to Cultivate Beauty* (pamphlet; n.p., 1893).

9. Pamela Herr and Mary Lee Spence, eds., *The Letters of Jessie Benton Frémont* (Urbana: Univ. of Illinois Press, 1993), 466; Joseph H. Thatcher credit ledger, 1880–1885, Portsmouth Atheneum, Portsmouth, N.H. For formulas, see Charles E. Hamlin and Charles Warren, *Hamlin's Formulae, or Every Druggist His Own Perfumer* (Baltimore: Edward B. Read & Son, 1885), 60.

10. James H. Hutchinson, "On Two Cases in Which Cerebral Symptoms Were Produced by the Use of White Lead as a Cosmetic," *Philadelphia Medical Times* 4 (17 January 1874): 242; P. V. Schenck, "Chronic Lead Poisoning Following the Use of Cosmetics—with Cases," *St. Louis Courier of Medicine and Collateral Sciences* 1 (1879): 506–18; L. A. Sayre, "Three Cases of Lead Palsy from the Use of a Cosmetic Called 'Laird's Bloom of Youth,'" *Transactions of the American Medical Association* 20 (1869): 563–72.

11. Martin Freeman in *Anglo-American Magazine* (1859), quoted in Dorothy Sterling, ed., *We Are Your Sisters* (New York: Norton, 1984), 214. See Graham White and Shane White, *Stylin': African-American Expressive Culture from Its Beginnings to the Zoot Suit* (Ithaca: Cornell Univ. Press, 1998).

12. See Crane & Co. advertisement, *Washington Bee*, 25 May 1901; Hartona advertisement, *Colored American Magazine* (January 1901): 242.

13. See the use of the term "makeup" in Robert Tomer, *The Bazar Book of Decorum* (New York: Harper, 1876), 130–31.

14. See David Scobey, "Anatomy of the Promenade: The Politics of Bourgeois Sociability in Nineteenth-Century New York," *Social History* 17 (January 1992): 203–27; William R. Leach, *Land of Desire: Merchants, Power, and the Rise of a New American Culture* (New York: Pantheon, 1993). For a theory of performance and identity, see Judith Butler, *Gender Trouble* (New York: Routledge, 1990).

15. Zona Gale (1885) quoted in Ella Matson Andrews, arr. *Century of Fashion* (TS,

Lombard, Ill., 1909), n. pag., Sophia Smith Collection, Smith College. On the rise of fashion, see Banner, *American Beauty;* Claudia Kidwell and Margaret Christman, *Suiting Everyone: The Democratization of Clothing in America* (Washington, D.C.: Smithsonian Inst. Press, 1974).

16. Guild quoted in David Jaffee, " 'One of the Primitive Sort': Portrait Makers of the Rural North, 1760–1860," in Steven Hahn and Jonathan Prude, eds., *The Countryside in the Age of Capitalist Transformation* (Chapel Hill: Univ. of North Carolina Press, 1985), 110. Hammond, *Diary of a Union Lady,* 84–85; H. J. Rodgers, *Twenty-Three Years Under a Sky-Light, or Life and Experiences of a Photographer* (Hartford: H. J. Rodgers, 1872), 173. Abigail Solomon-Godeau, "The Legs of the Countess," *October* no. 39 (Winter 1986): 77; Marszalek, *Miss Emma Holmes,* 84–85, 210. On mirrors, see Kasson, *Rudeness and Civility,* 166.

17. Alan Trachtenberg, *Reading American Photographs* (New York: Hill & Wang, 1989), 14–70; Elizabeth Anne McCauley, *A. A. E. Disderi and the Carte de Visite Portrait Photograph* (New Haven: Yale Univ. Press, 1985). On tintypes, Edward M. Estabrook, *The Ferrotype, and How to Make It* (Cincinnati: Gretchel & Hyatt, 1872). See also "Photographic Eminence," *Humphrey's Journal* 16 (15 July 1864): 93; "Photographic Albums," *GLB* 64 (February 1862): 208.

18. Trachtenberg, *Reading American Photographs,* 40; William Welling, *Photography in America: The Formative Years, 1839–1900* (New York: Crowell, 1978), 66; *The Ferrotyper's Guide* (New York: Scoville Manufacturing Co., 1873), 84. See also "Chip," *How to Sit for Your Photograph* (Philadelphia: Benerman & Wilson, [1872]).

19. Mrs. A. M. Richards, *Memories of a Grandmother* (Boston: Gould & Lincoln, 1854), 13; *Photographic Art-Journal* 1 (August 1851): 212. See also Harold Francis Pfister, *Facing the Light: Historic American Portrait Daguerreotypes* (Washington: Smithsonian Inst. Press, 1978), 21–22; C.A.H., "Daguerreotypes," *GLB* 63 (August 1861), 110.

20. Henry Peach Robinson, *The Studio; and What to Do in It* (New York: Scoville Manufacturing Co., 1885), 120; James F. Ryder, *Voigtländer and I: In Pursuit of Shadow Catching* (Cleveland: Cleveland Printing & Publ. Co., 1902), 232. See also *The Art-Union* 10 (1848): 238; S. D. Humphrey, *American Hand Book of the Daguerreotype* (1858; reprint, New York: Arno, 1973), 50; Levi L. Hill, *A Treatise on Daguerreotype* (1850; reprint, New York: Arno, 1973), 57–58.

21. Robinson, *The Studio,* 117. *New York Times* (1885) quoted in Jeanne Moudoussamy-Ashe, *Viewfinders: Black Women Photographers* (New York: Dodd Mead, 1986), 14. Rodgers, *Twenty-Three Years Under a Sky-Light.*

22. Olive Logan, *Apropos of Women and Theaters* (New York: Carleton, 1869), 135. On performance and makeup, see Olive Logan, *The Mimic World and Public Exhibitions* (Philadelphia: New World, 1871), 78–79, 570. On women performers, see Allen, *Horrible Prettiness;* Faye Dudden, *Women in the American Theater* (New Haven: Yale Univ. Press, 1996).

23. "Cartes de Visite," *American Journal of Photography* (April 1862): 17. On celebrity photographs, see "Photographic Eminence," 93; Logan, *Mimic World,* 219. For an album that mixed family and celebrity photographs, see Swain Family Album, Visual Studies Workshop, Rochester, New York.

24. "Photographs of a Few Celebrated Artists," *American Journal of Photography* 9 (1863): 565; *Humphrey's Journal* 12 (15 February 1861), 305. For actresses in cosmetics ads, see *Harper's Bazar* 14 (2 July 1881): 430–31; Mrs. C. Thompson, Mrs. Langtry's Secret of Beauty trade card, Cosmetics, WCBA. On lighting, Richard Hudnut, *Twentieth Century Toilet Hints* (New York, 1899), 28, Strong Museum, Rochester. On tableaux vivants, S. L. Louis, *Decorum: A Pratical Treatise on Etiquette and Dress* (New York: Union Publishing House, 1882), 361.

25. Brown, Sherbrook & Co., *Scrap Book for Homely Women Only* (Boston 1884), 68; A. I. Mathews & Co., *Hints on Various Subjects Connected with Our Business* (Buffalo, 1856), 79. *Julian Eltinge Magazine and Beauty Hints* (1913), 60, Scrapbook 182, Robinson Locke Collection, New York Public Library.

26. On women as consumers, see Ellen Garvey, *The Adman in the Parlor* (New York: Oxford, 1996); Susan Strasser, *Never Done: A History of American Housework* (New York: Pantheon, 1982), 242–62.

27. Zion City General Stores catalog (Chicago, 1907), 16–18; Chicago House Wrecking Co., *The Price Wrecker*, Catalog #167 (1912), 700, Dry Goods, WCBA. See also Siegel, Cooper & Co., *Original and Household Recipes* (Chicago: S. Ettlinger, n.d.), CHS; Brown, Sherbrook, *Scrap Book for Homely Women Only*, 68. On expenditures, *TR* 1 (June 1916): 12; 1 (May 1916): 22–23. On secret use of cosmetics, see Irenaeu P. Davis, *Hygiene for Girls* (New York: D. Appleton, 1899), 172.

28. *LHJ* 8 (September 1891): 12. On readers' letters, see Helen Woodward, *The Lady Persuaders* (New York: Ivan Obolensky, 1960), 106. Mary Ellen Waller [Zuckerman], "Popular Women's Magazines, 1890–1917" (Ph.D. diss., Columbia University, 1987), warns of methodological problems with these sources.

29. For wholesalers, see W. H. Schiefellin & Co., *General Prices Current of Foreign and Domestic Drugs, Medicines, Chemicals .'. .* (New York, March 1881); McKesson & Robbins, *Prices Current of Drugs and Druggists' Articles* (New York: Thitchener & Glastaeter, 1872); Peter Van Schaack & Sons, *Annual Price Current* (Chicago: J. M. W. Jones, 1899). On merchant druggists, Hance Brothers and White, *How to Be a Druggist; How to Make Money on and by Agreeable Trifles* (Philadelphia, 1892), 8, 13–14; Edward Kremers and George Urdang, *Kremers and Urdang's History of Pharmacy*, 4th ed. (Philadelphia: J. B. Lippincott, 1987), 290–301. On distribution, see Alfred D. Chandler, Jr., *The Visible Hand: The Managerial Revolution in American Business* (Cambridge: Harvard Univ. Press, 1977), ch. 7.

30. MPA, *Proceedings of the Fifteenth Annual Meeting* (New York, 1909), 25. Sears, Roebuck, and Co., *Catalog*, no. 105 (Chicago, 1897). See also the catalogues of R. H. Macy & Co., 1877–78, 1884–85; B. Altman & Co., 1882–1912 ser.; John Wanamaker, 1893–94, 1899–1900, all in Dry Goods, WCBA. On department store merchandising, see Leach, *Land of Desire*, 15–150.

31. Ozonized Ox Marrow Company advertisement, *Voice of the Negro* (June 1905); Lyon Manufacturing Co. pamphlets, Patent Medicine, WCBA. The early growth of the trade can be gleaned from ads in the *Washington Bee*, 1882–1905; *Colored American Magazine* (1900–09); *Voice of the Negro* (1904–07). See also National Negro Business League, *Report of the Second Annual Convention* (1901), 29; *Re-*

port of the Sixth Annual Convention (1905), 67–75, 119–21. On advertising, G.A. Sykes, "The Advertising of the Colored Race," *PI* 8 (1893): 340–42; Vanessa Broussard [Simmons], "Afro-American Images in Advertising, 1880–1920" (M.A. thesis, George Washington University, 1987).

32. On the Richmond entrepreneurs, *Richmond Planet*, 1895–1901; *Washington Bee*, 11 May 1901; personal communication, Greg Kimball, Valentine Museum, Richmond, Virginia, 2 November 1994.

33. Mary P. Welch letter, "Should Women Paint" contest, *Baltimore Sun*, 25 August 1912.

34. *Madeleine: An Autobiography* (1919; reprint, New York: Arno Press, 1980), 60, 151; Syracuse Moral Survey Committee, *The Social Evil in Syracuse* (Syracuse, 1913), 54; personal communication, Maia Harris, on interviews with Storyville residents, 4 October 1993. On prostitution, see Ruth Rosen, *The Lost Sisterhood: Prostitution in America, 1900–1918* (Baltimore: Johns Hopkins Univ. Press, 1982).

35. *New York World*, 5 January 1890, 16. See also Marquise de Fontenoy, *Eve's Glossary: The Guidebook of a Mondaine* (Chicago: Herbert S. Stone, 1897), 44.

36. Louise de Koven Bowen, "Our Most Popular Recreation Controlled by the Liquor Interests: A Study of Public Dance Halls" (1912), in *Speeches, Addresses and Letters of Louise de Koven Bowen Reflecting Social Movements in Chicago*, vol. 1 (Ann Arbor: Edwards Brothers, 1937), 243. See also Ruth True, *The Neglected Girl* (New York: Survey Associates, 1914), 50–55, 66–67. For a general discussion, see Kathy Peiss, *Cheap Amusements: Working Women and Leisure in Turn-of-the-Century New York* (Philadelphia: Temple Univ. Press, 1986), 56–87.

37. Maggie Trebet letter, "Should Women Paint?" contest. Macy's manager quoted in Elaine Abelson, *When Ladies Go A'Thieving* (New York: Oxford Univ. Press, 1989), 107, 250. Edna K. Wooley, "Mere Man Opposes Woman's Vanities," *Milady Beautiful* (July 1915): 27. On Newark police, "Policewomen Wash Off the Paint," *National Police Journal* 3 (January 1919): 13. Mary Odem, *Delinquent Daughters: Protecting and Policing Adolescent Female Sexuality in the United States, 1885–1920* (Chapel Hill: Univ. of North Carolina Press, 1995), 181–82. For the larger controversy over female behavior, James R. McGovern, "The American Woman's Pre–World War I Freedom in Manners and Morals," *Journal of American History* 55 (September 1968): 315–33; Lewis A. Erenberg, *Steppin' Out: New York Nightlife and the Transformation of American Culture, 1890–1930* (Westport, Conn.: Greenwood, 1981).

38. *LHJ* 29 (January 1912): 5; Vox Fueri letter, "Should Women Paint?" contest; *Dry Goods Economist* (1901), quoted in Abelson, *When Ladies Go A'Thieving*, 56. See also *TR* 1 (April 1916): 15; 5 (June 1920): 28; 3 (September 1918): 14.

39. On the Cooper Union debate, see "Artificial Beauty Wins Girl Votes," *Marinello Messenger* (April 1914): 30.

40. Isabel V. Reitz, Mrs. C. H. Lears, Jessie Barclay, Eva Dorsey Carr, Mrs. Nan M. Vanaman letters, "Should Women Paint?" contest.

41. "Artificial Beauty Wins Girl Votes."

42. Nicketti McMullen, M. O. Burns, Mrs. W. F. Wild letters, "Should Women Paint?" contest.

43. Mrs. W. S. Farmer, Mrs. William Pimes, Mrs. A. L. Waranch letters, "Should Women Paint" contest.

44. James Harvey Young, *Toadstool Millionaires* (Princeton Univ. Press, 1967), 54.

45. On changing cosmetic products, see *LHJ* 6 (December 1889): pt. II, 2; Charles E. Hamlin and Charles Warren, *Hamlin's Formulae, or Every Druggist His Own Perfumer* (Baltimore: Edward B. Read & Son, 1885), 60–61; Emma Elizabeth Walker, "Cosmetics," *Reference Handbook of the Medical Sciences* clipping (n.d.), Emma Elizabeth Walker Papers, Sophia Smith Collection, Smith College. For makeup techniques, cf. Madame Edith Velaro, *How to Use Cosmetics* (New York: L. Boeker, 1886), 5–6; Charles D. Hess, *Practical Handbook on Dermatology* (Rochester: Youthful Tint Manufacturing Co., n.d.), Cosmetics, WCBA, 29.

46. Brown, Sherbrook, *Scrap Book for Homely Women Only*, 66–67; M. Stein Cosmetic Co., *How to Make-Up* (pamphlet, n.d.), 4, Special Collections, Fashion Institute of Technology, New York; Hess Co., *Art of Making Up*, 7th ed. (Rochester, NY: James Conolly, 1916), 7, 11; Max Factor, Jr., "Forty Years of Making Hollywood's Glamour Girls More Glamorous" ([1950]), ch. 3, 6; ch. 6, 4, MFPG.

47. Anne O'Hagan, "The Quest of Beauty," *Munsey's* 29 (June 1903): 409. See also Anne Hard, "The Beauty Business," *American Magazine* 69 (November 1909): 79–90; Banner, *American Beauty*, 212–25.

CHAPTER THREE

1. On beauty culture as a "vulgar" trade, see *Marinello Messenger* (November 1916): 1; NNBL, *Report of the Fourteenth Annual Convention* (1914), 211–12. For an overview of women's labor history, see Alice Kessler-Harris, *Out to Work* (New York: Oxford Univ. Press, 1982).

2. E. Burnham, *The Coiffure: Catalog No. 37* (Chicago, [1908]), 4, Hair, WCBA. On Williams, NNBL, *Report of the Sixth Annual Convention* (1905), 119–21. On black women in early beauty culture, see Loren Schweninger, *Black Property Owners in the South, 1790–1915* (Urbana: Univ. of Illinois Press, 1990), 85.

3. See *Trade-Marks for Perfumes, Toilet Articles, and Soaps* (New York: Associated Manufacturers of Toilet Articles, 1925), a compilation of all trademarks in this class registered by the U.S. Patent Office to 1924. My tally is probably low, as it omits individuals who used initials instead of first names. For information about other women entrepreneurs, see L. W. Alwyn-Schmidt, *American Almanac of Hairdressing-Beauty Culture 1922* (New York: Professional Yearbook Co., 1922). For examples of patents, see Julie Desmarques Young, No. 116,786, 4 July 1871; Harriet Fish, No. 67,182, 30 July 1867, Records of the U.S. Patent Office.

4. On Adams, see Lois Banner, *American Beauty* (Chicago: Univ. of Chicago Press, 1983), 214. Marie Mott Gage, *How to Cultivate Beauty* (pamphlet; n.p., 1893), 29, CHS; alumnae records, Vassar College Archives.

5. Harriet Hubbard Ayer trade card, Cosmetics, WCBA; Frances E. Willard and

Mary A. Livermore, *A Woman of the Century* (1893; reprint, Detroit: Gale Research, 1967), 41. See also Bernard A. Weisberger, "Harriet Hubbard Ayer," in Edward T. James, ed., *Notable American Women, 1607–1950*, vol. 1 (Cambridge: Harvard Univ. Press, 1971), 72–74; Henry E. Hamilton, "Harriet Hubbard Ayer," *Personal Reminiscences of Henry E. Hamilton* (TS, [1915]), CHS.

6. See Albro Martin, "Elizabeth Arden," in James, ed., *Notable American Women*, vol. 1, 32–33; "I Am a Famous Woman in This Industry," *Fortune* 16 (October 1938): 58–65, 142–54; Alfred Allan Lewis and Constance Woodworth, *Miss Elizabeth Arden* (New York: Coward, McCann & Geoghegan, 1972).

7. Cf. Rubinstein's autobiographies in *The Art of Feminine Beauty* (New York: Horace Liveright, 1930), and *My Life for Beauty* (London: Bodley Head, 1965). See also Jo Swerling, "Beauty in Jars and Vials," *New Yorker*, 30 June 1928, 20–23; Allison Gray, "People Who Want to Look Young and Beautiful," *American Magazine* 94 (December 1922): 32–33, 161–64; Maxene Fabe, *Beauty Millionaire: The Life of Helena Rubinstein* (New York: Thomas Y. Crowell, 1972); Patrick O'Higgins, *Madame, An Intimate Biography of Helena Rubinstein* (New York: Viking Press, 1971).

8. "Woman Says Poro College Is Hers to Last Penny," *St. Louis Post-Dispatch* clipping (1927), in box 262, CAB; these papers contain extensive correspondence with Malone and other materials related to Poro. For biographical information, see Bettye Collier-Thomas, "Annie Turnbo Malone," in Jessie Carney Smith, ed., *Notable Black American Women* (Detroit: Gale Research Inc., 1992), 724–27; Jeanne Conway Mongold, "Annie Minerva Turnbo-Malone," in Barbara Sicherman et al., eds., *Notable American Women: The Modern Period* (Cambridge: Harvard Univ. Press, 1980), 700–702; Gwendolyn Robinson, "Class, Race, and Gender: A Transcultural Theoretical and Sociohistorical Analysis of Cosmetic Institutions and Practices to 1920" (diss., Univ. of Illinois at Chicago, 1984), 347–76.

9. The most reliable biographies of Madam C. J. Walker are A'Lelia Perry Bundles, *Madam C. J. Walker, Entrepreneur* (New York: Chelsea House, 1991); Charles Latham, Jr., "Madam C. J. Walker & Company," *Traces of Indiana and Midwestern History* 1, no. 3 (summer 1989): 28–36, both based closely on archival sources in the Madam C. J. Walker Papers [MCJW]. See also Robinson, "Gender, Race, and Class," 377–410; "Madam C. J. Walker: Two Dollars and a Dream" (video documentary, Stanley Nelson & Associates, 1988). Also useful is "America's Foremost Colored Woman," *The Freeman* [Indianapolis], 28 December 1912.

10. See *Madam C. J. Walker Beauty Manual*, 3rd ed. (Indianapolis: Madam C. J. Walker Co., 1940) for content of products and description of the process; also Latham, "Madam C. J. Walker," 29. On the contested origins of the systems, see Collier-Thomas, "Annie Turnbo Malone," 724–25.

11. "Wealthiest Negro Woman's Suburban Mansion," *New York Times Magazine*, 4 November 1917; Walker Manufacturing Co. to Commissioner of Internal Revenue, 2 January 1923; G. S. O. memo, 19 April 1921, Financial Statements and Audits, MCJW.

12. Teresa Catherine Gallagher, "From Family Helpmeet to Independent Professional: Women in American Pharmacy, 1870–1940," *Pharmacy in History* 31 (1989): 60–77.

13. Bertha C. Benz to "Dear Friend," form letter [1890], James King Wilkerson Papers, Special Collections Library, Duke University. Lewis and Woodworth, *Miss Elizabeth Arden*, 108; A'Lelia P. Bundles, "Madam C. J. Walker—Cosmetics Tycoon," *Ms.* (July 1983): 93; Albert Anderson, "The Amazing Inside Story of the Malone Case," *The Light and Heebie Jeebies* 3, no. 13 (19 February 1927): 14–22, box 262, CAB; Weisberger, "Harriet Hubbard Ayer," 73.

14. Anthony Overton, "The Largest Negro Manufacturing Enterprise in the United States," in NNBL, *Report of the Thirteenth Annual Convention* (1912), 99. On black drugstores and retailing, see W. E. B. DuBois, *The Negro in Business* (1899; reprint, New York: Arno, 1968), 7–8; NNBL, *Report of the Sixth Annual Convention*, 67–75. On salesmen, Timothy B. Spears, *100 Years on the Road: The Traveling Salesman in American Culture* (New Haven: Yale Univ. Press, 1995).

15. California Perfume Company, Depot Agent's Contract, 28 August 1899, in Cosmetics, WCBA. George Gaspar, "The California Perfume Company," *Collector's Showcase* 6, no. 6 (July/August 1987): 62–67.

16. Benz to "Dear Friend"; Bertha Benz to Miss Prim, 21 February 1893, James King Wilkerson Papers. Flora M. Jones advertisement, *LHJ* 8 (February 1891): 32.

17. G. S. O. memo; George S. Olive, The Mme. C. J. Walker Manufacturing Co., Inc., Report on Examination, January 1, 1918, to August 31, 1919, Financial Statements and Audits, MCJW.

18. For examples of these techniques, see Anne Hard, "The Beauty Business," *American Magazine* 69 (November 1909): 86–87; Elizabeth Hubbard, *Beauty, How Acquired and Retained* (New York: n.p., 1910); Cocroft Laboratories, *The Success Face Lifters* (n.p., n.d.); and W. E. Forest, *The Manual of Massotherapy: The Use of Massage Rollers and Muscle Beaters* (New York: Health-Culture Company, 1898), Cosmetics, WCBA.

19. Madame Josephine LeFevre, *LeFevre's Toilet Aids* (n.p., [1890]), 3, Cosmetics, WCBA. On these developments, see Banner, *American Beauty*, 210–12; American Hairdresser, *A Century of Service: A Hundred Year History of the Beauty Profession* (New York: Service Publ., 1978), 13–14.

20. On Harper, Karen Thure, "Martha Harper Pioneered in the Hair Business," *Smithsonian* 7 (1976): 94–100; personal communication, Jane Plitt, 18 December 1995. On Marinello, see *Cosmeticians Exchange* 2 (September 1913); *Milady Beautiful*, October 1914, 2; September 1922, 13, in SHSW. On franchising, see Thomas S. Dicke, *Franchising in America: The Development of a Business Method* (Chapel Hill: Univ. of North Carolina Press, 1992).

21. F. B. Ransom to Mrs. A. C. Burnett, 10 September 1918, Walker Mfg. Co. General Correspondence, MCJW. See also "America's Foremost Colored Woman"; NNBL, *Report of the Fourteenth Annual Convention* (1913), 210–12. On Malone's incentive plan, see PORO Publicity Department to Associated Negro Press, 27 December 1924, box 262, CAB. For a superb discussion, see Nicole Woolsey Biggart, *Charismatic Capitalism: Direct Selling Organizations in America* (Chicago: Univ. of Chicago Press, 1989).

22. Mrs. Gervaise Graham, *Story of Your Mirror* (Chicago, [1910]), 3, in Mrs. Gervaise Graham, Cosmetics, American Medical Association Historical Health Fraud and

Alternative Medicine Collection, American Medical Association, Chicago. Harriet Hubbard Ayer, *Beauty: A Woman's Birthright* (Pond's pamphlet, 1904), Inactive Accounts, Correspondence and Memoranda, 1940–70, JWT.

23. B. S. Cooban, "Two Profitable Specialties," *Bulletin of Pharmacy* 15 (November 1901): 463. See also "Druggists' Supplies," in William Borsodi, ed., *Advertisers Cyclopedia of Selling Phrases* (New York, 1909), 367–78. On patent medicine advertising, see Jackson Lears, *Fables of Abundance* (New York: Basic, 1994), 88–99.

24. Madame Yale, *Science of Health and Beauty* (n.p., [1893]), insert, 4, Cosmetics, WCBA. B. & P. Wrinkle Eradicators ad proofs, 55A (1903), 464G (1905), book 379, NWA.

25. Walker quoted in Bundles, "Madam C. J. Walker—Cosmetics Tycoon," 92. On Pinault, Frances E. Willard, *Occupations for Women* (New York: Success Co., 1897), 397.

26. Yale's biographical claims are in *Science of Health and Beauty;* Jean N. Berry, Wellesley College Archives, personal communication, 18 June 1992, states that Yale never attended the college. Madame Edith Velaro, *How to Use Cosmetics* (New York: L. Boeker, 1886), 27–38; Ida Lee Secrest registered beauty preparations under the name Madame Velaro.

27. "I Am a Famous Woman," 58; Carl A. Naether, *Advertising to Women* (New York: Prentice Hall, 1928), 30–31; J. W. Rafferty memo, 14 August 1935, Elizabeth Arden, National Broadcasting Company Records, SHSW. On Arden as an employer, see Helen Nash interview, 16 February 1990, Cover Girl Make-up Advertising History Collection, 1959–1990, Archives Center, NMAH; Lewis and Woodworth, *Elizabeth Arden*, 193–200, 204.

28. Helena Rubinstein, "The Beauty Specialist's Place in the Community," *Beauty* 1 (December 1922): 31; Hambla Bauer, "Beauty Tycoon," *Colliers*, 4 December 1948, 16; Swerling, "Beauty in Jars and Vials," 20; Gray, "People Who Want to Look Young and Beautiful," 33. On Arden's politics, see Lewis and Woodworth, *Miss Elizabeth Arden*, 167, 282; on Rubinstein's, *Career Women of America* (New York: Cultural Research Publishers, 1941), 55. O'Higgins, in *Madame*, 181, suggests Rubinstein's discomfort with being seen as "too Jewish"; Lewis and Woodworth, 88, indicate that Rubinstein's Jewish origins and Arden's anti-Semitism contributed to their rivalry. They quote Arden (without documentation): "To be Catholic or Jewish isn't chic. Chic is Episcopalian."

29. NNBL, *Report of the Thirteenth Annual Convention*, 154–55; *Report of the Fourteenth Annual Convention*, 210–12. See also Latham, "Madam C. J. Walker," 30; testimonials to Walker's character, 21 December 1912, Advertisements, MCJW.

30. Flora Jones, "Blush of Roses" circular (n.d.), in author's possession; *American Perfumer* 1 (May 1906): 10; Bell Mann Perfumery Co., *Specialties for Ladies and Gentlemen* (Chicago, [1876]), 6.

31. Yale, *Health & Beauty*, 4; Helena Rubinstein advertisement, *Town & Country*, 20 May 1915, Cosmetics, WCBA.

32. Susanna Cocroft to Ethel Vining, letters, instructions, and booklets, 1913–1914, in author's possession.

33. Madame Caroline, Ne Plus Extra Face Beautifier circular (New York, n.d.), Cosmetics, WCBA; Burnham, *The Coiffure*, 3, *Milady Beautiful*, October 1914, 8.

34. Madame Ruppert, *How to Be Beautiful* (New York: Herbert Booth King, n.d.), Scrapbook 18, BCL; Yale, *Science of Health and Beauty*, 75, 80.

35. Madame Ruppert advertisement, *American Jewess* 1 (July 1895): 213; on cosmetics, see 1 (April 1895): 32–33; *Die Deutsche Hausfrau*, April 1911, 32.

36. Susanna Cocroft, *A New Method of Physical Culture for the Face* (Chicago: Grace-Mildred Culture Course, 1912), 14; Mrs. R. W. Allen, *New Price List and Illustrated Catalog* (Detroit, [1890]), 15; Yale, *Science of Health and Beauty*, 7; Cocroft Laboratories, *The Overnight Way to a New Complexion* (n.p., n.d.), 1, Cosmetics, WCBA.

37. Yale, *Science of Health and Beauty*, 26; Mrs. C. Thompson, *Thompson Coiffure* (New York: Brentano Bros., 1879), 42–43, BCL.

38. *Marinello Magazine*, 3 (September 1914): 5. On Yale and the Woman's Building, see Jeanne M. Weimann, *The Fair Women* (Chicago: Academy, 1981), 507–10 (quote on 510); Madame M. Yale, *Guide to Beauty* (Buffalo: Richmond Lithographic Co., n.d.), 3, Personal Grooming Aids, BCL.

39. Yale, *Science of Health and Beauty*, 5, 6; "Miss Cocroft Tells How to Build a Neck," *New York Times*, 21 April 1915; Cocroft testimonial, 24 July 1903, in author's possession. On feminist views of beauty, see Banner, *American Beauty*, 86–105; William R. Leach, *True Love and Perfect Union: The Feminist Reform of Sex and Society* (New York: Basic, 1980), 213–60.

40. Lewis and Woodworth, *Miss Elizabeth Arden*, 92–93, 105–106. Rubinstein, *My Life for Beauty*, 60; James True, "Policies that Built World-Wide Sales for Helena Rubinstein," *Sales Management* 24 (22 November 1930): 298–99, 325–27. On ad expenditures, Periodical Publishers Association, *Nationally Established Trademarks* (New York, 1934), 13, 75.

41. Marie Cane to Madam C. J. Walker, 21 May 1918, Orders, MCJW. "Hints to Agents" ([1915]), Walker Manufacturing Co. Records, MCJW; *Madam C. J. Walker Beauty Manual*, 1st ed. (Indianapolis: Walker Manufacturing Co., 1928), 208; "A Great Woman," *The Crisis* 18 (July 1919): 131.

42. Mamie Garvin Fields, *Lemon Swamp and Other Places* (New York: Free Press, 1983), 188, 218; Elizabeth Clark to Madam C. J. Walker, 8 June 1918, Orders, MCJW.

43. Lubertha Carson to Madam C. J. Walker, n.d.; Grace Clayton to Walker, 14 June 1918; [author illegible], Pilgrim Health and Life Insurance Co., to Walker, 7 May 1918, Orders; "Instructions to Agents before 1919" (TS), Walker Manufacturing Co. Records; Belinda Bailey to Walker, 8 June 1918, Orders, MCJW.

44. "Instructions to Agents before 1919"; agent quoted in Bundles, "Madam C. J. Walker—Cosmetics Tycoon," 93. For earnings of top agents, see Payroll sheets and reports, 1915–1917, Walker Manufacturing Co. Financial Records, and Journals, 1919–1926, MCJW; NNBL, *Report of the Fourteenth Annual Convention*, 210–11. On black women's wages and occupations at this time, see Jacqueline Jones, *Labor of Love, Labor of Sorrow* (New York: Basic, 1985), 79–195.

45. Annie Bell to "My Dear Friend," 1918; Alice Clark to Madam C. J. Walker, 30

April 1918; Ethel Cornish to Walker, 30 April 1918; Rosa M. Anthony to Walker, 12 May 1918, Orders, MCJW.

46. Beatrice E. Crank to Madam C. J. Walker, 5 June 1918; Maggie Branch to Walker, 7 May 1918; Sallie Adams to Walker, 4 May 1918, Orders, MCJW.

47. M. P. Burleigh to F. B. Ransom, 8 June 1918, Orders, MCJW. "Sara Spencer Washington," in Smith, ed., *Notable Black American Women*, 1224; Joseph J. Boris, ed., *Who's Who in Colored America 1928–29*, 2nd ed. (New York: Who's Who in Colored America Corporation, 1929), 71, 385.

48. "Welcome into the PORO Organization!" (n.d.), box 262, CAB. "Instructions to Agents before 1919"; Ransom to Burnett. Useful for understanding Walker's social milieu is Darlene Clark Hine's *When the Truth Is Told: A History of Black Women's Culture and Community in Indiana, 1875–1950* (National Council of Negro Women, 1981).

49. National Association of Colored Women, *Minutes of the Eleventh Biennial Convention* (1918), 22, 93, 101, 308, Records of the National Association of Colored Women's Clubs, 1895–1992, microfilm ed. (Bethesda: University Publications of America, 1993). Walker also spoke at the Eighth (1912), Ninth (1914), and Tenth (1916) Biennial Conventions. On hairdressing in colleges, see F. B. Ransom to Mabel Marble, 17 January 1917; Ransom to James A. Booker, n.d., Walker Mfg. Co., General Correspondence, MCJW; Louis R. Harlan and Raymond W. Smock, eds., *The Booker T. Washington Papers*, vol. 13 (Urbana: University of Illinois Press, 1984), 30.

50. *Poro Hair & Beauty Culture* (St. Louis: Poro College, 1922), 8, 13; *'Poro' in Pictures* (St. Louis, 1926), 44; "Personal History of Annie M. Turnbo Malone" (TS, [1938]), Poro College Miscellaneous Pamphlets, CHS; *Southwestern Christian Advocate* quoted in Robert T. Kerlin, *The Voice of the Negro 1919* (1920; reprint, New York: Arno, 1968), 167–68.

51. Early press release on Madam Walker, n.d., Walker Mfg. Co. Press Releases, MCJW; "Welcome into the PORO Organization!" On Walker Clubs see Ransom to Burnett; on problems with adulteration and labeling, see "Hints to Agents" ([1915]), Walker Mfg. Co. Records, MCJW. For other agent clubs in Chicago, see Ford S. Black, *Black's Blue Book: Directory of Chicago's Active Colored People and Guide to their Activity* (Chicago, 1916), 87, and (Chicago, 1921), 28.

52. Press release, 1st Walker Convention 1917, 2, Walker Mfg. Co., Press Releases, MCJW. On Walker's political affiliations, see Bundles, *Madam C. J. Walker*, 73–87; Robert A. Hill, ed., *The Marcus Garvey and Universal Negro Improvement Association Papers*, vol. 1 (Berkeley: Univ. of California Press, 1983), 345; Alfreda M. Duster, ed., *Crusader for Justice: The Autobiography of Ida B. Wells* (Chicago: Univ. of Chicago Press, 1970), 378–79; "Wealthiest Negro Woman's Suburban Mansion"; *Chicago Defender*, 31 May 1919. On the first Poro convention, see *Chicago Defender*, 12 June 1920.

53. Helena Rubinstein, "Manufacturing—Cosmetics," in Doris Fleischman Bernays, ed., *An Outline of Careers for Women* (New York: Doubleday, Doran, 1928), 331.

54. Rubinstein, "Beauty Specialist's Place," 31.

55. Yale, *Science of Health and Beauty*, 33.

CHAPTER FOUR

1. Clyde B. Davis, "80 Years!", *TR* 16 (April 1931): 51; Robert S. Lynd, "The People as Consumers," in U.S. President's Committee on Social Trends, *Recent Social Trends in the United States,* vol. 1 (New York: McGraw Hill, 1933), 889, 905. This growth is discussed in James H. Collins, "The Beauty Business: It Makes the Things to Make You Beautiful," *Saturday Evening Post* 197 (22 November 1924): 14, 141ff; Paul W. White, "Our Booming Beauty Business," *Outlook* 154 (22 January 1930): 133–35; "Cosmetics: The American Woman Responds," *Fortune* no. 11 (August 1930), 29–43, 92–100.

2. "Women in Business III," *Fortune* 13 (July–December 1935): 81; Stephen L. Mayham, *Marketing Cosmetics* (New York: McGraw-Hill, 1938), introduction. On the new business methods and culture, see Jackson Lears, *Fables of Abundance: A Cultural History of Advertising in America* (New York: Basic, 1994); William R. Leach, *Land of Desire: Merchants, Power and the Rise of a New American Culture* (New York: Pantheon, 1993); Roland Marchand, *Advertising the American Dream: Making Way for Modernity* (Berkeley: Univ. of California Press, 1985); Susan Strasser, *Satisfaction Guaranteed: The Making of the American Mass Market* (New York: Pantheon, 1989); Richard S. Tedlow, *New and Improved: The Story of Mass Marketing in America* (New York: Basic, 1990).

3. MPA, *Proceedings of the Fifteenth Annual Meeting* (New York, 1909), 64. On the decline of old U.S. firms, Theodore Ricksecker, "American Perfumery: Its Growth and Possibilities," *American Perfumer* 2 (May 1907): 48. On Hudnut, see obituary, *New York Times*, 31 October 1928; D. K. Healy, "How a New Cosmetic Family Was Introduced," *PI* 167 (14 June 1934): 72–73. On French cosmetics, M. L. Wilson, "Why 'France' and 'Perfume' Are Synonymous," *PI* 135 (13 May 1926): 49–50; Helen M. Caldwell, "1920–1929: The Decade of the French Mystique in the American Perfume Market," in Terence Nevett et al., eds., *Marketing History: The Emerging Discipline* (Fourth Conference on Historical Research in Marketing, Michigan State Univ., 1989), 259–72.

4. James Harvey Young, *Toadstool Millionaires* (Princeton: Princeton Univ. Press, 1967), 46; Ellen Gruber Garvey, *The Adman in the Parlor: Magazines and the Gendering of Consumer Culture, 1880s to 1910s* (New York: Oxford Univ. Press, 1996), 11.

5. "Account Histories: Pond's Extract Company," 16 January 1926, in Inactive Account File, Chesebrough-Pond's, JWT.

6. *TR* 10 (October 1925): 64; *TR* 2 (July 1917): 26; Norbert A. Witt, *The Noxzema Story* (New York: Newcomen Society, 1967).

7. Claude C. Hopkins, *My Life in Advertising* (New York: Harper & Bros., 1936), 193–95.

8. Untitled autobiography, 9 October 1925, 2, box 1; see also "Dear Mr. Anderson" (n.d.), box 2, and other materials in CW. Armand ad proof 87F (1917), Book 386, NWA. W. H. Wiseman, "A Business Founded on the Good Will of Dealers," *Sales Management* 15 (14 July 1928): 85–86, 112.

9. Max Factor, Jr., "Forty Years of Making Hollywood's Glamour Girls More Glam-

orous" (TS, [1950]), ch. 1, 5. On Max Factor's early years, see newspaper interviews with Factor; William Hardwick, "Max Factor, Background and History" (TS, May 1977); "Interview with Bob Salvatore, Max Factor (Museum), Hollywood, California," by Kathleen McDermott, Winthrop Group, Inc., with Ed Rider, Procter & Gamble (TS, 16 February 1993); press releases and correspondence, MFPG; exhibits and newspaper clippings at MFMB.

10. Davis Factor to V. E. Meadows, 31 December 1926, Internal Correspondence, box 113, MFPG. On marketing, see Max Factor, Jr., "Forty Years," ch. 6, 4; Davis Factor to S. E. Umunsetter, 7 February 1927, Internal Correspondence, box 113; "Max Factor Chronology" and "Max Factor Product Introductions," MFPG. On the influence of Factor's children, see William Hardwick, "Max Factor," 13, 18. For early advertising, see Max Factor Sales Corporation, *Max Factor's Society Make-Up* (portfolio, 1929); Advertising Collection, MFPG; ad lineage and costs in Publishers Information Bureau, *National Advertising Records* (Chicago, 1926–29).

11. "Contribution of Dorothy Dignam, Writer" (1959), n. pag., box 1, DD. On stock formulas, see Francis Chilson, *Modern Cosmetics* (New York: Drug and Cosmetic Industry, 1934), 15–16; Everett G. McDonough, *Truth About Cosmetics* (New York: Drug and Cosmetic Industry, 1937), 79. On one harmful additive, see "Radium in Toilet Preparations," *TR* 3 (January 1919): 33.

12. On production, see Chilson, *Modern Cosmetics,* 189, 362. On the workforce, see Herman Goodman, *Cosmetics and Your Skin* (New York: Medical Lay Press, 1929), 29; Elisabeth D. Benham, "The Woman Wage Earner: Her Situation Today," U.S. Department of Labor, Women's Bureau *Bulletin* no. 172 (Washington, D.C.: GPO, 1939), 6. On private-label houses and brands, see Roland Cole, "Another Company Drops Private Brands and Lifts Profits," *PI* 134 (4 February 1926): 85–86; "Showing Indoor Girls How They Can Have Outdoor Complexions," *PI* 157 (24 December 1931): 70–72.

13. Louis Bader and Sidney Picker, *Marketing Drugs and Cosmetics* (New York: D. Van Nostrand, 1947), 37.

14. Phyllis Lewis, "Dramatizing the Window Display," *TR* 9 (May 1924): 44. See Correspondence, 1907–1925, O. N. Falk & Son Records, SHSW. On point-of-purchase merchandising, see Arthur Bennett, "Dealer Help and the Retail Clerk," *TR* 6 (December 1921): 25–26. For a superb history of these techniques, see Leach, *Land of Desire,* 39–90.

15. For a general history, see Daniel Pope, *The Making of Modern Advertising* (New York: Basic, 1983); Robert Jay, *The Trade Card in 19th Century America* (Columbia: Univ. of Missouri Press, 1987); James D. Norris, *Advertising and the Transformation of American Society* (New York: Greenwood, 1990), 47–60.

16. *J. Walter Thompson News Bulletin,* no. 37 (5 March 1917): 2, Publications: Company Newsletters, JWT. Donald S. Cowling, "Toilet Goods Buyers Are Demanding Nationally Advertised Goods," *PI* 145 (15 November 1928): 53, 56. Crowell Publishing Company, *National Markets and National Advertising* (New York: Crowell, 1929); White, "Booming Beauty Business," 133–35; *TR* 14 (April 1929): 44; Curtis Publishing Co., *Advertising in Ladies' Home Journal and Other Women's Publications 1927* (Philadelphia: Curtis, 1928), 30.

17. John Reber, Speech to American Manufacturers of Toilet Goods (TS, 21 April 1931), 3, in American Perfumer and Essential Oil, National Broadcasting Company (NBC) Records, SHSW. "Radio Case Histories" (n.d.), Information Center, JWT; Frank A. Arnold, *Broadcast Advertising: The Fourth Dimension* (New York: J. Wiley & Sons, 1931), 177–80; *TR* 13 (June 1928): 7, 72; Emmons C. Carlson to W. G. Young, 15 February 1933, Lady Esther, National Broadcasting Company (NBC) Records, SHSW. See also Susan Smulyan, *Selling Radio: The Commercialization of American Broadcasting, 1920–1934* (Washington: Smithsonian Inst. Press, 1994).

18. See Publishers Information Bureau, *National Advertising Records* (February 1926); this monthly series documented advertising placements by company and product, detailing locations, cost, and size of ad in major national media.

19. Helena Rubinstein, "Manufacturing—Cosmetics," in Doris Fleischman Bernays, ed., *An Outline of Careers for Women* (New York: Doubleday, Doran, 1928), 330. See also Mayham, *Marketing Cosmetics*, 93.

20. "Account Histories: Odo-Ro-No," Inactive Account File, JWT. Lester B. Colby, "What Princess Pat Has Learned about Selling to Women," *Sales Management* 30 (1 June 1932): 232–33, 256; Jean Jordeau Inc. and Bertha E. Levy, Docket no. 2012 (1932), Federal Trade Commission Records, Record Group 122, National Archives.

21. Catharine Oglesby, *Fashion Careers American Style* (New York: Funk & Wagnalls, 1935), 126, 127; Helena Rubinstein, *My Life for Beauty* (London: Bodley Head, 1965), 71–72.

22. "I Am a Famous Woman in This Industry," *Fortune* 16 (October 1938): 154.

23. Mrs. J. H. P. Coleman, "Manufacturing Hair Preparations," in NNBL, *Report of the Thirteenth Annual Convention* (1912), 64. For a sense of this activity, see Ford S. Black, *Black's Blue Book: Directory of Chicago's Active Colored People and Guide to their Activity* (Chicago, 1916), 7–8, 14, 34.

24. Obituary, *Chicago Bee*, 7 July 1946. Anthony Overton, "Largest Negro Manufacturing Enterprise in the United States," in NNBL, *Report of Thirteenth Annual Convention*, 96–100; Albon L. Holsey, "Negro Business," *Messenger* 9 (November 1927): 321. For biographical information, see "Anthony Overton," *Journal of Negro History* 32 (July 1947): 394–96.

25. Information about Barnett and Kashmir is in CAB, box 262, Manuscript Division, and boxes 3–4, Prints and Photographs, CHS. See also Linda J. Evans, "Claude A. Barnett and the Associated Negro Press," *Chicago History* 40 (Spring 1985): 44–56.

26. *Colgate Shavings* 3 (November–December 1923): 9, in Soap, WCBA. See also Walgreen's advertisement, *Chicago Defender*, 1 March 1919.

27. Boncilla advertisement, *Pittsburgh Courier*, 1 March 1924. American Products Company, *Zanol Products Catalog* no. 20 (Cincinnati, 1922), 33, 45; J. E. McBrady & Co., *The Great Central Market* (Chicago, [1915]), n. pag., CHS; J. E. McBrady advertising card, Cosmetics, WCBA.

28. "Patronize Your Own Fallacies," *Messenger* 6 (September 1924): 281.

29. "Plough Co. Opens $5,000,000 Plant," Associated Negro Press Release, 21 June

1951, box 261, CAB. For an "official" history, see *Memphis Commercial-Appeal,* 5 December 1954, in vertical files, Memphis-Shelby County Information Center, Memphis, TN.

30. *Memphis Commercial-Appeal,* 10 April 1957; Robert A. Sigafoos, *Cotton Row to Beale Street: A Business History of Memphis* (Memphis: Memphis State Univ. Press, 1979), 94, 299–300. For Plough's advertising strategy to blacks, see H. M. Gissom, Southern Advertising Agency, to *Indianapolis Recorder,* 20 October 1922, George P. Stewart Papers, Indiana Historical Society; Albon L. Holsey to Claude A. Barnett, 25 October 1930; Barnett to Holsey, 4 March 1933; Barnett to Annie M. Malone, 8 February 1929, CAB. On ads to whites, see Bruce Crowell, "Plough Chemical Repackages Entire Line as 1929 Campaign Breaks," *Sales Management* 18 (13 April 1929): 73.

31. F. B. Ransom to Kashmir Chemical Company, 20 March 1920, box 262, CAB; F. B. Ransom, "Manufacturing Toilet Articles," *Messenger* 5 (December 1923): 937. Formation of National Negro Cosmetics Manufacturers Association, untitled typescript, 1917, Walker Mfg. Co. Records, MCJW. On difficulties in organization, see Ransom to Kashmir, 18 March 1920; Kashmir to Ransom, 19 March 1920, box 262, CAB. On mass-market tactics, Barnett to Holsey, 4 March 1933.

32. "We the undersigned agents" to F. B. Ransom, 22 April 1918, Internal Correspondence; Advertising Dept. to "Madam," October 1920, Advertisements, MCJW. For Poro, see Monroe N. Work, ed., *Negro Year Book 1921–22* (Tuskegee: Tuskegee Institute, 1921), 15; "We advertise in the following papers," 24 March 1924, box 262, CAB. For Walker, Correspondence to F. B. Ransom concerning Walker Co. Advertisements; Journals, 1919–1926; Distribution of Invoices, 1919–1925; Louis W. George to F. B. Ransom, 4 August 1918, MCJW. On cosmetic lines, "Madam Walker Increases Line of Toilet Articles," *Indianapolis Recorder,* 15 March 1919; *Poro Hair and Beauty Culture Handbook* (St. Louis, 1922), 37.

33. "Madam Walker Increases Line of Toilet Articles"; *Walker News* 3 (July 1930): n. pag., Press Releases. On Tan-Off, Madam C. J. Walker Manufacturing Co., *Year Book and Almanac 1924;* for sales, Walker Mfg. Company Sales by Dealer, MCJW.

34. *The Independent* clipping, n.d., box 262, CAB; Barnett to Holsey, 4 March 1933.

35. Claude A. Barnett to Annie Malone, 8 February 1929, box 262, CAB. For Walker Company's decline, Charles Latham, Jr., "Madam C. J. Walker & Company," *Traces of Indiana and Midwestern History* 1, no. 3 (summer 1989): 34; LeRoy W. Jeffries, "The Decay of the Beauty Parlor Industry in Harlem," *Opportunity* 16 (February 1938): 49–52.

36. *American Perfumer* 2 (April 1907): 25; Tre-Jur advertisement, *TR* 9 (September 1924): 30–31. Weeks to Roy O. Bakerink, 2 August 1929; *Armand Broadside* ([1925]), 12, box 1. See also "Armand's Position with Reference to Traveling Representatives" (n.d.), box 2, CW.

37. "Secrets of 'Making Up' Movie Stars," *Dallas Morning News,* 26 February 1928, clipping, MFMB; Alice L. Tildesley, "How Would You Like to Be Beauty Doctor to All the Screen Stars," *Philadelphia Public Ledger,* clipping, Hill Street Store,

box 113, MFPG. On Factor's public image, "Interview with Bob Salvatore," 12, 20.

38. Carl Weeks to "Boys and Gentlemen," 25 January 1935, 8; "One Woman's Story" (TS, n.d.); "Comments from One Woman's Strange Story" (TS, n.d.), box 2, CW.

39. Beatrice Mabie advertisement, *TR* 16 (July 1931): 19. "Memo, Sales Force, E.P.H. James," 24 May 1928, Helena Rubinstein, Inc.; Lady Esther Serenade continuities, 17 January 1933, 29 January 1933, 11 July 1934, Lady Esther, NBC Records. Helen Woodward, *It's an Art* (New York: Harcourt, Brace, 1938), 343. On this practice, see "Answer, 23 July 1930," in Cheri (1930), Docket #1850, box 1236, Federal Trade Commission Records, National Archives.

40. Helen Woodward, *Through Many Windows* (New York: Harper, 1926), 302–26 (quote on 305).

41. "Beauty Culturist of International Repute Sponsors Nationwide Beauty Contest," *St. Louis Argus* clipping, 1925, in Black Cosmetics File, Community Life Division, NMAH. For Hightower and Golden Brown, see R. L. Polk & Co., *Memphis City Directories*, 1915–17, 1921–27; Hessig-Ellis, Ser. No. 139,680, *Official Gazette of the U.S. Patent Office*, vol. 283 (8 February 1920): 357; Ser. No. 207,354, vol. 332 (3 March 1925): 8; Claude A. Barnett to Albon Holsey, 29 October 1930; Harold Gilbert to Associated Negro Press, 12 November 1927; Barnett to Golden Brown, 1 June 1937, CAB. For comments on Golden Brown, see *Negro World*, 27 June 1925, 7; *New York Age*, 2 March 1929.

42. Aminta Casseres, "Agencies Prefer Men!" *PI* (August 1927): 35, 84–87; cf. Mary Louise Alexander, "Opportunities for Women in Advertising Agencies," *News-Bulletin of the Bureau of Vocational Information* 1 (15 November 1923): 1. Marchand, *Advertising the American Dream*, 25–51; Jennifer Scanlon, *Inarticulate Longings: The Ladies' Home Journal, Gender, and the Promises of Consumer Culture* (New York: Routledge, 1995). On women in print media, see Mary Ellen Waller [Zuckerman], "Popular Women's Magazines, 1890–1917" (Ph.D. diss., Columbia University, 1987).

43. "Contribution of Dorothy Dignam, Writer"; Woodward, *It's an Art*, 214.

44. Sam Meek quoted in "Ruth Waldo," Sidney Bernstein Papers, Personnel Information; on Resor's centrality, see *J. Walter Thompson Company News*, 10 January 1964, Officers and Staff Members, Biographical Information; James Webb Young to Mr. Peck, 18 March 1963, Correspondence and Histories, Inactive Account Files, Andrew Jergens Co., Howard Henderson Files, JWT.

45. "Ruth Waldo—Business Biography and some personal description" (n.d.), 2, in Sidney Bernstein Papers. For feminists, see Women file, Sidney Bernstein Papers; "To all members of the staff," 19 October 1918, Domestic-NYO-Review Board, Information Center Records; employment applications of Ruth Becker, Mildred Holmes, Ruth Lamb, Frances Maule, Josephine Schain, Therese Olzendam. See also Scanlon, *Inarticulate Longings*, 169–96.

46. Helen Resor, Stockholder's Affadavit (20 March 1924), 69; "Women in Advertising," Bernstein Papers; Frances Maule, "The 'Woman Appeal,'" *J. Walter Thompson News Bulletin*, no. 105 (January 1924): 6–7; Casseres, "Agencies Prefer Men," 84. For examples of the woman's viewpoint, see Carl A. Naether, *Adver-*

tising to Women (New York: Prentice Hall, 1928). For an opposing position, see Daniel Starch, *Principles of Advertising* (Chicago: A. W. Shaw, 1923), 346, 352–60.

47. Clipping, *Chicago Post* (January 1920), and "Silhouettes" (n.d.), in Dorothy Dignam scrapbook, DD.

48. This circulation is apparent in JWT personnel files and employment applications; Mary Margaret McBride, *How to Be a Successful Advertising Woman* (New York: McGraw-Hill, 1948), 225–44; Catharine Oglesby, "Women in Advertising," *LHJ* (October 1930): 23.

49. N. W. Ayer, "Why Are There So Many Charming Women Today?" *Advertising Advertising* (1927), N. W. Ayer Archives; Elizabeth Colt Kidd, "How to Advertise Cosmetics and Toiletries," in Blanche Clair and Dorothy Dignam, eds., *Advertising Careers for Women* (New York: Harper, 1939), 92.

50. "Account Histories: The Pond's Extract Company," Armour and Company, Pond's Extract Soap advertisements, Soap, WCBA.

51. "Account Histories: The Andrew Jergen's Company—Woodbury's Facial Soap," 12 April 1926, 1, 3, Inactive Account File, Andrew Jergens, JWT.

52. On women's magazines, see Helen Woodward, *The Lady Persuaders* (New York: Ivan Obolensky, 1960); Waller, "Popular Women's Magazines, 1890–1917"; Scanlon, *Inarticulate Longings;* Garvey, *The Adman in the Parlor.*

53. Loring A. Schuler talk, 26 May 1930, 6, Monday Evening Meetings, USA and International Offices: New York Office, JWT; Curtis Publishing Co. "Analysis of Editorial Content," *Bulletin* ([1927]), Curtis Publishing Co. Records, Special Collections, Van Pelt Library, University of Pennsylvania. *Delineator* 64 (July 1904): 1–6. Hazel B. Stevens, "An Inquiry into the Present Contents of Women's Magazines as an Index to Women's Interests" (M.S. thesis, Columbia University, 1925), 37, 53, 81.

54. Mary Farmer Stempel, "The Woman's Page in the Smaller Cities" (M.S. thesis, Columbia University, 1929), 27; *TR* 13 (May 1928): 10–11; Curtis Publishing Co., *Advertising in Ladies' Home Journal,* 30.

55. *J. Walter Thompson News Bulletin,* no. 84B (25 March 1922): 15. *Redbook* advertisement, *TR* 13 (May 1928): 10. Woodward, *Lady Persuaders,* 9–10; Woodward, *It's an Art,* 47, 307–11.

56. "Pond's Spring 1921 newspapers" memo, 6 January 1921, Research Reports, reel 52, JWT; *Milady Beautiful* (December 1922): 12–13.

57. *TR* 7 (December 1922); "Beauty Through the Air," *TR* 12 (February 1928): 65. See also Louise Paine Benjamin, "Keeping the Faith," *TR* 21 (April 1936): 21; *Mademoiselle* 7 (May 1938): 48–49, 71.

58. JWT to Miss Poupeji, 30 January 1923, Toilet Preparations Investigation (1923), Research Reports, reel 59, JWT; Rebecca Stickney, "The Cosmetic Urge," *Advertising and Selling* 11 (31 October 1928): 21. On market research, see Waller, "Popular Women's Magazines, 1890–1917," 167–202.

59. LeBlume Import Co. advertisement, *TR* 7 (March 1923): insert; Nathan Benjamin Zimmerman, "Tut-Ankh-Amen in Three New York Newspapers" (M.S. thesis, Columbia University, 1923), 10, 16, 28. Edna Wallace Hopper advertisement (n.d.),

Competitive Advertisements, JWT. For the suntanning tie-in, DuBois, "What Is Sun-tan Doing to Cosmetics?" *Advertising and Selling* 13 (12 June 1929): 64, 67. On movie tie-ins, Frank H. Williams, "How the Movies Can Help You Sell More Toilet Goods," *TR* 14 (June 1929): 49. See also Charles Eckert, "The Carole Lombard in Macy's Window," in Jane Gaines and Charlotte Herzog, eds., *Fabrications: Costume and the Female Body* (New York: Routledge, 1990), 100–21.

60. Dave [Davis Factor] to Abe [A. B. Shore], 31 March 1927, Internal Correspondence; Dave to Abe, 11 June 1927, LA 350, Interoffice Correspondence, Hill Street Store, box 113; Max Factor release records, MFPG.

61. Cutex Investigations, "Report on Cutex Demonstration" (29 August 1921), n. pag., Research Reports, reel 38, JWT.

62. Carl Weeks, "The Following Is a Write-up" (n.d.), box 2, CW. E. W. Bartram to O. N. Falk & Son, 31 December 1917, Falk & Son Records.

63. C. M. Lindsay, "A $10,000 Beauty Show," *TR* 7 (May 1922): 37. *TR* covered many such "beauty events": see, e.g., 9 (May 1924): 52; 11 (August 1926): 47–49; 13 (August 1928): 28, 74.

64. Mayham, *Marketing Cosmetics*, 160–66; Florence Wall, *The Principles and Practice of Beauty Culture* (New York: Keystone, 1941), 655. Catharine Oglesby, "The Fashion Touch in Selling," *TR* 13 (December 1928): 24–25; Randolph Nelson, "Enlisting the Stylist in Behalf of Toilet Goods," *TR* 13 (March 1929): 26; Waldon Fawcett, "Color Coordination and Its Cosmetic Complex," *TR* 15 (September 1930): 42, 105. On style organizations, see Oglesby, *Fashion Careers American Style*, 29–33; Leach, *Land of Desire*, 308–19.

65. MPA, *Minutes of the Twenty-seventh Annual Meeting* (New York, 1921), 24–25; "The Psychology of the Package," *TR* 3 (March 1919): 20; Randolph Nelson, "The Craze for Color," *TR* 13 (June 1928): 68; Dorothy Cocks, "How Marinello Modernized," *Printed Salesmanship* 52 (January 1929): 407. On package design, see Adrian Forty, *Objects of Desire: Design and Society from Wedgwood to IBM* (New York: Pantheon, 1986), 62–93.

66. Bertina Foltz, "Beauty Is as Fashion Does," *TR* 21 (September 1936): 29.

67. S. E. Peacock, "Comments from Convention Report, 2–5 February 1930," box 1, DD; Philip De Angelis to Carl Weeks, 28 March 1930, box 1, CW. The Symphonie campaign is documented in CW; ad proofs, 1930, book 382, NWA; Symphonie advertising samples and promotion booklet, DD; "Armand Capitalizes Fashion by Anticipating It," *PI* 151 (29 May 1930): 131–32. On the "charm decade," see John Labatta, "The Return to Feminine Charm," *LHJ*, May 1930; Curtis Publishing Co., *Bulletin* no. 120 (July 1930), Curtis Publishing Co. Records.

68. "SYMPHONIE December 1930," box 1, CW.

69. On this practice, see Mayham, *Marketing Cosmetics*, 97–106; Cowling, "Toilet Goods Buyers Are Demanding," 54.

70. John Allen Murphy, " 'Hidden' Demonstrators Unfair to Consumer and Advertiser," *PI* 125 (13 December 1923): 3–6; on Macy's, *TR* 13 (September 1928): 23.

71. Frank Dahlberg to Weeks, 1 September 1929, box 1; "I Am in Rebellion" (n.d.); "From CW January 14th from NY" to William C. Weeks (n.d.), box 4, CW.

72. "A Cosmetic Demonstrator Tells How to Beat the Demonstration Game," *Advertis-*

ing and Selling 21 (October 12, 1933): 16. "Findings From Two Weeks in Toilet Goods Department in Bloomingdale's Department Store" (20 November 1923), Research Reports, reel 59; "Report on Three Weeks Spent Demonstrating Cutex at Abraham and Strauss' in Brooklyn" (9 September 1921), 3, Research Reports, reel 38; *J. Walter Thompson News Bulletin*, no. 43 (16 April 1917), 1. On rumor-mongering, see "Account Histories: Cutex" (1926), 11, Inactive Account Files, JWT.

CHAPTER FIVE

1. *TR* 8 (May 1923): 38; Nell Vinick, *Lessons in Loveliness* (New York: Longmans, Green, 1930), 5.
2. For an overview of these trends, see Martha Banta, *Imaging American Women: Idea and Ideals in Cultural History* (New York: Columbia Univ. Press, 1987); Rosalind Rosenberg, *Beyond Separate Spheres: The Intellectual Roots of Modern Feminism* (New Haven: Yale Univ. Press, 1982); Sheila Rothman, *Women's Proper Place: A History of Changing Ideals and Practices* (New York: Basic, 1979); Lewis A. Erenberg, *Steppin' Out: New York Nightlife and the Transformation of American Culture, 1890–1930* (Westport, Conn.: Greenwood, 1981); Carroll Smith-Rosenberg, "New Woman as Androgyne," in *Disorderly Conduct: Visions of Gender in Victorian America* (New York: Oxford Univ. Press, 1985), 245–96.
3. Armand ad proof, *Normal Instructor,* 1930, book 686, NWA. See also J. W. Watkins, Garda ad proofs, DD.
4. Frances Maule, "The 'Woman Appeal,'" *J. Walter Thompson News Bulletin* no. 105 (January 1924): 1, 2. See also Frances Maule, "How to Get a Good 'Consumer Image,'" *J. Walter Thompson News Bulletin*, no. 84 (March 1922): 9–11, in Periodicals, JWT.
5. Edith Lewis, "A New Kind of Beauty Contest," *J. Walter Thompson Co. News Letter* 11, no. 32 (March 1929): 1; Pond's ad proofs, *Good Housekeeping,* November 1923; *American Weekly,* 25 November 1923; and *New York American,* 27 January 1924, Chesebrough-Pond's, Advertising Collection, JWT.
6. *The Story of Pond's* (TS, 1937), 10, Inactive Account Files, Chesebrough-Pond's, Inc., Account Histories, JWT.
7. See Minutes, Special Production and Representatives Meeting, 9 April 1928, 4, New York Office Staff Meetings; *Story of Pond's;* "Account Histories: Pond's Extract Company" (18 January 1926), Inactive Account File, Chesebrough-Pond's, Account Histories; "Interview with Margaret King Eddy and Sidney R. Bernstein" (19 November 1963), 11, RG3, Sidney Bernstein Papers, JWT. For ads, see *LHJ,* February 1924, October 1925, and November 1925, Chesebrough-Pond's, Advertising Collection.
8. "Account Histories: Pond's Extract Company," 6; Minutes, Special Production and Representatives Meeting, 19. On signing up endorsers, see Pond's, "To secure data" (TS, n.d.), Testimonial Advertising, Information Center Records, JWT. On endorsers' looks, see Helen Woodward, *It's an Art* (New York: Harcourt,

Brace, 1938), 86; Alva Johnston, "Testimonials, C.O.D.," *Outlook and Independent* 157 (18 March 1931): 398–99.

9. Cf. Pompeian advertisements, *Woman's Home Companion*, November 1909, and *Pictorial Review*, October 1923. Everett G. McDonough, *The Truth about Cosmetics* (New York: Drug and Cosmetic Industry, 1937), 5.

10. See Maybelline advertisements in *Photoplay* and *True Story*, 1920–1925.

11. Edith Lewis, "The Emotional Quality in Advertisements," *J. Walter Thompson News Bulletin* no. 97 (April 1923): 13.

12. Virginia Lee, *The New Way to Beauty* (n.p.: Virginia Lee, Inc. 1929): 3. Armand ad proofs, nos. 11592, 11993 (1929), book 382, NWA.

13. Boris Glagolin, *Every Day Make-Up* (Milwaukee: Gutenberg Publishing Co., 1935), 157. Armand ad proof no. 9299 (1929), book 382, NWA. Armand Company, *Find Yourself* (n.p., 1929); "In the 1929 'Find Yourself' campaign," box 2, CW. See also Hazel E. Gray, "The 'Voice' of the Skin," *TR* (July 1931): 24–25. For a classic analysis, see Warren I. Susman, " 'Personality' and the Making of Twentieth-Century Culture," in *Culture as History* (New York: Pantheon, 1984), 271–85.

14. *A Short History of Mademoiselle: The Magazine for Smart Young Women* (New York: Street & Street, [1940]), 8. On the promise of transformation, see Jackson Lears, *Fables of Abundance* (New York: Basic, 1994), 56–63.

15. Dorin advertisement, *TR* 4 (August 1919): 10.

16. Countess Ceccaldi, *Secrets and Arts of Fascination Employed by Cleopatra, the Greatest Enchantress of All Time* (Tokolon Co. pamphlet, n.d.), 7, in Cosmetics, WCBA. Zip advertisement, *TR* 9 (April 1924).

17. Advertising scrapbook, Ruth DeForest Lamb Atkinson Papers, Vassar College. "The Armand Beauty Test Packet" (1926), book 384, NWA. On the impact of these ads, see Helen Woodward, *Through Many Windows* (New York: Harper, 1926), 252–53.

18. Marinello advertisement, *Milady Beautiful* (November 1922). "In the 1929 'Find Yourself' Campaign."

19. Wilson Flagg, *Analysis of Female Beauty* (Boston: Marsh, Capen, & Lyon, 1833), 31–32; Sir James Clark, *The Ladies' Guide to Beauty* (New York: Dick & Fitzgerald, 1858), 78.

20. On Cleopatra, see, e.g., Ceccaldi, *Secrets and Arts of Fascination;* Kashmir Chemical Company records, box 262, CAB. On the commerce in exoticism, Robert Rydell, *All the World's a Fair: Visions of Empire at American International Expositions* (Chicago: Univ. of Chicago Press, 1984); Lears, *Fables of Abundance*, 103–4, 149–50. On ethnic stage makeup, see M. Stein Cosmetic Company, *How to Make-Up* (New York, n.d.), in Special Collections, Fashion Institute of Technology; Hess Company, *The Art of 'Making-Up'* (Rochester, NY: James Conolly Co., 1916), 38.

21. Max Factor Make-Up Color Harmony Charts (Hollywood: Max Factor Studios, 1937); Max Factor, "The Art of Motion Picture Make-Up" (TS, n.d.), 4–5, MFPG. See also Esther Andrews, "Selling the Personality," *TR* 7 (September 1922): 27.

22. Armand ad proof, no. 10039 (1929); "The Armand Beauty Test Packet"; Armand, "To Look Your Loveliest" ad proof, *LHJ* (June 1926), book 384, NWA.

23. Armand *Jewish Daily Forward* advertisement, book 384, NWA; see also Jewish Daily Forward, *The Fourth American City: The Jewish Community of New York* (New York, 1927). *La Opinion* [Los Angeles], 26 October 1928, clipping, MFMB.

24. Helen Macfadden, *Help Yourself to Beauty* (New York: Macfadden, 1939), 129; *Faces as Typed by Eddie Senz of Paramount Studios; A Study in Face Values* (New York: Better Vision Institute, 1940), n. pag., Cosmetics, WCBA. See also Lois Banner, *American Beauty* (Chicago: Univ. of Chicago Press, 1983), 206.

25. "Armand Redesigns Packages; Creates Chain Store Line and Expands Its Field," *Sales Management* 38 (15 February 1936): 240.

26. Southern Flowers ad proof, no. 31 (1924); Nadine Advertising portfolio (1926), package 1, DD; cf. Nadine advertisements, *Pittsburgh Courier* (4 July 1925, 27 June 1925). Albert F. Wood, *The Way to a Satin Skin* (Detroit, 1923), 8–9, Cosmetics, WCBA; Pond's Investigation, "List of Skin Bleaches," Information on Certain Drugs and Cosmetic Products ([1931]), Research Reports, reel 53, JWT.

27. Harrison Vogt, "It's the Skin, Not the Clothes, This Year," *TR* 14 (July 1929): 21. On the industry's slow response, see Marie DuBois, "What Is Sun-tan Doing to Cosmetics," *Advertising and Selling* 13 (12 June 1929): 19.

28. Desti advertisement, *TR* 7 (February 1923): insert; Tre-Jur advertisement, *TR* 13 (February 1929): 35; Courtenay D. Marvin, "The Bleach Season Is On," *TR* 13 (October 1928): 28; Donald S. Cowling, "Will the Vogue for Tan Last?" *Printers Ink Monthly* 19 (August 1929): 32.

29. *Messenger* 7 (January 1925): 34.

30. Katherine Albert, "Remodel—Hollywood Fashion," *Good Housekeeping* 97 (October 1933): 172; Macfadden, *Help Yourself to Beauty*, 143; Eddie Senz, "Making Faces," *Mademoiselle* 5 (September 1937): 60. "Intelligent Use of Powders," *TR* 5 (April 1920): 21; Vinick, *Lessons in Loveliness*, 86.

31. "Charm vs. Glamour," *Hollywood Mirror* 1 (July 1935): 15; Max Factor Studios, *The New Art of Society Makeup* (Hollywood, 1928), 9.

32. Dorothy Cocks, *The Etiquette of Beauty* (New York: George H. Doran, 1927), 192. For Tangee, "Bad Taste in Advertising" (7 January 1936), 20, J. Walter Thompson Forum, USA and International Offices, JWT; "Men and Lipsticks," *PI* 161 (29 December 1932): 13. *The Secret of Charm and Beauty*, Book III (New York: Independent Corporation, 1923), 33.

33. *Secret of Charm and Beauty*, 19; Colgate advertisement, *Pictorial Review* (May 1924): 30; *Vogue's Book of Beauty* (New York: Conde Nast, 1933), 22.

34. Bernice Peck, "You Can Take It with You," *Mademoiselle* 6 (May 1938): 48–49. See also Vinick, *Lessons in Loveliness*, 47, 90; *Vogue's Book of Beauty*, 60–62.

35. Ruth Murrin, "Make a Picture of Yourself," *Good Housekeeping* 100 (May 1933): 112; *Vogue's Book of Beauty*, 85–86; Dr. Joseph Franklin Montague, "Let's Make Up and Have Friends," *TR* 21 (October 1936): 34; McDonough, *Truth about Cosmetics*, 5.

36. "Frances Ingram on Personality," *Radio Digest* 25 (October 1930): 77, 89.

37. Elizabeth Arden ad, *McCall's*, October 1928, 71. On Tre-Jur, *TR* 10 (February 1926): 5–7. See also "Cosmetic Advertising and Pretty Girl," *PI* 155 (9 April 1931): 100. On Depression-era advertising, see "Cosmetic Skin," *PI* 167 (10 May

1934): 33–36; Roland Marchand, *Advertising the American Dream: Making Way for Modernity* (Berkeley: Univ. of California Press, 1985), 285–333.

38. *Vogue's Book of Beauty,* 86; Armand ad proof, #11594, box 382, NWA; Ruth F. Wadsworth, *Charm by Choice* (New York: The Woman's Press, 1930), 78; Sylvia of Hollywood, *"No More Alibis!"* (Chicago: Photoplay Publ. Co., 1934), 123; Ceccaldi, *Secrets and Arts of Fascination,* 12; Margaret T. Kenyon, "A Lesson in Loveliness," *Good Housekeeping* 81 (July 1925): 177. McDonough, *Truth about Cosmetics,* 7.

39. "Will He-Men Ever Be a Good Market for Scented Cosmetics," *Sales Management* 40 (15 January 1937): 110, 114. See also Milwaukee Journal, *Consumer Analysis of the Greater Milwaukee Market* (Milwaukee, 1923), 31.

40. See, e.g., Patricia Marks, *Bicycles, Bangs and Bloomers: The New Woman in the Popular Press* (Lexington: Univ. Press of Kentucky, 1990), 131; Marquise de Fontenoy, *Eve's Glossary: The Guidebook of a Mondaine* (Chicago: Herbert S. Stone, 1897), 50–51; E. M. Woods, *The Negro in Etiquette: A Novelty* (St. Louis: Buxton & Skinner, 1899); Theodore Dreiser, *Sister Carrie* (New York: Doubleday, 1900). On masculine ideals, Anthony Rotundo, *American Manhood* (New York: Basic, 1994).

41. George Chauncey, *Gay New York: Gender, Urban Culture and the Making of the Gay Male World 1890-1940* (New York: Basic, 1994), 50–56.

42. "The Male Face," *Fortune* 15 (May 1937): 156. On men and beauty culture, Madame Edith Velaro, *How to Use Cosmetics* (New York: L. Boeker, 1886), 28; Allison Gray, "People Who Want to Look Young and Beautiful," *American Magazine* 94 (December 1922): 33.

43. "The Male Face," 156. *Journal of Commerce* quoted in P. H. Erbes, Jr., "The Eyes Have It," *PI* 190 (2 February 1940): 23. Pond's Consumer Investigation, Chester and Providence, C-39, Research Reports, reel 52, JWT. C. B. Bailey, "Men Are Buying Every Cosmetic Except Rouge and Lipstick," *TR* 15 (December 1930): 51. See also Mary Pickford bookmark advertisement (1917), Cosmetics, WCBA; "Account Histories: Vauv Company" (19 December 1925), Inactive Account Files, Account Histories, JWT.

44. *Spokane Review* quoted in *TR* 10 (September 1925): 61.

45. Gillette advertisements, *Town and Country* (1909–1910), *Country Life in America* (December 1910); Colgate, "How to Shave Yourself" (brochure, 1897), all in Barbering, WCBA.

46. J. Curley and Brothers, "Curley's Easy-Shaving Safety Razor" ([1896]), Barbering, WCBA; J. B. Williams advertisement, *American Magazine* 105 (April 1928): 103. Richard Porter, "Cosmetics for Men," *Aromatics* 13 (August 1930): 17, 76.

47. For ads addressing men and women, see Pompeian advertisement, *Cornhill,* 16 May 1914; *Saturday Evening Post,* 16 March 1912, 49. On Cutex inquiries, see "Cutex, Third Meeting of Class," *J. Walter Thompson Class Meetings* (January–June 1920), 70. On mascara, cf. Mrs. R. W. Allen, *New Price List and Illustrated Catalogue* (n.p., [1890]); *TR* 5 (June 1920): 28. For the gendering of cosmetics, see the *Reader's Guide to Periodicals,* which listed articles on men's cosmetics under "toilet goods" until the 1960s.

48. *TR* 12 (March 1928): 60; 11 (October 1926): 61. See also *TR* 7 (May 1922): 21; 9 (February 1925): 49, 52; 11 (May 1926): 41–42.
49. "The American Male Likes to Smell Nice Too," *Business Week*, 9 May 1953, 148. On tinted powder, *TR* 12 (May 1927): 66. On powder puffs, Bailey, "Men Are Buying Every Cosmetic," 51; Maurice Levy Talc-Pad advertisement, *TR* 12 (February 1928): 14.
50. "Selling Idea of Florian Line," 10 October 1925, 2, box 2, CW; Carl Weeks, "Why Armand's New Line Is Marketed Separately," *PI* 148 (11 July 1929): 68; Charles Muller to Carl Weeks, 9 February 1929, box 1, CW. On men's use of Symphonie, see Alice B. Bosshard to Carl Weeks (n.d.), box 3, CW.
51. "For Men Only! Florian Toilet Goods," *PI* 152 (17 July 1930): 33–34, 36; Weeks, "Why Armand's New Line," 69–70.
52. *Fortune* 11 (January 1935): 132; 11 (June 1935): 173; 12 (December 1936): 182; Fougere Royale advertisement, *Esquire* 1 (January 1934): 145. "Will He-Men," 110.
53. Carl Weeks, "Cosmetic Laws" (1932), 10, box 3, CW.

CHAPTER SIX

1. *TR* 5 (May 1920): 40. Business Week, *The American Consumer Market* (New York: McGraw-Hill, 1932), n. pag.
2. Market research is a problematic historical source for consumers' attitudes and behavior. Methods of data collection and analysis varied greatly, and findings, intended to influence advertisers and manufacturers, need to be viewed skeptically. I have relied most heavily on studies that used random samples, door-to-door interviewing, and reported qualitative as well as quantitative information. These data are suggestive, not definitive.
3. Allison Gray, "People Who Want to Look Young and Beautiful," *American Magazine* 94 (December 1922): 33; Beth Brown, "Chicago—The Convention City," *TR* 9 (August 1924): 46. See also *TR* 8 (April 1923): 33.
4. Representatives Meeting Minutes, 9 August 1927, New York Office Staff, USA and International Offices, 9–10, JWT. Nell B. Nichols, "Women's Search for Beauty" and "Analysis of Women Interviewed in Topeka, Kansas" (September 1923), Research Reports, reel 59; Pond's Extract Company, "Consumer Investigation in Columbus, O." (November 1927), 4–6, 16–17; "Consumer Investigation in Chester and Providence" (June 1927), 6, 16–17, P-49, Research Reports, reel 52; "Investigation on the New Pond's Cream Jar Hartford–Providence" (June 1933), Research Reports, reel 53, JWT. See also Paul W. Kearney, "Two Billions for One," *TR* 10 (April 1925): 43, 47.
5. "Outstanding Facts on Investigation in Small Towns in Indiana," *J. Walter Thompson News Bulletin* no. 42 (9 April 1917): 2, Publications, JWT; O. N. Falk & Sons Records, SHSW. See also Luliette Bryant, "Cosmetics in the Country," *Beauty* 1 (December 1922): 35, 79; "What Do Our Rural Neighbors Buy," *J. Walter Thompson News Bulletin* no. 120 (March 1926): 12.

6. *TR* 11 (January 1927): 52; Farm Journal and Farmer's Wife, *Cross Country Inventory, no. 6: Cosmetics-Drugs* (n.p., 1941), 7–8. See also Pond's Extract Company, "Consumer Investigation in Circleville, Ohio and the Farming Sections" (November 1927), 4–5, Research Reports, reel 52, JWT. "Farmer's Daughter Big User of Cosmetics and Drugs," *Sales Management* 37 (15 August 1935): 147, shows a significant discrepancy between city and farm women's cosmetics use in the mid-1930s.

7. Ruth S. Becker, "Cosmetics—From Behind the Counter," *J. Walter Thompson Newsletter* no. 194 (15 December 1927): 527. "Consumer Investigation in Chester and Providence," 16; Pond's Extract Co., "Complete Statistical Summary of College Girls, Circleville Women, Farm Women" (November 1927), 5, 30–31, Research Reports, reel 52, JWT; Erwin, Wasey & Co., *The Buying Power and Brand Preferences of the American College Student*, no. 603 (n.p., July 1931).

8. Nichols, "Women's Search for Beauty," 10.

9. Vincent Vinikas, *Soft Soap, Hard Sell* (Ames: Iowa State Univ. Press, 1992), 8–14; Cincinnati Office, "An Analysis of Subscription Circulation of Forty-four Magazines in Metropolitan Cincinnati, 1923," Research Department, Correspondence and Memoranda, JWT; Curtis Publishing Co., *City A and City B* (Philadelphia, [1926]), Curtis Publishing Company Records, Special Collections, Van Pelt Library, University of Pennsylvania. Robert and Helen Lynd, *Middletown* (1929; reprint, New York: Harcourt, Brace, & World, 1956), 239–42.

10. "Findings from Two Weeks in Toilet Goods Department in Bloomingdale's Department Store" (20 November 1923), 3, Research Reports, reel 59; Cincinnati Office, "A Plan for the Future Growth of the Jergens-Woodbury Business" (24 October 1931), 14, Research Reports, reel 45, JWT; Fraser V. Sinclair, "The Farmer's Wife Comes to Town," *TR* 5 (April 1920), 25. See also Mary E. Hoffman, *Buying Habits of Small-Town Women* (Kansas City: Ferry-Hanly Advertising Co., 1926), 31, 34; Milwaukee Journal, *A Survey of the Milwaukee Market on Cosmetics and Accessories* (Milwaukee, 1923), 31. On price appeals, see Michael Schudson, *Advertising: The Uneasy Persuasion* (New York: Basic, 1984), 11.

11. Research Department, "Small Town and Rural Investigation among Subscribers to *People's Home Journal*" (February 1925); Research Department, "Rural and Small Town Investigation, Indiana" (February 1925), 137; Research Department, "Rural and Small Town Investigation, Putnam County, New York" (1923), Research Department Reports, JWT. Modern Magazines, *Fourth Survey of Beauty: A Study of Cosmetic Buying Trends* (New York: Dell, 1934); *Short Cuts for the Beauty Shop* (Pasadena: Chap Book Press, 1933), 48.

12. "Analysis of Fifty-Two Questionnaires for Pond's Cream" (10 November 1920), 4, Research Reports, reel 52; Pond's Investigation, "Tentative Conclusions" (4 November 1931), Research Reports, reel 53, JWT.

13. Nichols, "Analysis of Women Interviewed," 8, 46. "Woodbury's Facial Soap Investigation of Southern Debutantes" (23 September 1925), n. pag., Research Reports, reel 45, JWT. See also "Consumer Investigation in Columbus," 37, 40–41.

14. "For the Andrew Jergens Company, Woodbury's Facial Soap, National Campaign 1926," 4, Inactive Account Files, Andrew Jergens Co., Howard Henderson Files,

JWT; "Woodbury's Facial Soap Investigation among Chicago University Girls" (May 1925), 13, 22, Research Reports, reel 45, JWT. See also A. W. Urquhart, "How We Can Help One Another," MPA, *Proceedings of the Twenty-seventh Annual Meeting* (New York, 1921), 29.

15. "Woodbury Facial Soap Investigation among Smith College Students" ([1924]), 15; "Woodbury Facial Soap Investigation Among Michigan University Students" (February 1925), 14–16, Research Reports, reel 45, JWT; "Investigation among Chicago University Girls," 15.

16. *TR* 13 (November 1928): 23; Milwaukee Journal, *A Survey of the Milwaukee Market*, 98–117, 134–55, 198–221. See also Scripps-Howard Newspapers, *Market Records; A Home-Inventory Study of Buying Habits and Brand Preferences of Consumers in Sixteen Cities*, vol. 1 (n.p., 1938), 172, 180, 184, 188. For skin-care routines, "Consumer Investigation in Columbus," 4–5, 43–50; "Complete Statistical Summary of College Girls, Circleville Women, Farm Women," 30–36.

17. "Consumer Investigation in Columbus," 18, 37; Mrs. S. E. Baldwin to NBC ([December 1934]), Lady Esther, National Broadcasting Company Records, SHSW. "Consumer Investigation in Chester and Providence," C-39, P-39. "How 10,000 Housewives Rate Drug, Cigarette and Auto Ads," *Sales Management* 37 (15 August 1935): 148–49.

18. "Consumer Investigation in Chester and Providence," C-39; Jergens Co., "Consumer Investigation" (1929), 96, Research Reports, reel 196; "Toilet Articles Investigation Questionnaire by Mail" (February 1923), Research Reports, reel 59, JWT; "Investigation on the New Pond's Cream Jar." See also *TR* 10 (June 1925): 37; *J. Walter Thompson Newsletter* 10, no. 25 (15 December 1928): 1; Rebecca Stickney, "The Cosmetic Urge," *Advertising and Selling* 11 (31 October 1928): 21.

19. Nichols, "Analysis of Women Interviewed," 31, 6–7.

20. "McCall's—Interview with Miss Fillmore," Interviews with Experts on Skin (n.d.), Research Reports, reel 45, JWT; Nichols, "Analysis of Women Interviewed," 3, 31.

21. Nichols, "Analysis of Women Interviewed," 36, 19–20.

22. Pond's Investigation, "Tentative Conclusions," n. pag.

23. "Women Less Particular about Food Brands than Cosmetics," *Sales Management* 39 (20 October 1936): 652; Phyllis Lewis, "Making Salesmen of the Goods," *TR* 8 (July 1923): 36.

24. Dorothy Brewster Smith Dushkin diary, 1 March 1920, box 1, Sophia Smith Collection, Smith College; "Powder Puffs and Politics," *TR* 4 (January 1920): 50. See also *J. Walter Thompson Newsletter* 12, no. 32 (31 March 1929): 1; *TR* 9 (June 1924): 69.

25. Milwaukee Journal, *Survey of the Milwaukee Market;* "Consumer Investigation in Columbus," 4–5, 43–50; "Complete Statistical Summary of College Girls, Circleville Women, Farm Women," 30–36.

26. *Seattle Union Record*, 26 March 1925; 30 March 1925. Twenty letters on women's makeup ran in Ruth Ridgway's column from 26 March to 29 April 1925.

27. Ruth Field, "Report of Two Weeks Selling Experience in Toilet Articles Department at Lord and Taylor" (December 1923), 5, 13, 4, Research Reports, reel 59,

JWT; Blanche Snyder to M. C. Phillips, 11 March 1935, Skin Deep Correspondence with Readers, Publications—Books, Administrative Files, Consumers' Research, Inc. Papers, Special Collections and University Archives, Rutgers University Library. "Smart Set Magazine—Interview with Miss Waterbury," Interviews with Experts. See also Jergens Co., "Consumer Investigation," 93.

28. *Seattle Union Record,* 8 April 1925; 13 April 1925.

29. Nichols, "Analysis of Women Interviewed," 44, 47.

30. Violet Osler, "My Aids to Beauty," *Household Magazine,* February 1932, n.p.; "Harper's Bazaar—Interview with Mrs. McCommon," Interviews with Experts; "Popular Types, Shades and Brands of Rouge and Lipstick" (August 1932), Research Reports, reel 49, JWT.

31. "Findings from Two Weeks in . . . Bloomingdale's Department Store," 8; Field, "Report of Two Weeks . . . at Lord and Taylor," 12. William C. Weeks to Armand Salesmen, 26 September 1935, box 2, CW.

32. Boncilla Laboratories, Inc., *How Your Skin Is Actually Transformed* (Indianapolis, n.d.), Hagley Museum and Library. J. R. Watkins Co., *Watkins Timely Suggestions* (Winona, Minn., 1920), Cosmetics, WCBA.

33. *Seattle Union Record,* 26 March 1925. "Women Less Particular about Food Brands than Cosmetics," 652; "The Consumer Goes to Market—With What and for What?" *Sales Management* 34 (15 March 1934): 225.

34. *Seattle Union Record,* 8 April 1925; 24 April 1925.

35. "Gans, Watkins," "Gans, Montour Falls" cards (n.d.), box 25; Edith V. Enders, "Supplement to Cornell Reading-Course for Farmers' Wives," Discussion Paper (March 1905), box 24, College of Human Ecology Papers, Rare and Manuscripts Collections, Cornell University Library.

36. Nichols, "Analysis of Women Interviewed," 1, 6, 10, 13. On use of white powder, "Readers' Questions," *TR* 21 (June 1936): 40. On religious opposition to makeup, James Kenneally, "Eve, Mary, and the Historians," in Janet Wilson James, ed., *Women and American Religion* (Phila.: Univ. of Pennsylvania Press, 1980), 201.

37. Violet Osler, "My Aids to Beauty," n. pag. Ruth Field, "Report of Two Weeks . . . at Lord and Taylor," 12; Jergens Co., "Consumer Investigation," 93. See also "What Our Wild Young Women Really Think," *Beautiful Womanhood* 1 (September 1922): 53.

38. Christine Frederick, *Selling Mrs. Consumer* (New York: Business Bourse, 1929), 189; *True Story,* July 1919, 61; *Beautiful Womanhood* 2 (March 1923): 54. See also Pamela Haag, "In Search of 'The Real Thing': Ideologies of Love, Modern Romance, and Women's Sexual Subjectivity in the U.S., 1920–1940," *Journal of the History of Sexuality* 2 (April 1992): 547–77.

39. "Harper's Bazaar—Interview with Mrs. McCommon," Interviews with Experts.

40. "Delineator—Interview with Miss Martin," Interviews with Experts.

41. Nichols, "Analysis of Women Interviewed," 1–2, 5, 8–9, 42.

42. *Seattle Union Record,* 13 April 1925; Blanche V. Greenwood to M. C. Phillips, 30 January 1935, Skin Deep Correspondence.

43. Brown, "Chicago," 46. The Milwaukee Journal's *Survey of the Milwaukee Market,* the most extensive survey in my sample, found that less than 4 percent of women

used mascara and only 15 percent used lipstick in 1923. On the "tough" working-class women, see Marlou Belyea, "The Joy Ride and the Silver Screen: Commercial Leisure, Delinquency and Play Reform in Los Angeles, 1900–1980" (Ph.D. diss., Boston University, 1983), 309–10.

44. On making up in public, see *TR* 15 (August 1930): 52; "Woman's Leisure Time," *PI* (17 January 1935): 48; *Industrial Psychology Monthly* 2 (August 1927): 440. On Elder, see Raquel, *Turning Scents into Dollars* (New York, 1928), 9.

45. "Charm vs. Glamour," *Hollywood Mirror* 1 (July 1935): 15. "Men and Lipsticks," *PI* (29 December 1932): 13.

46. Margaret Parton, *Journey Through a Lighted Room* (New York: Viking, 1973), 26.

47. Anzia Yezierska, *Bread Givers* (1925; reprint, New York: Persea, 1975), 182. On Jewish women, appearance, and consumption, see Andrew Heinze, *Adapting to Abundance* (New York: Columbia Univ. Press, 1990), 89–104, 197–98.

48. "Interview with Irene, Hungarian, 18 years of age," and "Interview with Jolan, Hungarian, 20 years of age" (1939), box 31, Young Women's Christian Association (YWCA), National Board Archives, New York, Records File Collection, Sophia Smith Collection, Smith College. Mary E. Odem, *Delinquent Daughters* (Chapel Hill: Univ. of North Carolina Press, 1995), 175, 161. George J. Sánchez, *Becoming Mexican American: Ethnicity, Culture and Identity in Chicano Los Angeles, 1900–1945* (New York: Oxford Univ. Press, 1993), 265. On family conflicts, see Silvia S. Silverman, *Clothing and Appearance: Their Psychological Implications for Teen-Age Girls* (New York: Columbia Teachers College, 1945), 1–2.

49. Nichols, "Analysis of Women Interviewed," 37.

50. Latino ballad quoted in Belyea, "Joy Ride," 323. Children's Aid Association (Hampshire County, Massachusetts), *Annual Report* (1928), 18. See also "Interview with Caroline K," box 31, YWCA Papers.

51. Field, "Report of Two Weeks . . . at Lord and Taylor," 6; "Lipstick—Check at Walgreen's—Chicago, April 4, 1934," Research Reports, reel 196; Creative Organization Staff Meeting Minutes, 19 March 1932, JWT.

52. Gray, "People Who Want to Look Young," 32–33.

53. Quoted in Chris Rasmussen, "State Fair: Culture and Agriculture in Iowa, 1854–1941" (Ph.D. diss., Rutgers University, 1992), 294. O. S. Hubbard, "Beauty Contests for High School Girls," *School Life* 18 (September 1932): 3. On beauty pageants, see Lois Banner, *American Beauty* (Chicago: Univ. of Chicago Press, 1983), 249–70.

54. Herbert Blumer, *Movies and Conduct* (New York: Macmillan, 1933), 30, 31; Herbert Blumer and Philip M. Hauser, *Movies, Delinquency and Crime* (New York: Macmillan, 1933), 100–101, 115; Hazel Grant Ormsbee, *The Young Employed Girl* (New York: Womans Press, 1927), 82. Belyea, "Joy Ride," 309–10. For market research, see Modern Magazines, *Eighth Survey of Beauty* (New York: Dell, 1938), 6, 9; and *Ninth Survey of Beauty* (New York: Dell, 1939), 6, 10.

55. Motion Picture Autobiographies, Motion Picture Research Council Papers, Hoover Institution, K2, J2, G1, I2; transcripts provided by Kathryn Fuller, in author's possession; some are reprinted in Garth Jowett et al., *Children and the*

Movies: Media Influence and the Payne Fund Controversy (New York: Cambridge Univ. Press, 1996). Blumer, *Movies and Conduct,* 251. See also Jackie Stacey, *Star Gazing: Hollywood Cinema and Female Spectatorship* (London: Routledge, 1994); Miriam Hansen, *Babel and Babylon: Spectatorship in American Silent Film* (Cambridge: Harvard Univ. Press, 1991).

56. Motion Picture Autobiographies, M3; Paul G. Cressey, "Preliminary Generalizations upon the New York University Motion Picture Study" ([1932]), 3, Payne Fund Study, W. W. Charters Papers, Ohio State University; Blumer, *Movies and Conduct,* 154.

57. Gray, "People Who Want to Look Young," 32–33. Louise de Koven Bowen, "The Girl Employed in Hotels and Restaurants" (1912), in *Speeches, Addresses and Letters of Louise de Koven Bowen Reflecting Social Movements in Chicago,* vol. 1 (Ann Arbor: Edwards Brothers, 1937), 256. Adelaide K. Zitello, "Evaluation of Interviews of Twenty-one Second Generation Girls" (8 June 1939), 2, box 31, YWCA Papers. For discussions of job requirements, Susan Porter Benson, *Counter Cultures* (Urbana: Univ. of Illinois Press, 1986), 124–42, 236–38; Alice Kessler-Harris, *Out to Work* (New York: Oxford Univ. Press, 1982), 128–41; Dorothy Sue Cobble, *Dishing It Out* (Urbana: Univ. of Illinois Press, 1992), 127–31; Walter Licht, *Getting Work* (Cambridge: Harvard Univ. Press, 1992), 124–25, 136.

58. William Fretz Kemble, *Choosing Employees by Mental and Physical Tests* (New York: Engineering Magazine, 1917), 166–67; Theodosia Hewlett, "Guidance and the Commercial Graduate," *Occupations* 15 (December 1936): 222. Vocational Guidance Records, Smith College Archives. See also Licht, *Getting Work,* 95, 165.

59. *TR* 6 (November 1921): 27; Frances Maule, *She Strives to Conquer: Business Behavior, Opportunities and Job Requirements for Women* (New York: Funk & Wagnalls, 1936), 89, 136–37. See also Lisa Fine, *Souls of the Skyscraper* (Philadelphia: Temple Univ. Press, 1990), 61.

60. *Bulletin for Department Meetings* 20 (9 April 1928): n. pag., and *Talks to Waiters and Waitresses, Hotels Statler* (1939), 10, Statler Hotels Collection, Cornell University Library. *Long Lines* [American Telephone and Telegraph] 1 (February 1922): 8–9; (April 1922): 48; C. G. Hicks, "Packing Pickles in Patterns Aids Toilet Goods Sales in Pittsburgh," *TR* 14 (August 1929): 58, 110.

61. On the YWCA, see Northeastern Field Committee, "Reports of Camp Councils" (1915), 2, and "Reports of the Industrial Girls Club Councils" (New York, 1916), 21, box 16; "The Younger Girl in Business and Industry: A Girl Reserve Program" (New York, 1920), 18, box 27; "Report of the Industrial Dept. of the——— YWCA, Sept. 1929–June 1930," 118, box 26, YWCA Papers. On commercial colleges, see Fine, *Souls,* 176–77.

62. "The Symbolic Jacket," in Andria Taylor Hourwitch and Gladys L. Palmer, eds., *I Am a Woman Worker* (1936; reprint, New York: Arno, 1974), 22–23. Nichols, "Analysis of Women Interviewed," 39.

63. On school opposition to makeup, see *TR* 6 (January 1922): 31. On home economics enrollments, see John L. Rury, "Vocationalism for Home and Work: Women's

Education in the U.S., 1880–1930," *History of Education Quarterly* 24 (spring 1984): 22.

64. Helene Harmon Weis diary, 13 January 1939, Helene Harman Weis Papers, Schlesinger Library, Radcliffe College. For business-school cooperation, see *Curtis Bulletin* 112 (June 1929): n. pag., Curtis Publishing Co. Records; Helena Rubinstein, *The Art of Feminine Beauty* (New York: Horace Liveright, 1930), 29; Silverman, *Clothing and Appearance*, 7. For the cleanliness appeal, see *TR* 7 (February 1923): 27; Elizabeth Terhune, "America Learns to Brush" (1997, unpublished paper in author's possession); Vinikas, *Soft Soap, Hard Sell*. See also Carolyn Goldstein, "Mediating Consumption: Home Economics and American Consumers, 1900–1940" (Ph.D. diss., Univ. of Delaware, 1994).

65. Natalie Eileen Dunn, "An Exploratory Study of the Relationship Between a Cornell Freshman's Wardrobe and Her Orientation to College Life" (M.S. thesis, Cornell University, 1934), 12, 119. On beauty instruction, see "Cosmetics in Education," *TR* 21 (November 1936): 35; Hildegarde Fillmore, "Let's Look at the Younger Generation," *TR* 21 (August 1936): 17, 52. Louise Gibb, "Personal Appearance," *Occupations* 15 (March 1937): 528–30.

66. A. K. Getman et al., New York State Education Department . . . to District Superintendents, 27 March 1936, box 11, New York State College of Home Economics, College of Human Ecology Papers, Cornell University Library. Silverman, *Clothing and Appearance*, 1–2.

67. "Smart Set—Interview with Miss Waterbury." On expenditures, Thyra Samter Winslow, "Beauty for Sale," *New Republic* 169 (25 November 1931): 40–42. Curtis Publishing Company, *Consumer Purchase Survey: Selective Spending in Chicago-Providence-Denver* (April 1938), 23; New York Herald Tribune, *How New York Families Spend Their Money* (New York, 1939).

68. Ruth DeForest Lamb, *American Chamber of Horrors: The Truth about Food and Drugs* (New York: Farrar & Rinehart, 1936). On the importance of women's groups, see Lamb to C. Ray Cooper, 9 September 1937; Lamb to Mrs. Strauss, 21 November 1937, in Ruth DeForest Lamb Atkinson Papers, Vassar College.

69. M. C. Phillips, *Skin Deep: The Truth about Beauty Aids—Safe and Harmful* (New York: Vanguard Press, 1934). Mabel B. Moats to Phillips, 14 March 1935, Skin Deep Correspondence.

70. Nelle Mordoff to F. J. Schlink, 11 May 1940, Skin Deep Correspondence. See also reviews in *Baltimore Evening Sun*, 28 November 1934; *The Headlight* (Pennsylvania State College Library), April 1935, Skin Deep Reviews, Publications—Books, Administrative Files, Consumers' Research, Inc. Papers.

71. Shirley R. King to M. C. Phillips, 26 December 1934; see also Miss E. Oellame to Consumers' Research, 20 November 1935; Miss Josephine Diorio to Phillips, 19 May 1938, Skin Deep Correspondence.

72. Alice Breitenbach to M. C. Phillips, 18 February 1935; Mrs. Earl Kerwell to Consumers' Research, 6 July 1938; Barbara Bullock to Phillips, 20 August 1936, Skin Deep Correspondence.

73. Anna Hrivnak to M. C. Phillips, 31 December 1935; Mrs. E. Szilagyi to Phillips,

31 December 1936. See also Lucille Ingles to Phillips, 23 January 1935; Marcelle White to Phillips, 4 August 1936, Skin Deep Correspondence.

74. Agnes Hoffman to M. C. Phillips, 23 December 1935, Skin Deep Correspondence.

75. See, e.g., Winslow, "Beauty for Sale," 42.

CHAPTER SEVEN

1. Chandler Owen, "Good Looks Supremacy," *Messenger* 6 (March 1924): 80.

2. *Oklahoma Eagle*, 3 March 1928, clipping, box 262, CAB.

3. E. Azalia Hackley, *The Colored Girl Beautiful* (Kansas City: Burton Publ. Co., 1916), 36.

4. John H. Adams, Jr., "Rough Sketches: A Study of the Features of the New Negro Woman," *Voice of the Negro* 1 (August 1904): 323–26. See also Henry Louis Gates, Jr., "The Trope of a New Negro and the Reconstruction of the Image of the Black," *Representations* 24 (Fall 1988): 129–55.

5. Hackley, *Colored Girl Beautiful*, 36–37; *Voice of the Negro* 1 (August 1904).

6. Hackley, *Colored Girl Beautiful*, 29, 75. Concerns about dress and deportment appear throughout the Records of the National Association of Colored Women's Clubs, 1893–1992, microfilm ed. (Bethesda: University Publications of America, 1993); see especially National Association of Colored Women, *Proceedings of the Ninth Biennial Convention*, 1914; Fannie Barrier Williams, "The Dress Burden," *National Association Notes* (May 1913): 8–9. See also Hazel V. Carby, "Policing the Black Woman's Body in an Urban Context," *Critical Inquiry* 18 (Summer 1992): 738–55.

7. Mrs. Booker T. Washington, "The Tuskegee Woman's Club," *Southern Workman* (1920): 366. African Broadway described in Elizabeth Ewen and Stuart Ewen, *Channels of Desire* (New York: McGraw-Hill, 1982), 212. E. M. Woods, *The Negro in Etiquette: A Novelty* (St. Louis: Buxton & Skinner, 1899), 29, 34, 81.

8. Nannie Burroughs, "Not Color but Character," *Voice of the Negro* 1 (July 1904): 278.

9. Burroughs, "Not Color but Character," 277. On color hierarchies, see William B. Gatewood, *Aristocrats of Color: The Black Elite, 1880–1920* (Bloomington: Indiana Univ. Press, 1990), 151–70.

10. Anna Julia Cooper, *A Voice from the South* (1892; reprint, New York: Negro Univ. Press, 1969), 75; Burroughs, "Not Color but Character," 277. See also Fannie Barrier Williams, "The Colored Girl," *Voice of the Negro* 2 (June 1905), 402–403. On black women reformers, see Hazel V. Carby, *Reconstructing Womanhood: The Emergence of the Afro-American Woman Novelist* (New York: Oxford Univ. Press, 1987); Paula Giddings, *When and Where I Enter* (New York: Morrow, 1984).

11. *Crusader* 1 (June and July 1919), covers; *Chicago Defender*, 31 May 1919. The appearance of blue veins on the skin was considered a sign of "whiteness." On the politics of this period, see Wilson Moses, *The Golden Age of Black Nationalism, 1850–1925* (Hamden, Conn.: Archon, 1978).

12. George Schuyler, "Unnecessary Negroes," *Messenger* 8 (1926): 307; "Shafts and Darts: A Page of Calumny and Satire," *Messenger* 9 (July 1927): 230; *Black No More* (1931; reprint, Boston: Northeastern Univ. Press, 1989). Chandler Owen, "Good Looks Supremacy," 80. For Black-No-More advertisement, see *New York Age*, 16 July 1914.

13. Percival Burrows, "Give Me Your Votes" (1925), Walker Mfg. Co. Press Releases, MCJW. George Schuyler, "Madam C. J. Walker," *Messenger* 6 (August 1924): 256. See also ads in *Negro World*, 4 April 1925; 18 July 1925; 21 March 1925.

14. On the importance of the *Defender*, see James R. Grossman, *Land of Hope: Chicago, Black Southerners, and the Great Migration* (Chicago: Univ. of Chicago Press, 1989), 74–88. See also Frederick G. Detweiler, *The Negro Press in the United States* (1922; reprint, College Park, Md.: McGrath Publ. Co., 1968).

15. On cosmetic ads in black newspapers, see Guy B. Johnson, "Newspaper Advertisements and Negro Culture," *Journal of Social Forces* 3 (1924–1925): 706–709; Paul K. Edwards, *The Southern Urban Negro as a Consumer* (New York: Prentice-Hall, 1932), 185–87.

16. Francis Marion Dunford, "Conflicting Forces in Negro Progress," *Journal of Social Forces* 3 (1924–1925): 703; "That Bleaching Imposition," *Half-Century* 6 (April 1919): 3.

17. *Half-Century*, 11 (November 1921): 3. Mrs. J. H. P. Coleman, in NNBL, *Report of the Thirteenth Annual Convention* (1912), 67. Overton-Hygienic Company, *Encyclopedia of Colored People*, (n.p., [1922]), 8. Calls to boycott appear in *Crusader* 1 (September 1918): 7; 2 (September 1919): 10–11.

18. *Half-Century* 8 (February 1920): 17; 8 (April 1920): 17–18; 10 (May–June 1921): 17.

19. D. F. Nealon, *Report of Studies on Nadinola Bleaching Cream* (Paris, Tenn.: National Toilet Co., 1946), in University of Wisconsin Library. Cf. ingredients in Kashmir Chemical Company formulas, box 262, CAB; Overton-Hygienic Company product insert (n.d.), Medical Sciences Division, NMAH. On the effects of ammoniated mercury, see Gerald A. Spencer, *Cosmetology in the Negro* (New York: Arlain Printing Co., 1944), 46.

20. *Half-Century* 7 (November 1919): 21; 8 (February 1920): 17. Claude A. Barnett to Annie M. Malone, 8 February 1929, box 262, CAB.

21. Plough advertisement, *New York Age*, 11 January 1919; *Crusader* 1 (March 1919): 7; *Half-Century* 6 (February 1919): 13. *Chicago Whip* quoted in Dunford, "Conflicting Forces," 703.

22. *Pittsburgh Courier*, 7 April 1923. On the beauty of the New Negro Woman, see *Messenger* 6 (January 1924): 7, and covers, 1917–1925; cf. editorial on the "New Negro," *Messenger* 2 (August 1920): 73. See also "Types of Racial Beauty," *Half-Century* 6 (June 1919): 7.

23. One extant issue of the *Afro-American Journal of Fashion* (May–June 1893) appears in the Records of the National Association of Colored Women's Clubs (microfilm ed.). On Coston see M. A. Majors, *Noted Negro Women* (1893; reprint, Freeport, New York: Books for Libraries Press, 1971). For Madame Rumford's column, see *Colored American Magazine*, July 1901. On black women's maga-

zines, see Penelope L. Bullock, *The Afro-American Periodical Press 1838–1909* (Baton Rouge: Louisiana State Univ. Press, 1981), 166–93. On women's pages, see Detweiler, *Negro Press in the United States*, 105, 109.

24. *New York Age*, 23 July 1914; 6 August 1914. Golden Brown advertisement, St. Louis *Argus* clipping (1925), in African-American Cosmetics File, Community Life Division, NMAH. See also beauty contest clippings, box 261, CAB.

25. Overton-Hygienic, *Encyclopedia of Colored People*, 11.

26. For Poro, see *Pittsburgh Courier*, 25 March 1911, 1 November 1912; *Chicago Defender* 26 May 1917. For Walker, see *Crisis* 3 (January 1912): 130; 15 (December 1917): 99; 17 (March 1919): 256; *Messenger* 2 (July 1918): back cover; 2 (January 1918): back cover.

27. Claude Barnett, "Fly Out of Darkness" (MS autobiography, n.d.), 6, 8, box 406, CAB.

28. *Ibid.* Kashmir tearsheets, brochures, photos of posters, and product labels are in CAB, box 262, and Prints and Photographs, box 4, CHS.

29. Kashmir Chemical Co., *Nile Queen for Hair and Skin* (Chicago, 1919), 6–7, CAB. See also Kashmir Chemical Company, *Beauty, Health, Success, The Kashmir Way* (Chicago, n.d.), 8–9. For the new style of Walker ads, see the following in the *Messenger:* "Beauty's Synonym," 6 (August 1924): back cover; "Men Prefer Beauty," 9 (1927): 51; "From Boudoir to Beach," 6 (September 1924): 284–85.

30. Vere E. Johns, "Our Artificial Women," *New York Age*, 12 May 1934. Kashmir, *Nile Queen*, cover, and product labels.

31. "From Boudoir to Beach." See Hazel V. Carby, " 'It Jus' Be's Dat Way Sometime': The Sexual Politics of Women's Blues," in Ellen Carol DuBois and Vicki L. Ruiz, eds., *Unequal Sisters* (New York: Routledge, 1990), 238–49.

32. Walker advertisement, *Messenger* 7 (1925): 212. Kashmir advertisement, *Chicago Defender*, 22 February 1919.

33. "Aunt Pat's Forum," *Dallas Express*, 26 March 1921, quoted in Detweiler, *Negro Press*, 246. *Half-Century* 4 (June 1918): 14; 7 (October 1919): 11.

34. See, for example, *Crusader* 1 (February 1919): 19; 1 (April 1919): 19; 1 (May 1919): 19. *Negro World*, 9 January 1926; *Half-Century* 1 (August 1916): 14; 2 (January 1917): 8–9; 10 (May–June 1921).

35. *Madam C. J. Walker Beauty Manual*, 1st ed. (Indianapolis: Walker Manufacturing Co., 1928), 181; *Poro Hair and Beauty Culture* (St. Louis: Poro College, 1922), 24–25. "Types of Racial Beauty," 7. Walker advertisement no. 20 ([1920]), Advertisements, MCJW.

36. Plough advertisement, *Chicago Defender*, 29 May 1920; Golden Brown advertisement, *New York Age*, 7 February 1920.

37. "Betrayers of the Race," *Half-Century* 8 (February 1920): 3. Eulalia Proctor, "La Femme Silhouette," *Messenger* 7 (1925): 93; see also 34.

38. *Half-Century* 12 (February 1922): 21. See also "Betrayers of the Race," 3. For *Jewish Daily Forward* ad placements, see Walker Company ledger, sales distribution, August–September 1925.

39. Louis W. George, "Beauty Culture and Colored People," *Messenger* 2 (July 1918): 26.

40. Sarah Armstrong to Madam C. J. Walker, 29 April 1918; Marie Alexander Sykes to Walker, 27 April 1918, Orders, MCJW.

41. Annie Dervin to Madam C. J. Walker, 4 May 1918; Bessie Brown to Walker, 28 June 1918, Orders; Walker Company ledger, sales recapitulation, 1923–1932, MCJW.

42. On these variations in bleaching, see Spencer, *Cosmetology in the Negro,* 46; Overton-Hygienic, *Encyclopedia of Colored People,* 25, 27; *Half-Century* 4 (June 1918): 14; Leon A. Greenberg and David Lester, *Handbook of Cosmetic Materials* (New York: Interscience Publishers, 1954), 47.

43. Lillie Byrd to Madam C. J. Walker, 20 May 1918, Orders; Byrd quoted 1 Cor. 11–15: "If a woman have long hair, it is a Glory to her." Dora Bastce [?] to Walker, 8 May 1918; Marie Cane to Walker, 21 May 1918, Orders, MCJW. See also "What Poro has Meant to the Nation" (TS, [1925]), box 262, CAB.

44. Virgie Brown to Madam C. J. Walker, 21 June 1918; Mamie Bass to Walker, 10 May 1918, Orders, MCJW.

45. Helen Bell to Madam C. J. Walker, 5 June 1918, Orders, MCJW; O-zo-no ad, *Chicago Defender,* 1 March 1919.

46. Emmett J. Scott, comp., "Additional Letters of Negro Migrants of 1916–1918," *Journal of Negro History* 4 (October 1919): 455; see also 447. See Grossman, *Land of Hope,* 74–88.

47. F. B. Ransom to Mrs. A. C. Burnett, 10 September 1918, Walker Mfg. Co. General Correspondence, MCJW.

48. Scott, "Additional Letters of Negro Migrants," 451. See Grossman, *Land of Hope;* Peter Gottlieb, "Rethinking the Great Migration: A Perspective from Pittsburgh," in Joe William Trotter, ed., *The Great Migration in Historical Perspective* (Bloomington: Indiana Univ. Press, 1991), 70.

49. Emmett J. Scott, comp., "Letters of Negro Migrants of 1916–1918," *Journal of Negro History* 4 (July 1919): 315, 317.

50. M. L. Craft to Madam C. J. Walker, 26 April 1918, Orders, MCJW; James H. Collins, "The Beauty Business: It Makes the Things to Make You Beautiful," *Saturday Evening Post* 197 (22 November 1924): 14; Interview with Elizabeth Cardozo Barker, 19, Black Women Oral History Project, Schlesinger Library, Radcliffe College; H. A. Haring, "Selling to Harlem," *Advertising and Selling* 11 (31 October 1928): 17.

51. *Chicago Advocate,* 26 February 1921, quoted in Detweiler, *Negro Press,* 243. Mamie Garvin Fields, *Lemon Swamp, and Other Places* (New York: Free Press, 1983), 176. On proscribing rural customs, see Grossman, *Land of Hope,* 145–52; on urban style, Shane White and Graham White, *Stylin': African American Expressive Culture from its Beginnings to the Zoot Suit* (Ithaca, N.Y.: Cornell Univ. Press, 1998).

52. George, "Beauty Culture and Colored People," 26; *Outlook* (1904), quoted in Lorenzo J. Greene and Carter G. Woodson, *The Negro Wage Earner* (1930; reprint, New York: Russell & Russell, 1969), 93; Evelyn Northington, "About Cosmetics and Other Things," *Half-Century* 9 (October 1919): 11. On freedom bags, see Elizabeth Clark-Lewis, " 'This Work Had a End': African-American

Domestic Workers in Washington, D.C., 1910–1940," in Carol Groneman and Mary Beth Norton, eds., *"To Toil the Livelong Day": America's Women at Work, 1780–1980* (Ithaca, N.Y.: Cornell Univ. Press, 1987), 207. On urban employment for black women, see Jacqueline Jones, *Labor of Love, Labor of Sorrow* (New York: Basic, 1985).

53. For hair terminology, see Vertamae Smart-Grosvenor, "The Beauty Quest," *Essence* (May 1985): 155. Pauli Murray quoted in Gatewood, *Aristocrats of Color,* 180.

54. Hortense Powdermaker, *After Freedom: A Cultural Study in the Deep South* (1939; reprint, New York: Russell & Russell, 1968), 179, 180, see also 175–78. Horace Cayton and St. Clair Drake, *Black Metropolis: A Study of Negro Life in a Northern City* (New York: Harcourt, Brace, 1945), 495–504 (quotes on 499, 501, 503).

55. L. R. Stephens, "Black Girl," *Messenger* 8 (December 1926): 381. On changes in color hierarchies, see Gatewood, *Aristocrats of Color;* Harold R. Isaacs, *The New World of Negro Americans* (New York: John Day, 1963), 74, 80, 88. Lawrence Levine, *Black Culture and Black Consciousness* (New York: Oxford Univ. Press, 1977), 284–93.

56. Cayton and Drake, *Black Metropolis,* 503, 504.

57. Haring, "Selling to Harlem," 18; Edwards, *Southern Urban Negro,* 242.

58. LeRoy W. Jeffries, "Decay of the Beauty Parlor Industry," *Opportunity* 16 (February 1938): 49–52. "Sara Spencer Washington," in Jessie Carney Smith, ed., *Notable Black American Women* (Detroit: Gale Research Inc., 1992), 1224. Interview with Elizabeth Barker, 12. On Depression-era beauty shops, see Ethel Erickson, *Employment Conditions in Beauty Shops,* Bulletin of the Women's Bureau, no. 133 (Washington: GPO, 1935). On paying hairdressers with food, see Powdermaker, *After Freedom,* 180.

59. See Interview with Elizabeth Barker; Interview with Maida Springer Kemp, Black Women's Oral History Project. Compare *Apex News* 1 (1929); 8 (1936); 12 (January 1940). *Valmor and Sweet Georgia Brown Beauty Products, Catalog no. 22* (Chicago, 1936), in M. G. Neumann and Valmor Products, Docket no. 4866 (1943), Federal Trade Commission Records, Record Group 122, National Archives.

CHAPTER EIGHT

1. *New York Times Magazine,* 29 March 1942, 10–11; 26 April 1942.

2. J. C. Furnas, "Glamour Goes to War," *Saturday Evening Post,* 29 November 1941, 19; Max Factor, Jr., "American Women should be proud of that native heritage," press release, ca. 1940–45, MFPG. On pinups and American ideals, see Robert Westbrook, "I Want a Girl Just Like the Girl that Married Harry James: American Women and the Problem of Political Obligation in World War II," *American Quarterly* 42 (December 1990): 587–614.

3. *Drug and Cosmetic Industry* 50 (April 1942): 382–83. Maureen Honey, *Creating Rosie the Riveter: Class, Gender and Propaganda during World War II* (Amherst: Univ. of Massachusetts Press, 1984), 179.

4. Tangee advertisements, *LHJ* 60 (August 1943): 73; 61 (May 1944): 86. For a discussion, see Jane Gaines, "War, Women, and Lipstick: Fan Mags in the Forties," *Heresies* no. 18 (1985): 42–47.

5. Ruth Bayard Smith, "The Girls of Summer," *Boston Globe Magazine*, 7 August 1988, 50–51; Maurice Zolotow, "Boom in Beauty," *Saturday Evening Post*, 25 December 1943, 23; Karen Anderson, *Wartime Women: Sex Roles, Family Relations, and the Status of Women During World War II* (Westport: Greenwood, 1981), 60–61; "Minimum Civilian Consumer Requirements for Toilet Preparations," 2, War Production Board Policy File, box 1696, Record Group 179, National Archives.

6. Pratt and Read Aeronautical Division signs, NMAH; Katherine Archibald, *Wartime Shipyard: A Study in Social Diversity* (Berkeley: Univ. of California Press, 1947), 26.

7. Archibald, *Wartime Shipyard*, 21. On Victory Girls, see Anderson, *Wartime Women*, 103–11.

8. "Brief Supporting Toiletry and Cosmetic Order and Schedules, 29 June 1942," 2, War Production Board Records, box 174, Record Group 179, National Archives; *Business Week*, 25 July 1942, 72. On consumer attitudes, see "Survey of Baltimore Group," Cosmetics Questionnaire file, War Production Board Policy File; "Face Powder and Lipstick, Tops Among 'Indispensables,' " *PI* 199 (24 April 1942): 13–14.

9. See discussions in War Production Board Policy File; "Beauty Carries On," *Business Week*, 1 May 1943, 77; *Drug and Cosmetic Industry* 50 (April 1942): 380.

10. Max Factor, *Make-Up Artist Bulletin* (1949), MFPG; Toilet Goods Association, *Reports and Addresses of the Eighteenth Annual Convention* (New York, 1953), 30. On the postwar market, "Toiletries and Cosmetics," *Modern Packaging* 28 (October 1954): 108–10; David A. Loehwing, "Search for Beauty," *Barron's*, 20 August 1956, 3, 19–21; J. Richard Elliott, Jr., "Beauty Contest," *Barron's*, 29 August 1955, 3, 21–23; Marshall Beuick, "It Pays to be Friendly," *PI* 240 (1 August 1952): 25–27. On cosmetics use, Milwaukee Journal, *1922–1948 Silver Jubilee: Consumer Analysis of the Greater Milwaukee Market* (Milwaukee, 1948); E. O. Dille and E. E. Garrison, *Consumer Shopping Habits Regarding Drugs and Cosmetics*, Univ. of Tennessee Extension Series, vol. 25, no. 3 (Knoxville, April 1949).

11. See Richard Steven Tedlow, "An American Autocrat: Charles Revson and the Rise of Revlon" (M.A. thesis, Columbia University, 1971); Andrew Tobias, *Fire and Ice: The Story of Charles Revson* (New York: Morrow, 1976); "The Revson Story: He Knows What Women Want," *PI* 261 (15 November 1957): 52–56; Helen Golby, "Rise of Revlon," *Advertising and Selling* 56 (March 1947): 105–106, 170; Walter Goodman, "The Lipstick War," *Nation*, 21 January 1956, 49.

12. Toilet Goods Association, *Reports and Addresses of the Twenty-first Annual Convention* (New York, 1956), 30. See also *Reports and Addresses of the Twentieth Annual Convention* (New York, 1955). On consumer panels, see *BBDO News Letter*, 28 January 1946. On magazines, "Seventeen: A Unique Case Study," *Tide* (15 April 1945). Charles H. Brown, "Self-Portrait: The Teen-Type Magazine," *Annals of the American*

Academy of Political and Social Science 338 (November 1961): 13–21. On children's cosmetics, interview with Martin Greenfield, 24 November 1988.

13. Louis Bader and Sidney Picker, *Marketing Drugs and Cosmetics* (New York: D. Van Nostrand, 1947), 43–44; "American Women Spend $8.59 on Cosmetics," *Sales Management* 63 (15 July 1949): 72. On black women, cf. Dille and Garrison, *Consumer Shopping Habits*, 9, 13–19, 20–23, 30, 32; Philadelphia Afro-American, *The New Philadelphia Story* (Baltimore: Afro-American Co., 1946).

14. Howard Henderson, "Truth as a Constituent of Advertising" (8 December 1948), 6, Speeches, Howard Henderson Papers, JWT.

15. On Coty, *PI* 260 (19 July 1957): 38. On Bishop, Margaret Allen, *Selling Dreams: Inside the Beauty Business* (New York: Simon & Schuster, 1981), 50; Elliott, "Beauty Contest," 21–22.

16. Bader and Picker, *Marketing Drugs and Cosmetics*, 23. Ad proofs, box 25, Cover Girl Make-up Advertising History Collection, 1959–1990, Archives Center, NMAH.

17. Ralph Banay, "The Trouble with Women," *Colliers* 118 (7 December 1946): 21, 74–79. Eugene D. Fleming, "Psychiatry and Beauty," *Cosmopolitan* 146 (June 1959): 31, 33–34, 36. See also Murray Wax, "Themes in Cosmetics and Grooming," *American Journal of Sociology* 62 (May 1957): 592.

18. Henderson, "Truth as a Constituent of Advertising," 5; Revson quoted in "It's the Ad that Sells Cosmetics," *Business Week*, 31 December 1952, 64.

19. G. M. White, "Why I Like Women," *LHJ* 67 (November 1950): 61.

20. Revson quoted in Hughes, "The Many Sides of Revlon's Revson," *Sales Management* 86 (3 March 1961): 40, 41, 99; "Revson Story," 52, 56; Fire and Ice advertisement, *LHJ*, November 1952; Tedlow, "American Autocrat," 57.

21. "Remarks of Miss Van Davis," Toilet Goods Association, *Reports and Addresses of the Nineteenth Annual Meeting* (New York, 1954), 17–18; Tedlow, "American Autocrat," 56; Kay Daly, "How Do You Advertise Cosmetics to Women," *Advertising Age* 32 (22 May 1961): 102.

22. Interview with Geraldine Giordano; also interview with L. C. Bates Hall, George Poris, Cover Girl Make-up Advertising History Collection.

23. See, e.g., Wini Breines, *Young, White and Miserable: Growing Up Female in the Fifties* (Boston: Beacon, 1992), 92–110. On the media's mixed messages, see Susan Douglas, *Where the Girls Are: Growing Up Female with the Mass Media* (New York: Times Books, 1994).

24. On children's cosmetics, interview with Martin Greenfield; "Toiletries and Cosmetics"; "Fresh Impulse in Children's Toiletries," *Givaudanian* (June 1954): 3–6. For grooming instruction, see "Pond's Case History, Confidential for Senior Representatives" (5 May 1959), 23, 21, Howard Henderson Papers, JWT; *Cover Girl Beauty Notebook* (Baltimore, 1966), in Cover Girl Make-up Advertising History Collection.

25. Mary Norton, "What's Happening in the Teen World," *Cosmetics Fair* 1 (March 1967): 23–26; "Seventeen Survey," *Cosmetics Fair* 1 (July 1967): 17–18; University of Michigan Research Center, *Adolescent Girls* (Ann Arbor, 1957), 7–9, 13–16.

26. Stephen Birmingham, "Odds-on Bet: Next Woman You See Will Wear These," *Life* (18 April 1960): 126.

27. Jessie Bernard, "Teen-Age Culture: An Overview," *Annals of the American Academy of Political and Social Science* 338 (November 1961): 9–10; Blanche Linden-Ward and Carol Hurd Green, *American Women in the 1960s: Changing the Future* (New York: Twayne, 1993), 321.

28. See, for example, makeup advice in Helen Gurley Brown, *Sex and the Single Girl* (New York: Pocket Books, 1963).

29. Henry L. Jackson, "Slick and Span: Accessories for Service Men," *Collier's* 114 (23 December 1944): 44; William L. Schultz, "Shulton Toiletries' War Program: Nimble Package Changes, More Ads," *Sales Management* 50 (15 May 1942): 30. See also "How Seaforth Built He-Man Appeal into a Line of Toiletries," *Sales Management* 51 (15 December 1942): 34. The ways that appearance might mark class and status reversals in the armed forces is suggested in the film *The Best Years of Our Lives* (Samuel Goldwyn Productions, 1946). On "Asiatics," personal communication, Ed Janczyk and Clarence Peiss, 26 December 1988.

30. See *Modern Packaging* 15 (January 1942): 34–35; 23 (September 1949): 104–107; 24 (October 1950): 102–103; 28 (October 1954): 108–109, 112. For advertising, *Esquire* 25 (January 1946): 17, 189, 232. On Arden, "Sweet Smell of Growth Pervades Male Toiletries Field," *Advertising Age* 34 (22 July 1963): 56.

31. "The American Male Likes to Smell Nice Too," *Business Week*, 9 May 1953, 148, 152–53. Carolyn Tabori, "Men's Toiletry Market: How Lusty Is It Really?" *PI* 291 (12 November 1965): 15.

32. "Sweet Smell of Growth," 54; "Winning Consumers with Exotica," *PI* 288 (7 August 1964): 42. On masculinity in the period, see Barbara Ehrenreich, *The Hearts of Men: American Dreams and the Flight from Commitment* (Garden City, N.Y.: Doubleday, 1983).

33. "Boom in Grooming," *Sponsor* 20 (24 January 1966): 39; "$14 Million in TV to sell Colgate's Bond-Inspired 007 Line," *Broadcasting* 69 (23 August 1965): 31; "Winning Consumers with Exotica," 45; "Sweet Smell of Growth," 54.

34. See Joseph Hansen and Evelyn Reed, *Cosmetics, Fashions and the Exploitation of Women* (New York: Pathfinder, 1986), quotes on 75, 39, 51, 50, 53.

35. Gwendolyn Brooks, "A Bronzeville Mother Loiters in Mississippi. Meanwhile, a Mississippi Mother Burns Bacon," in *The Bean Eaters* (1959), reprinted in *The World of Gwendolyn Brooks* (New York: Harper & Row, 1971), 320.

36. "Integration Comes to the Beauty Business," *Ebony* 21 (August 1966): 140, 142–43. Annie S. Barnes, "The Black Beauty Parlor Complex in a Southern City," *Phylon* 36 (1975): 149–54. On the postwar market, see David J. Sullivan, "America's Negro Market Is Growing" (1945), and "Beauty Is Rose Morgan's Business" (April 1959), box 261, CAB; Philadelphia Afro-American, *New Philadelphia Story; Ebony* 30 (September 1975): 118, 120. On *Ebony*, see Dwight Ernest Brooks, "Consumer Markets and Consumer Magazines: Black America and the Culture of Consumption" (Ph.D. diss., University of Iowa, 1991).

37. On Rose Morgan, see Constance H. Curtis to Claude Barnett, 20 July 1954; on Brandford Models, *New York Post*, 31 July 1946, clipping; on segregated beauty

pageants and beauty shops, see clippings, all in box 261, CAB. On *Mademoiselle*, see Elizabeth White, "The Super-Customer for Cosmetics Goes Back to College," *Cosmetics Fair* 1 (July 1967): 13. Shirley Lord, "Everybody's All-American," *Vogue* 179 (February 1989): 312, 315.

38. *Amsterdam News*, 5 May 1962, quoted in Harold R. Isaacs, *The New World of Negro Americans* (New York: John Day, 1963), 96. Malcolm X, with Alex Haley, *Autobiography of Malcolm X* (New York: Grove, 1965), 62–65.

39. Phyl Garland, "The Natural Look: New Mode for Negro Women," *Ebony* 21 (June 1966): 143; Earl Ofari, *The Myth of Black Capitalism* (New York: Monthly Review, 1970), 43. See also Valerie L. Giddings, "African American Dress in the 1960s," 152–54, and Anna Atkins Simkins, "Function and Symbol in Hair and Headgear among African American Women," 166–71, in Barbara M. Starke et al., eds., *African American Dress and Adornment: A Cultural Perspective* (Dubuque: Kendall/Hunt, 1990).

40. Shirley M. Works to the editor, *Ebony* 21 (January 1966): 14; letters to the editor, *Ebony* 21 (April 1966), in response to "Are Negro Girls Getting Prettier?" *Ebony* 21 (February 1966); Garland, "The Natural Look."

41. Garland, "The Natural Look," 143, 144. Letters to the editor, *Ebony* 21 (August 1966): 12, 14.

42. On the Miss America protest, see Robin Morgan, "No More Miss America," in *Sisterhood Is Powerful: An Anthology of Writings from the Women's Liberation Movement* (New York: Random House, 1970), 584–88. See also Alice Echols, *Daring to Be Bad: Radical Feminism in America 1967–1975* (Minneapolis: Univ. of Minnesota Press, 1989), 92–96; Linden-Ward and Green, *American Women in the 1960s*, 319–33. Betty Friedan, *The Feminine Mystique* (New York: Norton, 1963).

43. Dana Densmore, "On the Temptation to Be a Beautiful Object" (1968), in Roberta Salper, ed., *Female Liberation* (New York: Knopf, 1972), 204, 207; Una Stannard, "The Mask of Beauty," in Vivian Gornick and Barbara K. Moran, eds., *Woman in Sexist Society* (New York: Basic, 1971), 200–201.

44. On the slowdown in sales, see "Cosmetics," *Forbes* (15 August 1974): 30. On natural cosmetics, see, e.g., Marcia Donnan, *Cosmetics from the Kitchen* (New York: Holt, Rinehart, and Winston, 1972); Connie Krochmal, *A Guide to Natural Cosmetics* (New York: Quadrangle, 1973). On children, see "Selling Make-Believe Make-Up," *Time*, 24 August 1981, 58.

45. Interview with Helen Nash, Cover Girl Make-up Advertising History Collection; "Cosmetics: Kiss and Sell," *Time*, 11 December 1978, 90.

46. Quoted in Linda Wells, "Face Value," *New York Times Magazine, pt. 2: Fashions of the Times*, 26 February 1989, 72.

47. Mary Kay Ash, *Mary Kay* (New York: Harper & Row, 1981), 30, 33, 41.

48. Interview with Malcolm MacDougall, see also interview with Peter Troup, Cover Girl Make-up Advertising History Collection.

49. Phyllis Furman, "Ethnic Haircare Marketers Battling for Shares," *Advertising Age* 58 (2 March 1987): S6. Patricia O'Toole, "Battle of the Beauty Counter," *New York Times Magazine*, 3 December 1989, 28.

50. Penelope Green, "World Hues," *New York Times Magazine*, 18 August 1991, 38; O'Toole, "Battle of the Beauty Counter," 30; Lord, "Everybody's All-American," 312. See also Anne-Marie Schiro, "For Skins of All Shades, New Cosmetics," *New York Times*, 15 May 1987; "Targeting Black Dollars," *Newsweek*, 13 October 1986, 54–55.

51. Marcelle Clements, "The Mirror Cracked," *New York Times Magazine*, 15 September 1991, 71.

52. Fairchild Publications, Market Research Division, *Fairchild Fact File: Toiletries, Cosmetics, Fragrances and Beauty Aids* (New York, 1990), 38; Fairchild Publications, Market Research Division, *Toiletries, Beauty Aids, Cosmetics, and Fragrances* (New York, 1980). See also "Cosmetics Seen as Next Step in Men's Toiletries," *Advertising Age* 36 (14 June 1965): 3, 92; "Macho Glop," *Time*, 16 June 1980, 72.

53. Callaway Ludington, "Marketing Know-How Sparks Sales in New York," *Women's Wear Daily* 157 (7 April 1989): MT6; Phyllis Fine, "How to Treat the Male Consumer," *Product Marketing* 14 (January 1985): 17; "Macy's Gaining with Men's Space," *Women's Wear Daily* 147 (13 April 1984): S12; Jane F. Lanae, "Clinique Moves Ahead Slowly but Surely," *Women's Wear Daily* 142 (19 April 1981): S22. Linda Wells, "Flirting with Men," *New York Times Magazine*, 9 April 1989, 64; Guerlain Terracotta advertising insert, *Elle* (April 1989); and "No Limits on Success for No Color," Max Factor press release, 19 August 1988, both in author's possession.

54. Quoted in Elizabeth Bugg, "Change Seen Sparking Fragrance Male Call," *Women's Wear Daily* 142 (10 April 1981): S34. On professional men, see *New York Times*, 18 August 1989: D5; Camille Duhe and Therese Myseiwicz, "Manpower: A Fashion Awareness Fuels Men's Market," *Product Marketing* 16 (September 1987): 12; J. R. Redd, "Trading Faces, the Latest Wrinkle," *Time*, 17 December 1984, 86. On gay men and cosmetics, Martin Greenfield to author, 28 December 1988.

55. Interviews with Sheri Colonel, Giordano, Cover Girl Make-up Advertising History Collection. For recent cosmetics use, see Fairchild Publications, *Fairchild Fact File*.

56. O'Toole, "Battle of the Beauty Counter," 28. On expenditures, see also *Wall Street Journal*, 15 September 1983; Robert Goldenberg, "Ethnic Products," *Drug and Cosmetic Industry* 136 (March 1985): 18; Packaged Facts, Inc., *Ethnic Haircare, Skincare and Cosmetics Market* (New York: Packaged Facts, December 1988). See also Barbara Nordquist and Charlean Hines, "Cosmetics in the African American Market," 173–77, in Starke, ed., *African American Dress and Adornment*.

57. bell hooks, *Black Looks* (Boston: South End Press, 1992), 71–72; and "Straightening Our Hair," *Zeta Magazine* 1 (September 1988): 33–37. Gerald Early, "Life with Daughters: Watching the Miss America Pageant," *The Culture of Bruising* (Hopewell, N.J.: Ecco, 1994), 271.

58. "In Appearances, a Sense of Racial Unity," *New York Times*, 15 September 1991. Natalie Beausoleil, "Appearance Work: Women's Everyday Makeup Practices" (Ph.D. diss., Univ. of California Los Angeles, 1992); Simkins, "Function and Symbol in Hair and Headgear," 169.

59. See Arlene Stein, "All Dressed Up, but No Place to Go? Style Wars and the New Lesbianism," *Out/Look* (Winter 1989): 34–44. For academic theory, see Judith Butler, *Gender Trouble: Feminism and the Subversion of Identity* (New York: Routledge, 1990); Diana Fuss, ed., *Inside/Out: Lesbian Theories/Gay Theories* (New York: Routledge, 1991). See also Diane Griffin Crowder, "Lesbians and the (Re/De)Construction of the Female Body," in Catherine Burroughs and Jeffrey David Ehrenreich, eds., *Reading the Social Body* (Iowa City: Univ. of Iowa Press, 1993): 61–84.

60. *Ithaca (N.Y.) Journal*, 17 January 1992; *New York Times*, 2 September 1994. Paulette M. Caldwell, "A Hair Piece: Perspectives on the Intersection of Race and Gender," *Duke Law Journal* (1991): 365–96.

61. "Cosmetics for Queers (Go GRRRRL)" home page, World Wide Web, 1994; Internet posting, feykay@cyberzine.org, 22 December 1994, in author's possession.

62. Naomi Wolf quoted in Lena Williams, "Girl's Self-Image Is Mother of the Woman," *New York Times*, 6 February 1992. See also Wolf, *The Beauty Myth* (New York: Morrow, 1991).

Illustration

Acknowledgments

Grateful acknowledgment is made to the following institutions and individuals for permission to publish material from their collections (their archive numbers, where applicable, appear in parentheses following the page number):

AM Cosmetics Company: 236.
A'Lelia Bundles/Walker Collection: 231.
Beauty Fashion Inc.: 127, 128, 129, 153.
Chesebrough-Pond's USA: 138, 139
Chicago Historical Society: 68 (ICHi-27073), 75 (ICHi-27079), 219.
Cornell University Library, Division of Rare and Manuscript Collections: 32 (left and right), 195.
Duke University Library: 138, 139, 157 (bottom).
Elizabeth Arden: 65, 157 (top).
Franklin D. Roosevelt Library: 197.
George Eastman House: 201 (top and bottom), 233.
Helena Rubinstein Foundation, Collection: Frontispiece, 65, 88.
Indiana Historical Society Library: 69 (M399/C2140), 76 (M399/C2225).
J. B. Williams Company: 162.
Stanley Katz: 131, 147.
Lake County (Ill.) Museum, Curt Teich Postcard Archives: 216 (top).
Lee Pharmaceuticals: 145.
Le Maykup, DeNielle Inc., P.O.B. 10, Station CDN, Montreal, Quebec, Canada H3S 2S3: 154, 240, 241.

Library of Congress, Prints and Photographs Division: 74 (top), 103, 187 (bottom); Farm Security Administration Collection, 199, 228, 229; U.S. Office of War Information Collection, 177, 243 (top and bottom).

Maybelline USA, Schering-Plough Corporation: 142.

Menley and James Laboratories: 157 (bottom).

National Archives: 236.

National Museum of American History, Archives Center, Smithsonian Institution: 143 (97-4190), 147 (89-14353), 152 (97-4191), 242 (88-17600/8); Warshaw Collection, 11 (97-8525), 35 (89-14351), 52 (88-1157), 74 (89-14354), 84 (97-4192), 111 (88-1134), 126, 161 (87-10516).

Kathy Peiss: 28, 43, 49, 83, 148.

Procter and Gamble Company: 115.

Revlon: 250.

Rutgers University Library: 179.

Schomburg Center for Research in Black Culture, Photographs and Prints Division, New York Public Library, Astor, Lenox and Tilden Foundations: 214.

Sherman and Associates: 165.

Smith College Library, Mortimer Rare Book Room: 159.

State Historical Society of Wisconsin: 131 (Whi[X3]50254), 150 (Whi[X3]50253).

Wadsworth Atheneum, Ella Gallup and Mary Catlin Sumner Collection Fund, Hartford: 59.

Index

Page numbers in *italics* refer to illustrations.